But if in your fear you would seek only love's
peace and love's pleasure,
Then it is better for you that you cover your
nakedness and pass out of love's threshing-floor,
Into the seasonless world where you shall laugh,
but not all of your laughter, and weep, but not all of
your tears . . .
Love has no other desire but to fulfil itself.
But if you love and must needs have desires, let these
be your desires:
To melt and be like a running brook that sings its
melody to the night.
To know the pain of too much tenderness.
To be wounded by your own understanding of love;
And to bleed willingly and joyfully.
To wake at dawn with a winged heart and give thanks
for another day of loving;
To rest at the noon hour and meditate love's ecstasy;
To return home at eventide with gratitide;
And then to sleep with a prayer for the beloved in
your heart and a song of praise upon your lips.

—Kahlil Gibran, *The Prophet*, 1923

Americans do not wake up in the morning longing for a balanced
budget. What we do long for cannot be put in material terms, because
it is not material. We're about to realize that our biggest problems,
and our most powerful solutions, are not outside us but within.

—Marianne Williamson, *The Healing of America*, 1997

D0451159

DEBRA LYNNE KATZ (California) is an internationally aclaimed clairvoyant reader, healer, teacher, and spiritual counselor. She holds a bachelor's degree in psychology and a master's degree in social work and is a former federal probation officer. She has studied at the top psychic training schools in the United States and has studied with the faith healers and infamous psychic surgeons in the Philippines. She was the host of Sedona, Arizona's most popular television show, *The Psychic Explorer*. Debra currently resides in Malibu, California, with her adorable son, Manny.

YOU ARE PSYCHIC

THE ART OF
CLAIRVOYANT
READING
&
HEALING

DEBRA LYNNE KATZ

Llewellyn Publications
Saint Paul, Minnesota

First Edition
First Printing, 2004

Cover design by Ellen Dahl
"Spiritual Gift" painting on cover © 2000 Mia Bosna, used with permission
Edited by Andrea Neff

Permission to reprint an excerpt from Manuel Lukingan's "Paypay" essay is gratefully acknowledged.

Library of Congress Cataloging-in-Publication Data (pending)
ISBN: 0-7387-0592-6

Llewellyn Publications
A Division of Llewellyn Worldwide, Ltd.
P.O. Box 64383, Dept. 0-7387-0592-6
St. Paul, MN 55164-0383, U.S.A.
www.llewellyn.com

Printed in the United States of America

Dedication

To my son, Manny:
I love you more than all the stars in the sky,
all the fishes in the sea,
even more than infinity,
and in spirit we will be together
throughout eternity.

Acknowledgments

Special Thanks

To the most profound miracle of my life, my son, Manny: If I loved you anymore than I already do, my heart might explode, but I'm willing to take the risk. To my generous twin sister, Amy Beth Katz, my earliest partner in PSI research. To my dear friend Thomas Bruce McArthur, whose unconditional love and support made the completion of this book possible and painless, and who is living proof that angels really do exist. To the spirit of Lewis Bostwick: We never met in the body, but your courage, creativity, and compassion will dwell in my heart and the pages of this manuscript forever. To Jim Tipton and Ben Faust. And to my most powerful of teachers, my students and clients: You have demonstrated that courage is not about being fearless, but rather continuing on despite the fear. You have given me three of the most sacred of gifts during the course of our work together: a mirror as a tool for shattering limits; much of the knowledge presented in this book; and an unshakable conviction that the human race is absolutely one worth fighting for. It's my most sincere hope that this manuscript will help you answer those questions we didn't have time to address.

My Spiritual Teachers

I'd like to acknowledge my most influential teachers: Chris Murphy, Robert Skillman, Denise Bisbiglia, David Pierce (Intuitive Way), John Fulton (The Aesclepion Healing Center), Wayne Rhodes, and the 1995–1997 staff and graduating class of the Berkeley Psychic Institute, including Michael Leach, Edith Fogel, and Melanie Griffin. Also the Philippine healers: Brother William Nanog, David Oligoni, Brother Lawrence, and June Labo. Also to all my students, clients, and colleagues in Sedona, Arizona, and to my beautiful and enthusiastic students in Los Angeles, including Lynne Dufrane.

My Cherished and Talented Clairvoyant Girlfriends

To Rachael Mai, Kazandra Martin, Francine Sheppard, Dr. Rev. Tracy Thiem, and Christie Thompson: Your unwavering support, faith, and spiritual communication has truly sweetened my existence. You are my Spirit guides in the flesh.

My Beloved Friends, Supporters, and Muses

To my dearest friends Raul Perena and Tony Carito, Thomas Bruce McArthur and his family, Darrah Waters, Paul Thomas, John Bernstein, Dusty Currin, Manuel Lukingan, Ruth and Gary (Seven Centers Yoga), Sandra de Bresser, Joy Ramerez and her family from Pagnasinan, Philippines, Dolorous Garside, Al Rise (Geronimo TV), Steve Leon, and Sharon Tate. Also thanks to Steven Ross (The World Research Foundation) and to the St. Vianny's Catholic Church in Sedona.

My Writing Teachers

Thanks to Dan Gordon and Stephan Schultze, who modeled self-discipline and determination and helped me see the rewriting process as an asset rather than a tragedy, and to the 2002 graduating class of the Zaki Gordon Institute for Independent Filmmaking. Also to Dr. D. Wilson (University of Utah School of Social Work, 1994) for making me write all those papers, and to my supervisors and coworkers from the Northern District of California United States Probation Office (1995–1997) . . . this is why I had to leave.

My Family

Thanks to my gorgeous twin sister, Amy Beth Katz; my not-so-little bro, Bradley Katz; my mother, Nedra Katz; my father, Robert, and his wife, Dotty Katz; Uncle Larry and Lisa Goldfine; Grandma Rose Goldfine; and of course to my son, Manny.

My Publisher

To the staff at Llewellyn Worldwide Publishing, including Ellen Dahl in the art department who designed the stunning cover of this book; my talented editor, Andrea Neff; and charming publicist, Steven Pomije.

My Creator

Whoever, whatever, wherever, why ever . . . Thank you for this gift called my life.

Thanks also to Danny (aka Crash) Kohler, a real-life superhero who reminded me that having fun is not just for kids.

Contents

Prologue

Within the first week of moving to Sedona, Arizona, and beginning my new career as a professional psychic at the Center for the New Age, I was blessed to find a wonderful woman named Sharon to babysit my infant son. Each morning, I would drop little Manny off at Sharon's home and say hello to her husband, Brian, who was usually slouched over a copy of the *Red Rock News*, gulping down a cup of coffee at the kitchen table. He was always courteous, but distant. One afternoon, Sharon confided in me that her husband did not believe in psychic phenomena and was convinced that all psychics were frauds. "Please give him a reading to show him that what you do is legitimate," she implored. I replied with a resounding "No."

I explained that the most unpleasant and difficult people to read are skeptics because no matter what you say, they will find a way to discount it, putting up a wall that takes tremendous effort to penetrate. "It's certainly not impossible to read a nonbeliever, but why should I waste my time on someone who really has a lot invested in maintaining a limited paradigm of himself and the world?" I wondered aloud. "It's a fact of life that there will always be people who have no belief or understanding of what I do and that is something I just have to live with if I want to be of service to those who really are open to receiving my help." Sharon pretended to agree with me.

The following Monday, I was greeted by Sharon's husband at the door. He advised me that his wife had run out to the store, and that I should wait for her in the den, where he was sorting through some paperwork. After a few minutes of silence, he muttered, "So how's business?"

"Fine," I answered cheerfully. A few more minutes of silence elapsed, and then he said, "So, you don't really believe in this psychic stuff, do you?" I tried not to feel insulted.

"Do you actually think I would be going to work day after day, working forty-plus hours a week, spending all this time away from my son, just to do something I don't believe in? Do you really think I would engage in a career that is based on lying to people?" I asked him, sounding a bit hurt, in spite of myself.

"Well, I believe that you think what you are doing is real, but I just don't see how it can be," he replied.

At this point I had two options. One was to remain silent, and the other was to tell him some stories. Since the first one has always been difficult for me, I opted for the latter.

When I was living in the Philippines, a businesswoman came to me for a reading. In broken English, she stated that she wanted to know about the future of her business. I did not know anything about her or the nature of her work and was a bit nervous about reading someone from such a different culture. The first image I saw was that of her looking around herself and then just focusing on a single point. This meant that she needed to focus her attention on one task.

"That is what I am struggling with," the woman complained. "Many opportunities have recently been presented to me. What should I focus on?"

"Well, I see you standing at a blackboard doing some kind of teaching or demonstrating. This seems to be related to providing jobs for people," I advised.

"Yes, that is true," confirmed the woman. "I hire and train salespeople to sell products door to door. But I really am not sure which product to sell." I then focused my attention on her products.

"I see a person rubbing something under her arms. It's a pink bottle, possibly deodorant, but I've never seen anyone in the Philippines use deodorant."

"Oh yes," said the woman. "I used to sell women's deodorant to the high-society women, but that was many years ago."

"Well, I also see a woman wearing an apron. No, it's not quite an apron. There is a woman's butt sticking out and someone is tying some strings around her waist very tightly. I think it's a girdle. I also see women putting on makeup."

"Yes, but that does not really help," the woman responded in frustration. "I used to sell girdles and now I am selling makeup. But my salespeople owe me thousands of dollars in products I fronted, and it has taken me years to get out of debt. I want to prevent this from happening again."

I looked to see what the problem was and saw an effeminate-looking man making fun of her, as if he did not respect her. I saw a heavyset woman with long hair go to one house and then leave in frustration, returning to her apartment where she sat down in front of the television.

"First of all," I began, lecturing the woman, "you need to get a much bigger backbone. Your employees know they can walk all over you and you won't do anything about it, so they don't respect you. I see that if you write a new policy and contract clearly outlining your expectations, and then authoritatively verbalize the repercussions of breaking the contract, you will initially lose some potential applicants, but the ones you hire will be more dependable.

"I also see you with a tough-looking man with big muscles who is knocking on some doors. It appears that hiring a man like this to help with collections will be helpful because even if you make progress with your weak demeanor, this man will instill more fear in your debtors than you ever will. It's also clear that some of your salespeople get easily discouraged, so they tell you they have been working all day when in fact they went only to one or two houses and then gave up and went home. So you need to train them not just in your office, but also in the field. Your problem is not your products, it's your management of your employees."

My readee acknowledged that she had a hard time asking people for the money they owed because she did not want them to dislike her. She confirmed that she was in the process of drawing up a new employee manual and that the tough-looking man I had seen was her cousin, whom she had recently hired as a debt collector. The effeminate man and the heavyset woman were both prior employees.

"You saw all that?" Sharon's husband still eyed me suspiciously. "How is that possible?" I ignored his question and continued my discourse, enjoying this opportunity to talk about my work.

Yesterday a woman came into my office. I knew nothing about her except her name. She looked like any other middle-aged tourist who visits Sedona. Her only question was, "Will my financial situation improve?"

I closed my eyes and began talking about the images flashing in my mind. I saw her with a tall, mustached man. She was leaning on his arm and he was taking money out of his wallet. I saw a flash of a whiskey bottle and then he hit her. In another image, she was washing the floor under his feet (a common image for me that indicates an imbalance in power). This man seemed like someone with whom she had recently been involved. I sensed that she had been relying on him for money. At this point in the reading, the woman acknowledged that this totally described her boyfriend, whom she had broken up with last week. He had helped support her, but had been abusive.

I directed my attention to see what type of work she did and I saw an image of her stripping off her clothes, exposing some sleazy lingerie. I then watched as she threw herself on top of a man who was fully dressed except for his trousers. The realization came into my head that she had engaged in prostitution. Afraid that I might insult her, I timidly asked if she had ever been a dancer.

"Yes," she added just as meekly.

"Umm, were you ever a prostitute?"

"Yes," she answered reluctantly, "but I don't do that anymore."

I then directed my attention to see what kind of work she would really like to be doing. However, nothing was coming to me. I had the realization that she really did not have any career goals; her focus was solely on finding a man who would take care of her. She again confirmed that this was correct.

I looked into the future and saw that she really was not going to be successful if she continued on the path of seeking "easy money" and that it was likely she would revert to her former profession of prostitution unless she made some changes in her attitude.

At this point I saw an image of her shooting a needle into her arm and I advised her that she would find more answers by seeking out the assistance of a drug or alcohol counselor rather than that of a psychic. She was clearly irritated by my comments, but acknowledged that she was still struggling with a drug problem.

"Hmm." Sharon's husband made no other comment, but his ears were perked up like a dog who hears his master approaching.

"Then there was the woman whose head was sticking out of the ceiling," I began.

"What!?!" Sharon's husband leaned forward in his chair. I laughed and continued my story.

Well, not really, but that was the image I saw when she asked if she was going to get a raise. She gave me no information about herself prior to the reading. However, I immediately saw her head sticking out of the ceiling and the walls squeezing in on her, which clearly indicated that she had outgrown her job. I was then surprised to see an overweight, balding man wearing a white jacket. He opened her blouse and was staring unabashedly at her breasts. He then passed through a door into what looked like a waiting room and, using a magnifying glass, examined the large breasts of several other blond women.

At this point I really didn't know what any of this meant, but I got the feeling that my readee was very disgusted with this man. Fearful that I sounded crazy, I stole a peek at my readee and found her enthusiastically nodding her head.

"That is my boss!" She exclaimed. "He is a plastic surgeon and most of his clients are women desiring breast enlargements. But I often get the feeling that he is being unprofessional by making sexual comments to me about his clients. I feel like he does not respect women and that he does not trust me enough to give me more challenging tasks, so the only way I'll stay there is if I get a big raise."

"So did you see her getting a raise?" Sharon's husband seemed to appreciate that story. I shook my head.

"I did not even look at her future because it was clear that she already knew she was going to leave this job and that remaining there would be counterproductive. The reason she came to me in the first place was not really to learn if she would get a raise but rather to have someone else confirm what she was experiencing in the present and, in a way, give her permission to leave."

"Hmm," Sharon's husband pondered. "From all those advertisements on TV about psychic telephone hotlines where you see a big-haired broad wearing lots of mascara telling some other dopey-looking woman that she is going to meet Prince Charming and have lots of brilliant children and a big house, I always thought psychics concentrated on the future—which really is not verifiable until the victim has shelled out some big bucks and the psychic has left town."

"Sure, there are frauds out there," I agreed. "But that has nothing to do with what I or so many other legitimate psychics are doing. Anyway, the future can be changed depending on a person's actions in the present. If you just look to the future without connecting it to the present or the past, it really does not help the person other than to alleviate some worries or to cause a lot more. But even lots of my first-time clients have the same misconceptions, so they will ask about one thing when they really are wondering about something else. Part of my job is to search for the 'right question' and answer that one. But I must be boring you."

"Oh, no, please continue."

Well, there was the couple I read just yesterday. The woman's only question was, "Do you see any upcoming career changes?" I immediately saw the image of her being buried under a stack of papers and tearing out clumps of her hair. This showed me that she was obviously overburdened and stressed at her current job. Next, I saw her absent-mindedly kicking around a can and then watering some flowers in a garden. This told me that she was going to be retiring soon. She was worried about having too much time on her hands, but she would eventually adjust and find solace in hobbies such as gardening. I sensed that she was worn-out from work and that her and her husband's financial situation was secure enough that she really did not need to work anymore. She confirmed that this was all true.

Suddenly, the wrinkled face of a white-haired woman intruded on my train of thought. The method of intrusion was similar to those of deceased people who had appeared uninvited in past readings.

"Did your mother or grandmother recently pass away?" I asked the woman.

Not wanting to disrupt my trance state by opening my eyes, I took her startled gasp as an acknowledgment that I was on to something. Suddenly I felt an intense wave of pain pass through my head, which told me that whomever I was looking at seemed to have suffered from some kind of head pain. Next, a strong wave of grief passed through me, causing tears to gush from my still-closed eyes. I felt the sadness coming more from my readee than from this deceased spirit.

"She says that you did everything you could have done and that you need to stop punishing yourself for not getting there soon enough. She also wants you to know that she is very proud of you—she always has been, but just was never able to express that properly."

At this point my readee began sobbing loudly. I took a few minutes to do some healing work on the deceased spirit by visualizing her surrounded by the light of God. I also asked one of my healing spirits to act as her guide from this world to the next.

"If you'd like, I can do some healing work to help you make some separations from your mother so that she will be freer to move on and you will be able to get on with your life."

I opened my eyes. The woman was shaking her head.

"No," she said. "I still need her with me. I'm not ready to let her go yet." She then turned to her husband and, wiping her eyes, scolded him. "See, this is why I did not want to ask her about my mother. How can we go out for dinner with mascara all over my face?!"

Her husband then confirmed that his mother-in-law had died from a mysterious head injury. They found her alive, collapsed and bloody on the floor, but by the time they reached the hospital, she had passed away. Part of the woman's grief was that she had always longed for her mother to tell her that she was proud of her, but until this moment her mother had kept those feelings to herself.

"Wow!" Sharon's husband exclaimed. "You really got all that from a reading? Okay, so let's say you are somehow able to pick up that information, although I really don't understand how that is possible. What is that healing work you talked about?"

"When I am performing a clairvoyant reading, what I am really doing is looking at energy," I explained. "This energy comes in the form of images, thoughts, sounds, feelings, etc. As soon as I start to look at the energy or image, it begins to change. When the woman began sobbing, this was not just an emotional release, but an energetic one. So if I wish to perform a healing on someone, say to help them release pent-up sadness or the energy of a deceased relative, all I need to do is manipulate the image through visualizing the release of whatever no longer serves my client, and then I watch the desired outcome take place. That is what is referred to as a 'clairvoyant healing.' Oftentimes, people can even physically feel what I am envisioning."

I then told him another story as an example.

A young woman came to me for a reading, desiring to know where she should live. I saw her carrying a stack of books and wearing a graduate's cap. I then saw a map of the United States, and northern California or Washington seemed to spring out of the map.

I then saw an image of a black-haired woman angrily scrubbing some dishes. There was something strange about her mouth, like it was moving very fast. There was a harshness about her that made it unpleasant to be around her even clairvoyantly! I sensed that this angry woman was very jealous of her daughter. I suddenly felt a sharp pain in my throat and realized that this woman had said many discouraging and hurtful things to her daughter throughout her life, and was now trying to get in the way of her daughter fulfilling her dreams by going to graduate school out-of-state. My stunned readee voluntarily acknowledged that everything I said was 100 percent correct.

My clairvoyant gaze then zoomed to my readee's throat. I immediately saw a deep, dark-red slash going through it, and sensed that if she made one wrong move, her head would fall off! Feeling an urgency to help this bright young woman and sensing that she would be open to some healing work, I visualized (imaged) that this foreign red energy was effortlessly pouring out of her throat, and that the space was filling up with her own energy, which I saw as a lighter shade of pink.

I did not tell her what I was doing, but suddenly she yelled out, "Oh my gosh, something is happening in my throat! It feels like someone's hands are inside my throat yanking out something awful!"

I admitted that I was in the middle of performing a healing on her throat, and she became very excited, saying she had been suffering from repetitive ailments like laryngitis and tonsillitis for much of her life and somehow had always sensed that this pain was related to the demeaning words of her mother.

Sharon's husband had now risen from his chair. "Well, I don't know if I really buy this healing work. It just does not make sense. But if you really are doing what you say, why is it that you can do these things that are impossible for everyone else? I mean, no offense, but what makes you so special?"

"That's my whole point. I am not so special!" I was happy to tell him. "Everyone has these abilities, even you! You just need to develop them."

"Oh, come on now."

"Yes," I persisted, totally forgetting about my earlier commitment not to try to convince him of anything. "I always had an interest in psychic phenomena and occasionally had spontaneous psychic experiences that I did not understand while growing up, but I never had the slightest inkling that someday I would be able to do what I do today. That all changed five years ago when I took a meditation class from a teacher who offered a free reading as part of the class. She not only was able to see intimate details of my past, but also effortlessly peered into my imagination and told me what my very own visualizations looked like. I asked her how I could learn to do the same thing, and one week later I was performing my first clairvoyant reading and learning how to control my God-given abilities to an extent I never dreamed was possible."

"So how did you learn?" he asked.

"The same way you learned your profession. I went to school. There are many schools in California and in the United States, even around the world, that can teach you how to develop your clairvoyance. I was able to start picking up information the very first time I attempted to do a reading, and I myself have seen close to a hundred other students go from having no idea what they were doing to giving me and others incredibly accurate and helpful clairvoyant readings in just a few months. Someday I intend to write a book so everyone will have access to this knowledge."

At this point, Sharon entered the room and, glancing from me to her bewildered husband (who was now pacing back and forth across the room, biting his knuckles), mischievously exclaimed, "Oh, I see you had some time to chat."

"Yes," I smiled. "We were just talking about boring things like work."

I handed her my napping baby and made a quick escape.

PART I

An Introduction to Your Psychic Abilities and Energy

CHAPTER I

Introduction

One night as I was doing some last-minute Christmas shopping, I heard a group of excited teenagers discussing the blockbuster film *Harry Potter and the Sorcerer's Stone* and the series of books by J. K. Rowling that have made her the second wealthiest woman in England. They were saying how cool it would be to attend the fictional Hogwart's School of Witchcraft and Wizardry, where Harry Potter discovers that he has extraordinary abilities that he never imagined existed but that occasionally exhibited themselves in startling and detrimental ways until he was taught to control these talents. I smiled to myself as I thought about the esoteric school of clairvoyance that I attended, and the one I later established in Sedona, where every day, every minute, was a new adventure, filled with discovery, drama, mystery, and challenges unheard of by most living beings. It still amazes and saddens me that I lived twenty-seven years of my life without the slightest inkling that I possessed clairvoyant abilities, and that there were schools that could teach me things that were not supposed to even be possible.

It's my dream that someday there will be no need for clairvoyant training schools because clairvoyant reading will be understood, encouraged, and taught by parents as well as teachers throughout our educational institutions. Unfortunately, we are not there yet. I hope this book will provide the initial wake-up call for the slumbering adults in the

United States who are still oblivious to their own clairvoyant abilities and talents and therefore unaware of their own true potential and that of their children. If I could send everyone to a clairvoyant training school, I would, but that is neither feasible nor really necessary. Instead, I am bringing clairvoyant school to you, in this book, which I am dedicating to the thousands of clairvoyant students and teachers out there who can attest to the validity and usefulness of the information and guidance you are about to receive.

This is the only book of its kind devoted to the specific psychic ability of clairvoyance, although the techniques presented herein will aid in the development and attainment of other spiritual/extrasensory abilities as well. This book is based on the truism that every person is a natural-born clairvoyant and healer, and with training, practice, and faith, anyone can learn to perform detailed and accurate readings. The simple techniques described here are *guaranteed* to lead to immediate results, provided that you, the reader, do your homework.

This book will travel with you on your path of psychic and spiritual development: from learning basic techniques, to coping with the challenges of being psychic in mainstream society, to braving the business world of professional reading. Most importantly, this book will help you recognize how you naturally and constantly employ your psychic abilities (clairaudience, telepathy, transmediumship, and clairsentience) and will help you understand how these abilities may be enhancing or hindering your life. This material will provide you with invaluable, empowering tools that you can use in your everyday life, for the rest of your life, for guidance, healing, protection, manifestation, and creativity. This book will answer many questions and bring hope to those of you who have been experiencing problems for which there are no "logical" solutions.

About the Author and Creation of this Book

I began my clairvoyant training in 1994 at the Berkeley Psychic Institute in Berkeley, California, where I underwent an intensive thirteen-month clairvoyant training program. Within one week of my training, which required us to attend class three hours a week and perform readings two to three times a week, I was accessing my clairvoyance for the first time in my twenty-seven years of existence in this lifetime. I was actually performing accurate and helpful readings, which was not uncommon for beginning students. Upon graduation, I went on to take classes and work with beginning clairvoyant students at the Aesclepion Healing Center in Marin County, California.

The Berkeley Psychic Institute was founded by a brilliant psychic healer and spiritual teacher named Lewis Bostwick. Lewis recognized that people were suffering from pain and distress as a result of their lack of awareness of themselves as Spirit. He traveled throughout the world studying and practicing a variety of religions and disciplines, such as Catholicism, Scientology, the Rosicrucian Order, and Philippine faith healing, all of which strongly influenced the development of his clairvoyant reading and healing techniques. He designed and perfected specific techniques that have served the thousands of students who practiced them, as well as the hundreds of thousands of people who have received psychic readings from these students. Lewis Bostwick "fathered" generations of clairvoyant teachers, many of whom went on to establish their own clairvoyant and healing institutes and training programs.

I began my clairvoyant training about two months after Lewis' death, and many of the techniques in this book were taught to me by his talented students. Robert Skillman, David Pierce (founder of Intuitive Way, a psychic training school), John Fulton (founder of the Aesclepion Healing Center), and Chris Murphy were a few of my most influential teachers. Lewis Bostwick believed in an oral tradition of teaching. While his school published its own magazine with articles presenting simple techniques and concepts, he never published a comprehensive manuscript on clairvoyant training such as I am doing here. I never received any written materials during my clairvoyant training and have none to refer to as I write this book. Lewis felt that whoever really needed the information supplied by his school would find their way there.

In the late 1990s, I left my job as a federal probation officer in Oakland, California, and moved to the Philippines for nine months, where I studied with the faith healers and psychic surgeons and eventually met Manuel, the father of my son. Manuel was a self-taught acupuncturist and together we traveled to remote regions and villages, healing and giving clairvoyant readings to the indigenous people who had no other access to medical care or counseling.

After the birth of our son in Las Vegas, where I began my teaching career doing workshops through a local spiritual organization called Spiritual Endeavors, I found my way to Sedona, Arizona, where I embarked on a career as a professional psychic and went on to establish the Sedona Psychic Training Center out of my home. The Sedona Psychic Training Center has never had an affiliation with the Berkeley Psychic Institute, although its curriculum was partially based on my own course of training from BPI and from the Aesclepion Healing Center, which was founded by one of Lewis' most talented students, John Fulton.

The Sedona Psychic Training Center offered intensive month-long training programs in order to fit the schedules and lifestyles of Sedona's transient population, unlike its predecessors, which offered a lengthy course of study of at least one year for students under the age of thirty-six and two years for older students (many older students require longer periods of study because they have more pictures, resistances, programming, etc., to work through, although this is not nearly as true today as it was twenty years ago when BPI was established).

My own thirteen-month course of clairvoyant training was a sacred experience of which I would not trade a single minute. It was perfect for who I was, where I was, and what I needed to achieve at the time; however, I began to realize that not everyone desired, could manage, or even needed such an intensive and demanding commitment. Most of my classmates at Berkeley had no prior psychic training; in fact, many had never had an identifiable clairvoyant experience in their life. However, in Sedona, Arizona, many of my friends and students had been exploring their spiritual paths for decades. They already had attained a certain level of intuitive development. These were people who would never have found their way into a yearlong clairvoyant training program because they were not beginning students and would not tolerate being related to as such.

Three months after my arrival in Sedona, I created a television program called *The Psychic Explorer: Adventures of the Spirit*, which aired on channel 17, Geronimo Communications, and later channel 18, the Arizona Channel. I was the host, producer, and director. Channel 17 was only equipped to produce and air four hours of programming at a time, so there were weeks where my half-hour to an hour program ran every four hours, all day and all night long. Whether or not anyone intended to watch my show, if they owned a TV in Sedona, there was no way they could avoid it!

On the show, I would teach clairvoyant reading and healing techniques and interview a variety of metaphysically oriented guests, several of whom were graduates of various clairvoyant training programs throughout the country. Sedona is a small town and I was constantly being approached on the street, in the grocery store, the video store, and even on hiking trails by people who expressed gratitude and a burning interest in learning more about their clairvoyance.

At the same time, during reading sessions, client after client would ask me questions about how to protect themselves, how to break agreements with ex-lovers, how to overcome their blocks to manifest or get more in touch with their own energies, how to communicate with their spirit guides, and how to develop their clairvoyance. Occasionally I would intuit that a yearlong clairvoyant training program was appropriate for a particular client, but more frequently I would find that teaching these clients a few specific techniques was all they really needed. It became more and more apparent that trying to teach these techniques in the course of ten minutes at the end of a reading was not going to cut it. Many clients asked for books on the techniques that I knew to be effective from direct personal experience and observation of classmates and, later, my own students. I felt helpless and discouraged that I could not refer them to such a book because to my knowledge a book of this kind did not exist. I realized that the only way I could provide these hungry people with the information they needed in a simple, concise, and practical manner was to write a book myself.

As I began work on the book you are now reading, my work with my clients became more pleasurable and less stressful because I knew that soon I would have a means to continue to help them long after our session together had ended. Soon I would have a way to help masses of people help themselves, which is really the key to long-term healing. Before I had even finished writing the second chapter of this book, I already had a long list of clients waiting for its publication.

In this book I will present the techniques that I learned through the various clairvoyant training schools and workshops I have attended and that I have found to work for myself, my classmates, and my students. There is not one word herein that does not represent my own truth based on time-tested personal experience. The process I have undergone during the past seven years of my own spiritual and clairvoyant development has been extremely challenging and, at times, stressful and painful. After only one month of my own clairvoyant training, I knew I would someday teach clairvoyance and healing, and I have approached every single reading and personal experience from the perspective that whatever I was learning was not just for myself, but for my future students. You, the reader of this book, are as much my student as those I have met face to face, and I am honored to share with you keys to knowing yourself and the universe in ways you may have never imagined.

Who Should Read This Book?

Whether you have a casual interest in psychic phenomena or a burning desire to develop your abilities, there is something for everyone in this book. The entertaining real-life stories, thought-provoking discussions, and easy-to-follow techniques will appeal to novices and gurus alike. The techniques are simple yet extremely powerful. In my workshops and classes, I have witnessed beginning students accessing their clairvoyance within a matter of minutes. Many professional psychics that I encountered and taught in Sedona who had been reading for decades were surprised and delighted to discover new methods of clairvoyant development and healing techniques that profoundly enhanced their work and particularly their own health and wellness.

This book offers explanations and insights into the energetic dynamics of relationships, communication, and physical and mental health that you may not find in any other manuscript. It is an eye-opening resource for anyone in a helping profession, such as therapists, counselors, social workers, nurses, psychologists, and even elementary school teachers. Not only will it give you insights into many of your clients' problems, it will also help you avoid and overcome burnout. What's more, it will provide you with techniques you can put into practice and share with your clients.

How to Utilize This Book

First I implore you to read this book with an open mind. This is not a research paper. There are no statistics and no reports of scientifically controlled experiments, although it could easily be the impetus for numerous experiments, and I encourage all readers to explore the plethora of psychic research that has been written about in journals and other books. The techniques presented here have been proven to work by thousands of students who have performed countless hours of readings over the past few decades. My purpose in presenting real-life examples is not to convince you of anything, but to illustrate certain ideas and concepts that I and many of my students have found to be true for ourselves.

If you read this book with an open mind, it will increase your awareness of yourself as a spirit and of the unseen forces around you that affect you, whether or not you choose to diligently practice the exercises. If you do practice the clairvoyant techniques, you will discover your clairvoyance. It is my belief that learning through experience is the only way to know truth. This book is designed to create a safe and effective learning environment so that you may have your own experiences leading to truth and greater enlightenment.

For those of you who are natural-born skeptics, I ask you to exercise patience, not just with this book, but with yourself. While skepticism is healthy and necessary in moderation, an unwillingness to even consider that there is more to life than what your eyes see can be detrimental to your health, relationships, and life in general, as I will illustrate in later chapters.

Fanatical skepticism, atheism, doubt, and negativity are dense energies in the form of programmed thoughts and emotional pain that block your abilities and prevent positive, nurturing experiences from gracing your life. The only way to work through these blocks is to ask the universe to bring you experiences that will open your mind, and then be patient and permit the answers to arrive in unexpected ways. I realize that asking the faithless to have faith is an oxymoron, but it is not impossible.

If you cannot suspend your judgment long enough to attempt to have an experience that might teach you something, then ask yourself what emotion (probably fear) is behind this resistance. Ironically, every single skeptic I have met that had such a vengeful resistance to the possibility of extrasensory perception was actually more sensitive and more naturally intuitive that the average human being. A quotation I read years ago in a book about past lives has always stuck with me: "It is no more amazing to have lived many lives than to live even one life" (author unknown). The fact that we humans exist at all is so mind-boggling and wondrous that to question the possibility of anything in this world is a wonder to me. What a miracle we all are regardless of our psychic abilities! If you so sincerely doubt the possibility that you are psychic, how can you even believe in your own existence?

For believers and skeptics alike, I suggest that you first read the book from cover to cover and then go back and practice the exercises. Many of the chapters build upon the preceding one, so reading them in chronological order will enhance your comprehension of the material. Of course, as with anything, there are no rules that apply to everyone. Some of you may be drawn to the book because of a single sentence;

intuitively opening the book to a particular page where a much-needed message is waiting may be all you ever need from it.

I recommend practicing the clairvoyant exercises and psychic tools as they are prescribed, since every step of each exercise is presented for a specific reason. However, if you feel uncomfortable with a particular exercise or are not getting results with continued practice, go within yourself and see what modifications you can come up with that will work better for your particular needs.

Common Questions

What is clairvoyance?

Clairvoyance means seeing clearly. It is the ability to access and decipher visual information through extrasensory means in the form of images or pictures. It does not involve the eyes, but rather the infinite universe behind the eyes. When you access your clairvoyance, you are using the same mechanics and parts of your brain that are active when you dream or use your imagination to visualize. If you have the ability to visualize anything, even something as simple as a circle, then you have clairvoyant ability. When you perform a clairvoyant reading, you relax your logical mind and let information in the form of images appear to you. Often you will obtain information that you could not possibly have obtained through logical or physical means.

Why would I want to learn how to do clairvoyant readings?

First and foremost, the reason to do clairvoyant readings is because they are fun! It is like sitting back and watching a movie unfold before your eyes, or dreaming while you are awake. You get to see all kinds of fascinating things, and access information firsthand about other people and yourself that you would otherwise never get to experience. Clairvoyant reading is like embarking on a great adventure: you are often surprised by the images that appear, and like a detective you work your way through clues in the form of pictures, sounds, colors, and feelings until you solve the mystery of what these images mean for the person you are reading.

Clairvoyance enables you to know your fellow men and women on an extremely intimate level. It enables you to tap into the deepest realms of the subconscious mind of yourself or of any creature, including your pets. It automatically turns you into the master of all time travelers: with your spirit as captain and your clairvoyance as your time machine, you can easily zoom from the past to the future (which you are really doing all the time anyway, just without awareness), enabling you to bring back immeasurable treasures of insight to your present body. Also, when you "read" energy, you can alter it, so having clairvoyant ability not only makes it possible to pick up information about people that they themselves aren't even privy to, it also makes it possible to help them heal, change, and grow.

A clairvoyant reading can be extremely beneficial for both the person receiving the reading (the readee) and the person performing the reading (the reader). Clairvoyant reading is a form of meditation. More than any other mental exercise, it forces you to concentrate, since the second that your attention wanders, you will stop accessing information and this will be immediately apparent to the reader and readee. Clairvoyant reading brings you into a state of relaxation and makes it impossible for you to continue to focus on your own worries.

When you clairvoyantly read other people, you naturally heal yourself. By the end of a session, you are often in a completely different frame of mind and emotional state than you were at the beginning. Disciplined use of your clairvoyance will send you sailing through vast oceans of perceptions, paradigms, experiences, challenges, and opportunities that were previously nonexistent, or at best were only murky shadows in your logical mind. Through doing clairvoyant readings you will process energy, break patterns and programming, and heal wounds and heartbreaks for yourself and the person you are reading faster and more easily than you ever would doing anything else in your life! Reading other people helps you gain insights into your own situation because you will be drawn to read people who are mirrors for yourself.

While reading yourself may be a bit trickier than reading other people (since it is harder to concentrate and you have more biases to work through), you'll find it very valuable when you need clarification about a relationship in your life or are wondering about an upcoming event, like the result of a job interview.

Through developing your clairvoyance, you will access your power in ways you never imagined. I use the term *power* in the sense of personal power, power over oneself. While clairvoyance can give you power over other people as well, as in some forms of black magic or voodoo, that is not a path I chose to pursue and one that will not be addressed in this book. Control over others is always fleeting and self-defeating because what you are usually trying to get from someone else is what is missing in yourself, or is based on uncomfortable emotions within your own body from which you are trying to escape. It is only when you find your own inner power and peace that you can be truly satisfied.

If people are not doing what you want them to do or are not giving you what you desire, go inward and ask yourself how you can change your own thoughts and actions in order to obtain the joy you seek. Otherwise, you are going to waste a lot of your own vital energy, hurt other people, probably incur some nasty karma, and in the end be no further from where you began. (Think about a time in your life when you tried to change someone's mind about something they felt strongly about, or when you manipulated them into doing something against their will. Is that person still in your life? Were the consequences lasting and fulfilling? Probably not!)

Along with increasing your personal power and confidence, clairvoyant development will help you access a higher form of learning: you will learn through direct experience rather than through regurgitation of someone else's information. You will be better able to discern fact from fiction, truth from lies. Clairvoyance can also be utilized to help access creative energies and ideas that can greatly enhance creative projects and artistic endeavors.

What is the difference between clairvoyant reading and spiritual counseling?

A clairvoyant reading is one of the most effective and easiest forms of therapy/counseling because the clairvoyant can immediately identify the client's core issues; uncover unconscious motivations, desires, dreams, and fears; and actually witness and thus validate the client's past and present external and internal experiences. An experienced clairvoyant can identify and bypass a client's defense mechanisms within a single session. He or she can see through the most convincing persona and reveal the true face behind the most deceptive mask.

Because information is accessed through extrasensory means, the usual pitfalls of traditional psychotherapy can be minimized or even avoided during a clairvoyant reading, provided the clairvoyant understands these may be present and is open to receiving and committed to sharing whatever information emerges. Some of these pitfalls include faulty or deceptive self-reporting by clients; a client's inability to communicate (due to age, interpersonal skills, or disability); erroneous identification of the problem or issue by the client and therapist; and the time-consuming and difficult task of establishing trust.

A doctor deals with the physical body. A psychotherapist deals with the psychological, cognitive, and emotional functioning of the individual. A social worker may deal with the psychological as well as social, family, political, economic, and community factors. A clairvoyant deals with all of these plus one additional and essential element: the spirit. A clairvoyant can see the spirits of humans, both living and deceased. Clairvoyants can see the spirits of animals, plants, and alien life forms. A clairvoyant can even see ascended beings such as Jesus and Buddha and, of course, the greatest spirit of them all, God (see chapter 21).

It is not only unfortunate but downright tragic that so many people (spirits) live their whole lives having no knowledge that they are something other than a physical body and mind. These people can never fully know their true self or who they really are because they are not in touch with their true essence. People who have no concept of their own spirit often suffer from depression and feelings of hopelessness and frustration, and their lives as well as the process of their death are riddled with pain and fear.

In order for a person to thrive, that person's spirit must be nurtured through recognition and validation. Clairvoyance is actually an ability of the spirit. A clairvoyant accesses information by connecting with a readee's spirit or the Universal Spirit and then brings this information into the physical and mental realms.

For many people, the first time they feel as if they have truly been "seen," recognized, understood, and respected for who they really are is during a clairvoyant reading. To give this gift to a fellow human being is one of the most rewarding aspects of performing a reading.

A clairvoyant reading is a powerful catalyst for self-awareness and growth not just because it has a psychological effect on a person but because it actually has an effect on one's energetic and psychical body. It can elicit an instantaneous change in perception for both the client and the clairvoyant. When a clairvoyant looks at energy, that energy responds with movement. So emotions and pain, which are energy, may instantaneously be released. When a clairvoyant focuses on those energies and wills them to behave in a certain way, a "clairvoyant healing" is being performed.

Why would anyone want to receive a clairvoyant reading?

People have a lot of misconceptions about what clairvoyant/psychic readings are all about. While they can be used to access information about the future, a good clairvoyant reading will also focus on you in present time and see what is working for you or what changes need to be made in order for you to create the type of future you would like to have. Readings can help clarify your feelings and experiences and dispel confusion. While they can tell you things you didn't know, more importantly they will often uncover thoughts and feelings that you were afraid to admit to yourself. Sometimes when a relationship is headed in the wrong direction, such as in a violent or abusive marriage, we need an objective witness who can say, "This is what's going on and it's not conducive to your well-being." When a psychic you have never met tells you the details of your life and how remaining in your current situation is detrimental to your self-respect and physical health, you really can't remain in a state of denial. Hearing the truth from someone who does not know you or your situation makes a much greater impact than hearing the same thing from your family and friends who may be biased and too emotionally involved in your situation.

Readings can be performed on couples and families as well as individuals. They can serve as an extremely powerful form of marriage or relationship counseling since the reader does not need to rely on self-reports of who is to blame. The reader can look at agreements and past lives between the couple and see what is working for them as well as what's not. He or she can communicate thoughts and feelings that one partner may have been unable to adequately and neutrally voice. A clairvoyant reader/counselor can also look to see where the masculine and feminine dynamics of each partner are in conflict or harmony.

Why would I want to do clairvoyant healings?

Whether you are aware of it or not, you already are healing people around you. Whenever you sympathize with someone, whenever you wish you could help or change or transform someone's pain and suffering, you are healing that person. Most people have never thought of themselves as a healer or sought this out as a profession, but we all (with the exception of sociopaths) have experienced a desire to help. When we have that desire, when we feel someone else's pain as our own, when we attempt to give them advice, when we pray for them or try to change them, when we become frustrated with them for being stuck in their lives, we are calling forth our healing energy.

This has both positive and detrimental effects on that person and on ourselves, as we will discuss in the next few chapters. When you understand the dynamics and effects of your own healing energy and abilities, you will be better equipped to make the conscious choice of what you would like to do with your energy (which dictates your mental and physical health). You can decide whether or not you want to share someone else's suffering and whether or not you want to take on or interfere with their karma and spiritual path. Instead of feeling helpless or drained and transmitting negative energy (in the form of worry or judgment), you can actually learn to consciously employ simple techniques that will likely have a useful effect on a person you care about. The purpose of learning how to heal is not just to help others, but to avoid healing in ways that are inadvertently dangerous to yourself and to those around you.

If I am so psychic, why don't I know it?

I still marvel at the fact that I could have lived most of my life without knowing I had any clairvoyant ability, or even knowing what clairvoyance is. Most people don't believe me when I tell them that they have the same ability that I and many of the best psychics out there have, because they mistakenly believe that if they did have that ability, they would surely know it. Well, how do you know if you have any ability? The only way is by attempting it. If you never attempted to sing, you would not know that you had a beautiful voice. If you never attempted to play the piano, you would not know that you have the ability, with training and practice, to play the piano. The same is true with clairvoyance. With knowledge of some simple techniques and a moderate dose of patience, practice, and discipline, anyone can access their clairvoyance.

Thanks to religious influences dating back to the time of the Inquisition, mainstream society has done its best to squelch any sign of psychic abilities and gifts in children (and its adult members) through techniques ranging from ridiculing and ignoring signs that a child is communicating through extrasensory means, to punishing and forbidding the child to ever speak of such matters. Between being burned at the stake in past lives and being laughed at by the people we love and depend on in this lifetime, it is no wonder that we have turned off our natural abilities to the point that we forget we even have them!

Even in today's modern world, many of the psychics I know feel they must remain "in the closet." Much like gay and lesbian people, many talented psychic readers and healers hide their activities, abilities, and true selves from their families, coworkers, and neighbors out of fear of being ridiculed, misunderstood, labeled, ostracized, and discriminated against. These closet psychics are some of the most dedicated, honest, loving, and concerned citizens on this planet, and it is a travesty that they feel they have to hide their good deeds in order to maintain their jobs or relationships with people who reject and fear their own spiritual abilities. I know many of these psychics. I was one of them.

Of course, there are some psychics and spiritual leaders out there who would rather maintain the illusion that they somehow have been given special gifts that set them above the average person. This is done by some to maintain power, prestige, and wealth, and by others out of ignorance. Also, many "followers" of psychic gurus prefer to believe that their designated human "God" is more powerful than they are and will do whatever they can to maintain this illusion in order to avoid taking responsibility for their own lives. Ironically (since they will tell you they are following a guru in order to reach enlightenment), this act of dependence can block them from reaching their fullest potential.

People often turn to gurus because to go it alone is sometimes a difficult, lonely, and uncertain path. Many people want to believe that a guru or specific religion has all the answers because the truth that no one really knows for sure what the heck is going on out there can be really scary. Gurus and spiritual teachers can be very helpful and sometimes essential to personal growth, provided the relationship between student and teacher is balanced and healthy.

Many spiritual groups throughout the ages have sought to control information similar to that shared in this book because they feared that people would not use it ethically or responsibly. It's my belief that people are already doing so much harm by using their abilities without awareness that far more people will benefit from understanding the information presented in this book than will misuse it. There are so many books in existence that directly address the subject of black magic, available to those with ill intentions, that there is no reason for anyone to bother trying to extract information for evil purposes from a text such as this one that is intended only to enhance people's lives.

The greatest enemy of awareness is fear. Many people have so much fear about what is behind the door to their own personal power and freedom that they choose to remain in the dark. The path of clairvoyance is a path of personal transformation, and transformation is not always easy, as you surely know. When you begin to open up to your clairvoyance, it is like bringing a bright lantern into an ancient cave. You may or may not like what you see. There may be breathtaking crystal formations or perfectly preserved hieroglyphics, or decaying mummies guarded by drooling, man-eating tigers! While you can dim the light or even turn it off, you can never totally forget what you saw during the period of illumination, or how it felt to see so clearly. This is one of the major reasons people shy away from exploring their psychic abilities.

Sometimes during my workshops I'll ask the audience, "If there were a stranger hiding in your house, would you want to know about it or would you rather he just stay hidden away so you wouldn't have to deal with him and feel the fear and anxiety that might arise from the awareness that he is there?" Most people respond that of course they would want to know about this stranger so that they could protect themselves and get rid of him. I wonder how many people feel the same way about all the "strangers" in the form of spirits or foreign energies that are lurking in their auras and chakras, playing havoc with their relationships and communication with others as well as their inner selves?

I choose to know what is really going on, no matter how ugly "it" is, so that I can choose whether or not I wish to keep "it" in my life. In this book you will learn how to turn on the light and then deal with or conquer anything you don't wish to have in your personal space. By using the techniques presented here, your fear will diminish because you will know that you really can handle just about anything lurking in the dark.

The path of clairvoyance is one that must be undertaken by choice and free will. Undoubtedly many readers are still questioning whether they have psychic abilities, or if they have them to the extent that I suggest. The only way I can convince you of this truth is to share the techniques that have not only been proven effective by myself, but by thousands of others. You must do the rest.

What kind of impact will this book have on my life?

Beware: this book is likely to bring about change in your life! Just as energy is moved and altered when a clairvoyant sees it during a reading, energy is also altered when you read books like this one. When energy moves, perceptions and beliefs begin to get shaken up. It's like an inner earthquake of the mind and emotional body. My teachers refer to this phenomenon as a "growth period." A growth period is actually a very exciting thing because it will turn you into more of who you really are and want to be and can get you back on your spiritual path.

However, while undergoing a growth period, you may experience extreme emotions (such as sadness, fear, or anxiety) and sometimes a short period of turbulence in various aspects of your life. This is because we live in the illusion that our thoughts are the truth. The more we believe in our convictions, the more secure we feel. As we release and move energy, our convictions may suddenly crumble—our security blanket may be snatched out from underneath us with little warning (consider this to be your warning!).

As our convictions metamorphose into newer and more productive ways of thinking about ourselves and the world around us, our behavior may change, which will elicit change and reactions in those around us. As energy moves, either from reading a book or giving or receiving clairvoyant readings and healings, many of the emotions and pain we have ignored and suppressed from birth (and sometimes even before birth) may surface so they can be released, assimilated, and processed in a healthier way. As this energy in the form of physical and emotional pain is released, we may experience it in the present and misinterpret it as having to do with something happening in the present. This is known in psychological terms as *transference*.

If your reaction to a present situation is more extreme than the situation logically warrants, this is a sign that your present situation is merely triggering emotions that you did not adequately deal with in the past. The best way to handle a challenging growth period is to recognize when you are in one, to stop resisting it, and then to enjoy the ride.

If you find yourself in a particularly difficult growth period and would like communication from professionals who understand what you are experiencing, there are numerous clairvoyant training centers with a caring staff and enthusiastic students throughout the United States that will be happy to discuss your situation for free or give you a reading or healing, in person or long-distance, for a very modest price (see chapters 24 and 25).

CHAPTER 2

You Are Already Using Your Psychic Abilities

I'm always amazed and saddened when someone tells me they have never had a psychic experience. We are all actually having psychic experiences every moment of our lives; we just don't realize that is what's happening. So many of our thoughts, feelings, bodily sensations, dreams, fantasies, anxieties, etc., are coming from sources outside ourselves, but we mistakenly believe that they are being generated from our own mind and body.

For many of you, it's only when you have a psychic experience that is obvious and clear-cut that you will consider the possibility that you are psychic. For example, you are thinking of a friend whom you have not heard from in years and a moment later she telephones you; or you have a dream about a male relative meeting some ill fate and the next morning you find out that he passed away during the night; or you ignore your "irrational" mother when she tells you she feels anxious about you leaving the house on a particular evening, and then you total your car in a strange accident that night.

Some people only consider the possibility that they are psychic when they have an extreme out-of-body experience, like where they see things in a room that they could only observe from the ceiling; or they undergo a miraculous healing from a fatal illness without having a clue that throughout the day their spirit is entering and leaving their body a thousand times; or that every week they are undergoing healings that have saved them from death on countless occasions.

If you gain nothing else from this book, I hope you will at least begin to consider the possibility that you are psychic, not just on rare occasions but all the time. Psychic abilities are spiritual abilities. As a spirit, you possess the same qualities often attributed to God. Spirits are creative; they are omniscient (all knowing) and omnipresent (everywhere at once). Your spirit has these abilities even when it is attached to a living body—your body. Some of these psychic/spiritual abilities can be classified as *clairaudience, transmediumship, telepathy* and *clairsentience*, all of which will be illustrated in this chapter.

Clairaudience is the ability to hear the thoughts of other spirits, both with and without bodies. Transmediumship is the ability of your spirit/energy to leave your body and to bring other spirits/energies into your body. Telepathy is the ability to send and receive thoughts through extrasensory means. Clairsentience is the ability to feel the emotions of others. When used consciously, these psychic abilities can assist you in understanding and healing yourself and others. When used unconsciously, as is so often the case, they may be the cause of much unnecessary confusion, pain, and suffering.

As identical twins, my sister Amy and I were constantly asked what we thought to be a very silly question: "If one of you is in pain, does the other one feel it?" We always answered this with an exasperated "No!" But almost twenty years later, I realized that not only was I feeling Amy's pain and emotions, I was feeling the pain and emotions of everyone around me. This concept was never introduced into our frame of reference because it was foreign to our parents, teachers, and the society we grew up in. The ability for one person to experience the feelings of another was possible only in the realm of fantasy, or mythical stories and dreams. According to our close-minded society, if you feel pain, there can be only one explanation for it: there must be something wrong within your own body. And, of course, we were taught that the only acceptable ways to get rid of pain are to wait and see if it disappears, go to the doctor and take medication, or undergo some kind of operation.

I began to understand the limitations and dangers of this paradigm soon after embarking on my clairvoyant training. Because clairvoyance does not involve the intellect, the only way to develop it is though direct practice. So I was thrown immediately into readings without having any preconceived notion of what would happen. For the first few months of my training program, I usually read with other students (see chapter 17). This is an excellent way to build your confidence as a psychic, because as a beginning clairvoyant student, you have very little trust in what you are looking at, and even less courage to speak up about it. This is true even though you may be seeing the same thing that the more advanced students are viewing. Inevitably, someone else in the reading will talk about the same thing you have been silently looking at or sensing, and this of course will increase your confidence and let you know that you are really psychic and not "just using your imagination."

Much to my surprise, I soon began to notice that not only was I seeing the same images as my fellow psychics, I was also feeling the same sensations in my body. For example, during one reading I began to feel a strong pressure on top of my head, as if someone were sitting on it. I was also experiencing some intense pain in my upper back and a constriction in my throat. As I was wondering what was wrong with me and trying to figure out if my health insurance would cover a doctor's visit for these ailments, the other students doing the reading began voicing similar complaints. Much to our relief, one of our teachers finally entered the room and stated: "You all might want to say hello to those religious family spirits that are pounding you over your heads. Also don't be surprised if you are having difficulty reading because there are a lot of energies in the room that don't want you to talk about what you are seeing. And by the way (addressing the readee), have you had some back problems lately because I can feel that is some pretty intense pain you are in!" As soon as the reading was over, all of my pain and discomfort vanished.

A few minutes before another reading, I suddenly felt a strange tingling in my gums. Again I wondered what was wrong with me. When the readee entered the room, she apologized, saying, "Forgive me if I look funny. I just had a root canal and the Novocain has not yet worn off." From these experiences, I began to understand that these bodily sensations were not really mine; rather, I was channeling them.

Clairaudience, Transmediumship, and Telepathy

Most people assume that every thought in their mind is their own, but sometimes this could not be further from the truth. Have you ever been struggling with some nagging problem or question, and just when you were about to give up all hope, a brilliant answer just seemed to land in your mind? Where do you think this came from? Sometimes we really give ourselves too much credit! Albert Einstein and many other brilliant scientists, artists, writers, inventors, etc., were never so vain as to think that they alone were responsible for the monumental ideas that often came to them in their dreams or upon awakening. I believe that these thoughts come from other spirits and people.

You probably have noticed that people to whom you are very closely "connected," such as a sibling, best friend, or your husband or wife, etc., will finish your sentence or ask a question that you were about to ask. Sure, sometimes this might just be because of the similarities between the two of you, but many times it has more to do with your psychic abilities.

My first conscious lesson in clairaudience, transmediumship, and telepathy occurred a few weeks into my clairvoyant training. Instead of feeling excited like I usually did before a reading, on this particular occasion I felt a strange sort of dread as I drove to the Berkeley Psychic Institute. Several times I came close to turning my car around and going home. I told myself that if I couldn't find a parking space immediately in front of the door, I would do just that. I felt nauseated as I parked a few feet from the entrance, and meandered inside.

I had already been sitting in front of our readee for about fifteen minutes and the only thing I could see was darkness. My usual cheerful mood was replaced with feelings of worthlessness and self-ridicule. "What am I doing here?" I chastised myself. "This is all a big joke. I don't really have any psychic ability. This is a waste of time!" On and on the conversation droned in my head until finally I heard the words, "You are a f***ing, stupid bitch." This surprising profanity was music to my ears, because I had the instant realization that the words somehow did not belong to me! While I do have a tendency to criticize myself, I never use this language (well, only if I'm stuck in traffic!).

Intuitively, I knew these harsh words were somehow coming from somewhere else. Since trying to "look" at the readee was not working, I redirected my attention to whatever it was that was sending me these thoughts. I immediately saw an image of two glowing, slanted eyes, and then suddenly my entire body was pierced with a bolt of electricity and I was thrown back in my chair.

This "lightning bolt" did not hurt as much as startle me, but again I was filled with excitement because it only further confirmed my suspicions. Spontaneously, I knew that whatever this energy or spirit was, it had been having an effect on the readee. Without waiting for my fellow student to finish whatever he was saying, I blurted out to the woman, "You have been struggling with self-esteem issues for a long time, and I think you probably have some very self-punishing thoughts on a regular basis."

For the first time she excitedly spoke up, "Yes, yes, that is the whole reason I came in for this reading. Sometimes I even hear voices telling me to hurt myself and I really think they might be spirits rather than the hallucinations my therapist thinks they are."

This early experience was very significant because it prompted me to pay attention to the source of my thoughts and bodily sensations, not just in my readings, but in my everyday life.

As these examples demonstrate, your self-esteem can be influenced by the way other people think and feel about you, or even how these other people think about themselves. For example, imagine you are sitting in a classroom. You are confident with the course material and things are going well for you in life in general. Suddenly a woman sits down next to you who is very worried about getting a good grade and is feeling very unattractive or unintelligent. Within seconds, you could easily absorb or match her energy and your own self-esteem could plummet dramatically, regardless of whether you even speak to her or notice her at all.

Most of you have had at least some experience with public speaking, even if it was just during a speech class in school. If you think back to it, your success or failure may have been directly proportional to the receptivity and accompanying energy of your audience, in that they may have healed you or psychically attacked you. The energy of nervousness and anxiety is not only contagious, it also has a snowball effect, so that you may actually be a confident public speaker but when surrounded by others experiencing stage fright, you might match their fear and have a much harder time delivering your speech.

The energy generated by angry groups of people, such as neo-Nazis, white supremacists, protesters, drunken fraternity students, etc., can be quite contagious and seductive. This accounts for how some individuals can commit heinous acts when in a group, but would never even think of engaging in such behavior on their own. History has shown that many individuals who have surrendered to a poisonous groupthink are so mortified by their own actions that they cannot bear to live with themselves afterward, and end up suffering from posttraumatic stress disorder or trying to commit suicide, as in the case of many Vietnam veterans.

In part 2 of this book, you will learn techniques to help you make a separation from other people's fear, anger, and negativity. These tools will help you maintain your composure and confidence during public speaking or in any challenging situation, and make it easier for you to understand when you are being influenced by sources outside yourself.

Clairsentience

While undergoing my clairvoyant training in the evenings, I was work-ing full-time as a federal probation officer. One day as I was walking down the hall, I felt a peculiar sensation in the back of my first chakra, the energy center located at the base of the spine. It felt kind of like a burning pain, but not exactly. I wondered what was wrong with me. A minute later, I was approached by an enraged attorney clenching my sentencing recommendation in his upraised fist. The closer he moved to me, the more severe the sensation in my lower back became. I realized that the two were related.

The next day I felt a similar sensation, only this time in front of my fourth chakra, or chest. A few minutes later I was approached by a hysterical woman who begged me to do something about her youngest son, who had just been sentenced to several years in prison. The longer I was in her presence, the more intense the burning in my chest be-came, until it was difficult to breathe. During both occasions, these sensations completely subsided as soon as my companions departed. Luckily, I realized that I was being affected by my psychic ability of clairsentience rather than by health problems in need of medication.

Soon I was able to predict with great accuracy the mood of the per-son I was about to encounter or the type of interaction we would have by paying attention to unexpected bodily sensations. I also began using this as a diagnostic tool in my healing work. However, this type of *clairsentient precognition* had its limitations since I still did not know the content of our future contact, or whom I would be encountering (for that kind of detailed information, I would need to sit down and do a clairvoyant reading). The most helpful aspect of my new awareness was that rather than be a victim to whatever sensations I was having, I now had the ability to sort out which feelings were mine and which be-longed to other people. Then, by employing some of the techniques I will share later in this book, I was able to alleviate the unpleasant sen-sations in a timely and effective manner.

At the same time that I was becoming aware of being affected by other peoples' emotions and thoughts, I also seemed to be getting more sensitive to them. I wondered how many times in the past I had felt pain or emotions and had assumed that they were my own, when they were not. I started investigating the complaints of my friends, family, and coworkers to determine whether or not they too might unwittingly be picking up foreign sensations (using their clairsentient abilities). I was surprised to discover how often this was in fact the case.

On one occasion, I was sitting next to my mother in the waiting room of a hospital while we waited for my cancer-stricken grandfather to undergo some tests. I was feeling stressed so I began to meditate and give my fifth chakra (the energy center in the throat) a healing. After several minutes I had the realization that my mother, who was silent beside me, was "matching" me. I knew she was literally feeling the pain that was coming out of my throat by sensing it in her own throat. I considered whether to mention this to her, but decided not to disrupt my meditation.

A minute later my mother loudly cleared her throat and exclaimed, "Damn it, I must be coming down with another cold. My throat is killing me." I then attempted to explain to her what was really happening, but alas, the concept was too foreign to her and she left for the pharmacy in search of medication to alleviate her pain. I felt very saddened by this because I wondered how many times she and hundreds of thousands of other people had taken unnecessary medications or had even undergone surgery for mysterious pain they had truly experienced but falsely assumed was their own.

Unfortunately, most other people in my "everyday life" also refused to even consider my assertions, even when I was able to present a clear and logical argument by demonstrating the true source of their discomfort. Luckily, I found comfort in my fellow clairvoyant students, who were making similar discoveries in their own personal lives as well as in our readings together.

Clairsentience is not just limited to pain, but to many other energies, including emotions, obsessions, and sexual arousal. Oftentimes in my readings, I will see that a person is experiencing an intense emotion, such as depression, anger, or anxiety, and then trace this emotion to the person's spouse or parent, who may be alive or deceased.

During another reading, I saw that my client was obsessed with losing his money, even though it seemed his financial situation was better than that of most people. This was affecting his relationship with his wife and his enjoyment of life. I traced this obsession to his deceased father, who had committed suicide at the time of the Great Depression. His father and some other punishing spirits were plugged into his third chakra, which caused him a lot of stomach pain. He acknowledged that he had suffered from intense pain in his abdomen for years, but the doctors had never been able to determine the source. He felt as if he were being punched in the stomach. I performed some simple healing work to help him release this foreign energy. One month later he called to tell me that for the first time in twenty years, the pain was gone and he was getting much more enjoyment from spending his money.

My students often ask me, "How can we tell if an emotion is our own or is originating in another person?" A sign that the emotion is not really yours is when it feels totally out of control, as if no matter what you do, you cannot change your mood. The depression or sadness you feel may seem so intense and agonizing that the only recourse seems to be death, even though logically you know you have many reasons to live. Another sign that the emotion is coming from an outside source is when there is no logical cause for this emotion. Confusion, disorientation, or the inability to think are also signs that someone else's considerations are in your head.

From readings and my own personal experience, I am certain that what psychologists term "free-floating anxiety" is just that: anxiety that is flowing freely from an outside source to an unsuspecting recipient. I have found that by searching for the creator of the anxiety (which can be done through simple inquiry or observation of your companions), the feeling will quickly dissipate and will have little effect on you. Unfortunately, many people do just the opposite: they become anxious about feeling anxious, and before you know it, they are off to the psychiatrist for a prescription of anti-anxiety medication.

Another sign that you are "channeling" someone else's emotion is if you find yourself getting angry for no discernible reason only when you are in that person's presence. For example, have you ever been in a perfectly happy mood, feeling great about yourself and looking forward to seeing someone, but then soon after spending time with that person, you suddenly felt irritated or even enraged, for no apparent reason? This may have happened on a number of occasions, with the same person. While there could be a number of reasons for this, one possibility is that you were picking up on that other person's unexpressed anger and actually channeling it through your own body.

From the plethora of clairvoyant readings I have done for couples, I have ascertained that this transfer of emotions occurs commonly in relationships involving a partner, often the male, who has difficulty expressing emotions such as depression or anger. The partner who gives herself greater permission to express emotions will inadvertently begin to channel and eventually outwardly express this repressed emotion of her partner. Since it doesn't really belong to her, she cannot deal with the emotion as effectively as she can with her own and may become quite imbalanced, even hysterical.

This common male/female dynamic has been utilized for centuries by emotionally repressed men in order to justify their superiority over the women they label as "irrational" or "overemotional." Ironically, if and when this type of person (again, often male) begins to take responsibility for the proper expression of his feelings and re-own them, his partner will consequently be freed from feeling the effect of his emotional energy, and both partners, along with the relationship, will reach a more harmonious state of equilibrium. As noted earlier, emotions are most often overwhelming when they are not our own.

Sexual feelings and emotions of joy and excitement are energies that can also be absorbed and transferred from one person to another. When two people are attracted to each other, they are often unconsciously exchanging sexual energies. Oftentimes they are not aware of the actual energy exchange; they merely feel aroused and conclude that there is something they like about the other person that is making their own body respond. Think back to a time when you felt aroused around a person with whom you had nothing in common and did not particularly like or find attractive. It is very possible that they were running their sexual energy through you and you interpreted it as your own. This likely led to feelings of confusion and perhaps to behavior that you later regretted.

From the numerous readings I have participated in, it is clear that sexual fantasies are an extremely potent energy force and can affect either the person being fantasized about or someone in close proximity to the fantasizer, as if the fantasy were actually occurring to them. Many times I have read someone who I saw had all the symptoms of a victim of sexual abuse or who appeared to be a victim of incest. When I described what the abuser looked like and when the abuse occurred, the readee immediately knew who and what I was talking about, only they insisted that the abuse had never actually physically occurred.

For example, one woman, whom I'll call Alice, had a father who was a subscriber to several pornographic magazines. He spent several hours each day locked in the family bathroom with these magazines while his wife was busy with the household chores. He carefully kept these magazines out of sight from his family, so his daughter never saw one until she was an adult. When she would inquire why her father was locked in the bathroom, her mother explained that he was having stomach problems. However, beginning at the age of seven, whenever she walked into that bathroom, she would have extremely explicit sexual fantasies about acts she had never witnessed or even heard about. These led to confusing but strong feelings of arousal, which then prompted intense feelings of shame and self-disgust. It was clear from my reading and her subsequent confirmations that she had been absorbing the sexual images and feelings that had been generated in the bathroom.

This story demonstrates the need for what I call responsible fantasizing. Sexual fantasies are natural and at times desirable, but they need to be monitored and controlled so that we do not accidentally influence other people, particularly our children.

CHAPTER 3

Energy and Your Body

As discussed in the previous chapter, we are constantly picking up information about our universe and other people through extrasensory perception. We do this by transmitting and absorbing information (in the form of pictures, images, emotions, and pain) through our physical bodies and various energy systems that correspond to our physical anatomy. Two of these energy systems are the aura and the chakras. While an in-depth discussion of these complex energy systems is beyond the scope of this book, having a basic understanding of their function and major attributes can help us understand how we process foreign energies, how we are influenced by them, and how we can have more control over them. When doing clairvoyant readings, it is helpful to be aware of these energy systems and of some simple characteristics of energy so that we can better navigate our way through a reading. Understanding various energy systems as they correspond to the physical body makes it easier to locate problem areas on a client's body, thus facilitating the process of clairvoyant healing.

Your Aura

Read any spiritual text from the Hindu, Buddhist, Sufi, and Cabalistic traditions and you will find universal agreement that human beings are

much more than a physical body. Our physical body is really only a
very small percentage of who and what we are. Our spirit is housed inside our body, but it flows far beyond the tenuous walls of our flesh.
The part of our spirit that surrounds the outside of our body is an energetic field that is often referred to as an *aura*.

This aura actually registers on physical instruments and its colors
can be seen through Kirlian photography. Your aura reflects everything
about your personality and experiences in this lifetime and in other incarnations. Clairvoyants can see the information in this energy field in
the form of colors and images. The aura consists of layers, or spiritual
bodies. Throughout the ages, there have been a number of spiritual disciplines and religions that describe the aura in a very similar fashion.
Typically it is thought that the aura has seven main layers, or bodies. In
Kirlian photography, these layers are not very distinct; the colors blend
together, sometimes completely covering up the subject of the photograph. The colors of the aura or other energies often unexpectedly
show themselves in regular photography as well.

For the purpose of doing a clairvoyant reading, it is helpful to distinguish between the layers of the aura, imagining that each layer is
separate and unique from the others. This makes it easier to navigate
your way through the complex system of information contained in
your readee's energetic field (see chapter 16).

In my experience, the first layer (the first auric body) often contains
information about the physical body since it is closest to the body. The
second layer corresponds to emotions and sexual energies. The third
layer often has information in it about power, control, and self-esteem.
The fourth layer seems to contain information about matters of the
heart and relationships. The fifth layer concerns communication. The
sixth layer contains information about how a person perceives himself
or herself. Finally, the seventh layer, farthest from the body but closest
to the outside world, often holds information about other people's perceptions as well as foreign energies that are entering and leaving the
aura. There may be additional layers that I have not experienced due to
my training and preconceived notions about the aura.

Your aura contains your own energy and energy from other people and the environment. Everything about you—everything you have ever been, ever thought, dreamed, experienced, felt, desired, as well as every relationship you have ever had—is recorded, stored, and transmitted through the aura. I hesitate to describe the aura in any detail because the best way to learn about it, as with anything, is through your own clairvoyant observation, experimentation, and experience.

Color

Clairvoyants see energy as color. Since the energy that makes up a person and their aura is constantly changing, the colors of the aura are always in flux. One day the first layer of the aura may be predominantly blue. The next day it may be green, depending on the person's emotions, actions, and the foreign energies affecting them.

There are numerous books on the aura that attempt to define the meaning of every color. I shy away from this because colors are symbolic representations and the meanings of symbols are derived from personal as well as universal experiences (the same could be said about dream interpretation). Two clairvoyants may see the same energy as the same color, as different shades of the same color, or as two completely different colors, depending on their life experiences. All information is filtered through the reader's life experiences, emotions, personality, biases, and MEI pictures (see chapter 4). This is true in every aspect of life, not just when performing a reading.

When communicating about energy, clairvoyants will discuss similar information but provide different perspectives. Clairvoyant #1 might see yellow in the first layer of the aura and see this as the readee's mother's energy, while Clairvoyant #2 may have a clear sense that he is looking at the readee's mother's energy, but to him it looks blue. Further probing or questioning of the colors may lead Clairvoyant #1 to say, "The yellow energy tells me that your mother is praying for you constantly and that she really cares about you," while Clairvoyant #2 might say, "The blue energy I am looking at tells me that your mother is worried about you and is trying to protect you, but this protection is blocking you." Clairvoyant #1 is unconsciously focusing on the energy of prayer because he and his own mother pray a lot. Clairvoyant #2 is picking up the energy of worry because he is presently working on moving his own mother's concerns out of his own aura so he does not have to be afraid to take certain steps in his life. Both clairvoyants are accurately picking up information that is useful for the readee to hear.

Sometimes I will see red in the first layer of a client's aura and I discover that it represents my client's anger. In another reading I will see red in the seventh layer and it represents a creative energy being generated from a love interest. I may never know why both appeared as red, but for the purpose of performing clairvoyant readings, the answer is completely inconsequential. When performing a reading, you must turn down and get out of your analytical/logical mind in order to see what is in front of you. If you see a particular color, the last thing you want to do is impose a preconceived interpretation on it. Instead, ask the color to show you an image of what it means. Then ask that image to tell you what it means. This process is fully described in chapters 13 and 14.

After performing several clairvoyant readings, you might begin to build a vocabulary of images and colors, but these are only springboards for further clairvoyant investigation. When I see white in someone's aura, it often represents transmedium energy or energy from disembodied spirits. Cancer also seems to resonate as a white color. When I see black in an aura, it often represents a lower vibration, one of interference or disease. However, both these colors can have infinite meanings and it would be irresponsible and negligent to make loose assumptions about them when performing a reading.

Characteristics of an Aura

The aura is stretchable. Sometimes it is only a few inches from the body, while other times it spans hundreds of miles. Each individual has a different way of carrying his or her auric field. Some people are more comfortable having it close to their physical body, but in certain situations will expand it, and vice versa. People who are more reserved and introverted tend to keep their auric field closer to their body than people who are outgoing. When your aura is out very far, you can be affected and effect the people who are sharing physical space with you. It is often helpful to call your aura more closely around you when you feel overstimulated, such as when you are stuck in traffic or in a crowd of people. It is possible to expand or contract the aura simply by visualizing this and stating your intent.

One of my clairvoyant friends spent a couple months living with me when she was in between apartments. She had a tendency to walk into a room and spread out her aura so that she could feel secure. Her aura would actually meld into the walls. This was highly irritating to me because she was taking over the space that I was already occupying. It felt as if I were being swallowed up by her thoughts and emotions so that I could not think of anything else but her. The first time I mentioned this to her, she admitted that her former psychic roommates had complained about this as well. With a gentle reminder, she could call her aura closer to her body through visualization.

I encourage you to play around with your aura in a variety of situations to see what feels most comfortable to you (and to your housemates!) and to help you become aware of your aura as well as to strengthen it. Flexing and contracting your aura is much like exercising the muscles of your body. As you exercise your aura through visualization, it will grow stronger and you will gain more control over your energy field as well as your clairvoyance.

Chakras

Within the aura are concentrated centers of energy that correspond to the body. These energy centers are known as *chakras*. Chakra is a Sanskrit word for "wheel" or "centers of radiating force." There are also several of these main energy centers that rise above the head into the aura, as well as in the hands and feet. Chakras appear to be strong connection points where the spirit and physical body meet, and like the aura, they contain a plethora of information.

My clairvoyant and healing experiences confirm that all illnesses actually start in the chakras, and if the chakras are not functioning properly, the corresponding organs within the body will be adversely affected. Many psychics, including myself, see these energy centers as very small spinning disks. When they are not spinning, this means there is an imbalance in the chakra or the energy flow of the body.

Personally, I do not usually see chakras in great detail. I don't have a technical/mathematical orientation or inclination and am more interested in the information stored in the chakra than its structure. You may be able to see chakras in richer detail and complexity. As you develop your clairvoyant abilities, I encourage you to look at chakras and every other energy system of the body and spirit for yourself.

The first chakra is located at the base of the spine and in women at the base of the cervix. It has to do with issues concerning survival of the body and connections to society. There is usually a first chakra connection or cord running between a mother and her baby. When my infant son is not feeling well, I will feel an intense pain in my first chakra.

According to the Ruth and Gary Marchak, the founders of the Seven Centers School of Yoga Arts in Sedona, Arizona, when the first chakra is malfunctioning, a person will have difficulty manifesting money and other things in life that they desire and need, whether it be fulfilling work, cash, or healthy relationships. In chakra yoga, which is a form of kundalini yoga, there are specific postures and movements that influence a particular chakra. Oftentimes, all it takes to rebalance the first chakra and begin to create abundance in one's life is to perform a series of exercises (physical or mental) on a consistent basis for about a week.

The second chakra contains information about emotions, power, and sex. It corresponds with the reproductive organs. When you are tuned in to your clairsentient abilities and you meet someone to whom you are physically attracted, or when being physically intimate, you can actually feel narrow cords of energy, like needles, going into your second chakra. The second chakra also corresponds to the psychic ability of clairsentience. Again, there are particular yogic movements as well as visualizations that can be used to increase the energy flow through this chakra.

In my readings, I have observed that prostate cancer is often a result of a loss of power and energy flow through the second chakra. Caroline Myss has a wonderful series of audiotapes called *Three Levels of Power and How to Use Them*, which I highly recommend. She explains that men who retire from lifelong careers seem to develop prostate cancer more frequently than those who continue to work. Men who retire suddenly are disconnected from the source of energy that fueled their sense of personal power and self-worth, which was their job. When they lose this power, their energy bleeds from their second chakra, thus causing physical problems.

Women who suffered from sexual abuse at an early age, as well as those who have experienced neglect, abuse, or extreme disappointment in intimate relationships or who have remained in an unhappy situation against the wishes of their heart, often develop ovarian cancer or some other disorder of the female reproductive system. In fact, out of the dozens of readings I have done on women who have had hysterectomies, I have never found an exception to this rule. Information regarding this history is always located in the second chakra, but may reveal itself in corresponding chakras as well.

The third chakra has to do with issues of control and self-esteem. People who are "Type A" personalities or "control freaks" tend to have stomach problems such as ulcers because their third chakra is in overdrive. Because the third chakra is responsible for energy distribution of the entire body, this is a very powerful chakra. When someone has their third chakra revved all the way up, it is like a stereo blasting music at a deafening volume, so that everyone in the vicinity is affected by it.

On the other hand, if this chakra is shut down or depleted of energy, a person will be lethargic and their very life may be in jeopardy.

They will also be extremely needy of other people's energy. People need energy in order to thrive and function. When someone's third chakra is not generating enough of its own energy, it will seek out that energy in others, like a magnet. Some of the most powerful people in the world operate this way, including spiritual gurus, religious and cult leaders, politicians, movie stars, and corporate leaders. Because they either lack their own energy or are performing monumental tasks that require an exorbitant amount of energy, they must rely on and be sustained by the help and energy of devotees, followers, fans, or a large staff.

Our energy systems can replenish themselves but we have a limited amount of energy at any given time. That is why we need to eat and sleep and relax. There are only so many creative projects, relationships, responsibilities and problems we can handle before our systems start to malfunction through physical, mental or emotional illness.

For a period of time, I was performing an unusually high number of clairvoyant readings on women who were trying to do too much in their lives (undoubtedly because that was one of my own issues). In every case the message was clear: we all needed to stop trying to do everything; rather, we needed to narrow our focus to the things in our lives that were in the greatest alignment with our life goals. This meant eliminating projects, jobs, activities, and relationships that were not directly helping us achieve these goals. It didn't matter whether these goals were general, such as having peace, or if they were as specific as publishing a book. When we try to do more than we have energy for, the energy gets so watered down that none of our relationships or projects receive the energy they need in order to be successful and enjoyable.

The third chakra distributes energy and is connected to the other chakras. Since developing my psychic abilities, I have noticed that when I hurt any part of my body, whether I stub my toe or slam my finger in a drawer, I can feel a tightening or aching in my third chakra. John Fulton, the director of the Aesclepion Healing Institute in San Rafael, California, suggests that if you are ever in a position to assist someone who is suffering from injury and potential shock, you should place your hand on their third chakra (solar plexus area) and gently tell the injured person to focus all of their attention on their body beneath your hand. What this will do is redistribute the energy that accumulated in the injured area and that is producing the pain and shock. As the person shifts their attention from the injured area to their third chakra, the pain will decrease. Focusing on the third chakra will also help the person's spirit (energy) reenter the body in the event that it got knocked out of it at the moment the injury occurred. The person will need as much energy as possible in order to heal. I've discovered that this technique works well with young children and even infants.

Some faith healers and psychic surgeons in the Philippines work solely on the patient's third chakra, regardless of the type or location of their ailment. They postulate, demand, visualize, and pray that all of the illness in the body collects in the third chakra, and then employ a variety of techniques to extract the illness or foreign energy from that chakra.

The fourth chakra corresponds with the heart and is concerned with affinity for oneself and others. People with disappointments over relationships, or who are perfectionists and tend to be very hard on themselves, often will have heart attacks because of the malfunctioning of energy in the fourth chakra. I have clairvoyantly observed that women who suffer from breast cancer often have felt stifled or disappointed in relationships, and may not have had permission to even acknowledge this to themselves. Women who have a martyr complex also seem vulnerable to breast cancer.

The fifth chakra corresponds with the throat and is involved in communication, both on physical levels and on telepathic levels. When people channel the voice or thoughts of other spirits (as in clairaudience), this is often the chakra that the spirit will plug into. Sore throats, laryngitis, neck pain, and headaches are often related to a disruption in the flow of energy to the fifth chakra. People who have difficulty communicating their feelings often exhibit these symptoms, and their fifth chakra is usually too closed or clogged.

Sometimes years of withholding communication will cause damage to the fifth chakra, while other times the communication problem is a result of a damaged chakra. Most damaged throat chakras contain foreign energies from a family member or significant other who had an interest in keeping this person quiet or who desires to control their communication. Well-intentioned parents often insert a sort of energetic dam into their baby's fifth chakra in order to quiet them down. Whether the energy is in the form of a verbal reprimand or a telepathic one, the child will receive the message that "expressing yourself is undesirable, irritating to others, or shameful," and as a result the fifth chakra will contract.

Setting limits for children is necessary, and an occasional reprimand is not going to do much damage, but parents can help maintain the integrity of their children's chakras by being aware of their own energies and making sure they do not use their energy to overwhelm the sensitive and unprotected chakras of their children. By creating a safe environment where children are encouraged to appropriately express their feelings (including anger at their parents), children will maintain healthy chakras and be less vulnerable to physical ailments throughout their lives. They will also become more competent and confident communicators and public speakers.

People who are unable to verbalize their emotions and communicate feelings of anger, disappointment, or frustration to others can never truly be in their own power, so the fifth chakra also has to do with issues of personal power.

The sixth chakra, also known as the *third eye*, is the center of clairvoyance. It is located in the center of the head, slightly above the eyes. When someone is curious about what you are thinking or doing or doesn't want you to see them, they will unconsciously plug into your sixth chakra. As with the fifth chakra, the sixth chakra is very sensitive to foreign energies. Children often learn to turn down their sixth chakras, and essentially turn off their clairvoyance at an early age, in order to avoid seeing what their parents don't want them to see.

Fortunately, it is fairly easy to clear out foreign energies, either through energetic healing work or by activating the sixth chakra through intent and use. I have witnessed numerous beginning clairvoyant students who could not "see" a thing due to a clogged sixth chakra turn into amazing psychics within a matter of weeks just by showing up for readings and attempting to use their clairvoyance. There have been a handful of students whom I personally read before they ever had an inkling that they possessed clairvoyant abilities (and would be using them someday soon), usually because no one had given them permission to use their sixth chakra to its full capacity. Less than a year later, after learning the techniques discussed in this book, each of these students gave me a phenomenal reading that exceeded even my own expectations.

The seventh chakra is located in the top of the head. It is the seat of the soul, with the bottom half of the spirit running from the top of the head down to the feet and the upper half of the spirit running from the feet to the head. The energy continues up to God or the part of ourselves that can be called our God self. The crown chakra is where you access spiritual information through "spontaneous knowing," and where your spirit exits and other spirits enter. This is the chakra that your guru, spiritual teacher, or people who want to have power over you will plug into. The seventh chakra is often depicted as a golden halo above the heads of figures like Christ and other saints and angels. When I am under surveillance, either by a policeman's radar or a video camera, I will feel pressure on my crown chakra, which lets me know I'd better slow down and behave myself!

In this book, you will learn to bring in your cosmic energy and your own energy through the seventh chakra. You will learn how to set and maintain your crown chakra at a vibration that is comfortable and pleasant so that you do not inadvertently "match" lower vibrations (see chapter 9). You will also learn how to tune in to the seventh chakra of your readee (which essentially is tuning in to their spirit and unique energy vibration/essence) so that you can effectively perform a clairvoyant reading (see chapter 14).

Did you ever play the game "Light as a feather, stiff as a board" when you were a child? In this game, one child pretends they are dead and imagines that they are as light as a feather and as stiff as a board.

At least two children kneel beside the "dead" person, and each one gently places two fingers of each hand beneath the body. One child sits at the crown chakra and places two fingers behind the head and makes up a story about how the person died. Then everyone repeats the words "light as a feather, stiff as a board," and at the count of three they attempt to lift the person off the floor, using only their two fingers.

I played this game countless times at slumber parties. On one occasion, my sister and I shocked and frightened ourselves by actually raising an extremely chunky fellow third grader above our heads, until we lost our concentration and dropped her. To this day I don't know if she ever forgave us!

I once attended a lecture by a healer who revealed the secret of this game. He told us that it has to do with tuning in to and aligning with the subject's crown chakra. He demonstrated this by inviting a few people to stack their right hands over one man's crown chakra. The man must have weighed at least 180 pounds and was sitting upright in a chair. The three people were instructed to visualize the same color for about thirty seconds. Then they each placed two fingers under the man's chair and effortlessly lifted the chair several feet. The healer informed us that this process would work even if the three people had aligned themselves with the crown chakra of someone other than the man they were lifting. Somehow, aligning with the powerful energy of a fellow human's crown chakra gives the other participants the energy, power, and strength to do extraordinary feats. This would make a very interesting research project for any of you scientists out there!

The hand chakras are associated with healing and are located on the inside palm of each hand (also the feet). The Taoist and other Chinese energy healers call these points "bubbling wells." After several years of doing psychic readings and healings and undergoing numerous psychic surgeries on my hand chakras in the Philippines, I can easily feel other people's pain through my hand chakras. This is helpful when it comes to identifying problem areas, and is particularly useful with babies and people who cannot easily communicate. The downside is that sometimes the pain is as strong and unpleasant as if it were my own. Luckily, some of the techniques suggested in this book, such as grounding, offer instant relief (see chapters 7–12).

The feet chakras are connected with the earth. A variety of energies enter and exit through the feet. One of my favorite faith healers in the Philippines, David Oligoni (aka "The Exorcist"), works primarily with the feet. I have received several healings from him and observed him heal at least sixty other people. During a healing, he invites you to lie on a table. He then gently touches your big toe with one or two fingers and then commands the demons in your body to exit. At first this seems ludicrous, until the most agonizing pain starts releasing out of your big toe! This pain usually lasts about a minute, but seems like a lifetime. It is just as intense as labor pains, if not worse! Supposedly, not only is a "demon" being excised, but you are being cleared of all the pain that the unfortunate spirit was plugged into.

During my first healing with David Oligoni, I became furious because I thought he must be using some sharp object to pierce my toe. I thought, "I did not come all this way to the Philippines just to be prodded mercilessly by this witch doctor!" The only thing restraining me from kicking him in the face was fear that the other onlookers would accuse me of being possessed! However, a year later, he picked me out of another group of students and invited me to assist him in a healing. He directed me to gently place my finger on the healee's toe while he clasped his fingers around mine. Soon the healee was not only screaming out in pain, but was muttering strange sounds and convulsing on the table. Since the healee was a trusted friend of mine, I knew this was no act.

A few weeks later, upon my return home, I was performing a simple aura healing on a clairvoyant friend (working around the third chakra) when I heard myself silently muttering the same words the exorcist had muttered to our helpless feet: "Get out, you demon, get out!" I wondered, could I actually be performing an exorcism? Then suddenly my friend screamed out in agony, "Oh my gosh, my toe! There is a horrible pain leaking from my toe!"

You can focus on the aura and the chakras during a reading to learn about a person or to heal that person (see chapter 16). Although there are plenty of books that have been written on these energy systems (a few of these are recommended in the bibliography), as I've already mentioned, the best way to learn about them is through your own direct perception, in readings and in meditation.

Out-of-Body Travel

Our spirit is constantly in flux. When a clairvoyant performs a reading on a client, she is reading a person's spirit. When the spirit is out of the body, the clairvoyant will not be able to adequately perform a reading unless she calls the spirit back into the body, or travels to wherever that spirit is located. Most of the time when I have difficulty focusing on a client at the beginning of a reading, or I find that my attention is wandering, it is because the client's spirit is out of the body or has wandered out of it during the course of the reading. This exodus usually occurs when the client is hitting pain levels as a result of the communication they are receiving. Beginning clairvoyant students will save themselves a lot of frustration if they can be aware of this energy dynamic. Calling someone's spirit or energy back into the body can be as simple as letting the person know they have wandered, touching them on the shoulders, or visualizing their spirit's return to the body.

On the other hand, when performing certain kinds of healings, it may be desirable to bring the client's spirit out of the body so the healer can clear the negative energy that is clogging up the communication between the spirit and the body. Imagine that you are cleaning your car and the floor mats; in order to get both of these clean you need to separate them for a while. During times of intense stress and pain, the last place our spirit wants to be is in the body (where the pain is being experienced), so the spirit will leave the body and travel to another person, place, or time. Usually it will eventually return to the body, but not always.

It is for this reason that sleep is so important. A person who is not feeling well will need, or desire, more sleep. During sleep, our spirit is particularly free to leave our body and reunite with its source to be replenished. At the same time, our body can release tension, pain, and foreign energies so that upon awakening, both body and spirit are reenergized and ready to deal with each other again. It has been well documented that people who go for periods of time, even as little as three days, with no sleep will hallucinate and have psychotic reactions. Some people with sleep disorders who could not sleep for several months have actually died from lack of sleep. In these rare cases, the body was a prison from which the spirit could not escape, and in a sense, the spirit starved to death because it could no longer sustain itself.

Our spirit can leave our body not just in sleep, but at any time. Many people are familiar with the term *out-of-body experience (OBE)*. This usually refers to an intense experience that occurs when you are awake but your spirit leaves your body and you become aware of this process. During this type of conscious OBE, a person will feel himself floating above his body and often realize that he is looking at his body from above.

Caroline Myss, in her outstanding audiotape series *Why People Don't Heal and How They Can*, tells an extraordinary story about a woman who was in a car accident. She was seriously injured and felt herself rise above her body until she was looking down at the accident scene. Suddenly she became aware of a passenger in a nearby car. The passenger was reverently praying for her. She noticed the license plate of the car, from her vantage point outside her body, and memorized it. Weeks later, after she was released from the hospital, she managed to trace the license plate and contact the passenger to thank her. The stunned passenger acknowledged that she had in fact witnessed the accident and prayed for the victims.

People are constantly having out-of-body experiences, they just are not aware of this fact. Even you, at this very moment, may be more out of your body than in it.

When you daydream or feel "spacey," you are traveling out of your body. Maybe you have been trying to solve a problem or have been rehearsing for an upcoming presentation. Maybe you were thinking about an attractive man or woman, or worrying about paying your bills, and before you realize it, hours have passed, you can't find your hairbrush or your car keys, and you have worn out the carpet from pacing back and forth.

Have you ever driven somewhere and upon arrival were shocked to realize that you could not really remember most of the drive? Or perhaps you intended to take a five-minute shower, but thirty minutes later you still have not even washed the shampoo out of your hair? Luckily, lots of us can at least function adequately enough when our spirit is busy elsewhere, but not always. Have you ever sat through a class and walked out without the slightest inkling of what was discussed? Wherever you were traveling to was much more interesting than what was happening in the classroom.

Every person has a different way of operating their body. Artists and writers tend to spend more time out of their body because this is where they have greater access to creative ideas. People who choose careers as policemen, firemen, surgeons, or accountants tend to spend more time in their body because they must constantly be focused on what is happening in their environment in the present moment. While these two types of people can complement each other's deficiencies, oftentimes their coupling is disastrous because they have a hard time understanding each other. Those of us lost in space (who can't get ourselves out of the house before noon) can be pretty maddening to deal with. However, those of you who try to cut in on our space travel time by imposing your rigid schedule and rules of organization can be equally annoying.

In cases of child abuse and neglect, it is common for the child's spirit to escape far from the body and to let other energies or spirits come in to operate the body. This is why there is a high correlation between child abuse and dissociative disorders such as multiple personality disorder. Epilepsy, catatonic schizophrenia, autism, senility, and many other disorders are related to the spirit's precarious relationship with the body. The fact that there are also biochemical or physical manifestations of these conditions in no way undermines the validity of this spiritual separation theory; unfortunately, modern medicine tends only to focus on the biological. While medications can placate parts of the brain enough to coax the spirit to integrate better with the body, taking pills without addressing the spirit's needs is like putting bandaids on an amputated limb.

A sign that part of your spirit has vacated the premises of your body is when you feel constant boredom or sadness, or like something is missing from your life but you can't figure out what it is. What is missing may be you!

Moving your spirit in and out of your body can be very simple. Oftentimes, all that is necessary is for you to focus on wherever you want your spirit to be, and then imagine and/or postulate that it is going to that desired location. Play around with this and notice the difference. Also, throughout the day, before you make an adjustment, close your eyes and ask yourself, "Where am I?" You are sure to get some amusing answers!

Healers of all traditions, from Native American shamans to East Indian gurus, have known about soul travel since the beginning of time. When I first met healer Manuel Lukingan at his acupuncture clinic in Baguio City, Philippines, he asked me to read some papers he had written in order to correct his English. I was surprised to find an essay entitled "Paypay," which translates in his dialect as "Calling for the Spirit Left Behind." I include it here with Manuel's permission because it corresponds so closely to the clairvoyant information I accumulated during readings prior to my arrival in the Philippines and demonstrates the universality of some of the concepts just mentioned regarding soul travel. This essay is based on stories told to Manuel by his "tribal elders" from Data, in the Mountain Province, where people still live in grass huts with no running water or electricity. He wrote:

Paypay: most victims of this strange illness are young children at an age where the emotional, mental and spiritual being is not formidable enough to protect itself. The victim's soul is said to have been left behind somewhere, sometimes in a physical location he previously occupied. Only a few people who are revered as psychic could see or understand the circumstances of how, when and where this occurred. Sometimes, the spirit of those victims is cordially invited or attracted by other spirits in other places as a result of being hurt by accident or cruelty, and the spirit is left behind. In these cases, the child will exhibit a depressed demeanor, engage in unusual crying, unusual sensitivity but zero communication, and suffer from standing body hair, and sleep and eating disorders. In these cases a healer, often an old woman, along with the parents, will return to the area where the child's spirit left, such as the seashore, and call it back by telling it how much it has been missed and promising it food and nurturance. Unfortunately this primitive practice that has helped so many people has been discarded by modern allopathic doctors who have no understanding of the spirit.

Retrieving your spirit, or energy, is often as simple as willing it so. Chapter 8 is devoted to techniques that can help you with this process. In some instances, help from a healer or spiritualistic therapist is needed, particularly when intense trauma resulted in the spirit's long-term departure, or when another spirit has taken over the body (see chapters 22–25).

Exchanging Energies

Clairvoyantly, I have seen that there are minute threads of energy, in the form of light, connecting everybody and everything together. Without these minute connections, we could not exist or communicate. The more intimate we are with a particular person, or the stronger our spiritual agreement, the larger or more dense these connections or cords of energy become.

Your energy has the ability to be immediately transported through space or time. When you have a thought, that thought is made of energy. Your thoughts are not just mental processes, but energetic ones.

When you think of someone else, it is because that person's energy has entered or is remaining in your own energetic field, or because your energy has just traveled over to that person, or has been there for a while. In a similar manner, when you think of your work at the end of the day, when you think about a project, when you remember the past or worry about the future, your energy has traveled and is engaging with these things. If we could be paid for all the hours that our energy and not just our physical body was at work, we would surely be wealthy! Your emotions and your pain are also energies that can travel outside of your body, sometimes even faster than you can experience them. These examples demonstrate how psychic abilities such as clairsentience, clairaudience, and clairvoyance are possible.

In order to be influenced by someone else's energy, or vice versa, it is not at all necessary that either the recipient or sender be aware of the energy exchange or its effects. Sometimes one or both parties will even consciously intend the opposite reaction, as is often the case when the energy of protection is involved. Many times I have read a person who was suffering from confusion, self-doubt, and anxiety about a course of action that they had previously felt very enthusiastic about. It soon became apparent that the source of these nagging emotions was nothing more than their silently nagging mother or sibling!

These relatives had perfectly honorable intentions and were attempting to "protect" their loved ones through prayer, visualization, or just their "love." But what was really happening was that the worries and fear behind the prayers and protection were what was being transmitted, so that my clients were suffering far more from this energy than from whatever misfortune their relatives were hoping to protect them from. In many cases, the relatives outwardly gave their blessings and said nothing to indicate that they were worried. This made it especially difficult for my clients to recognize and understand what was happening. Usually, the most difficult energies to deal with are the ones that come from family members and close friends who "love" us. Because we care about them and their opinions, we are much more vulnerable to their energy than even to some stranger who is consciously using his energy to harm us.

The point of being able to recognize when you are being affected by someone else's energy is not so you can then confront them or blame them or avoid them (although in some cases confrontation or avoidance may be the most advantageous course of action), but rather so you can do whatever is necessary to release the energy. Frequently, the moment I look at or point out the foreign energy in someone's aura, they will release it, provided they are no longer in agreement to having it there. This is basically what a clairvoyant healing is about (see chapter 21). However, sometimes people want to keep foreign energy in their body and energy field, despite the consequences, because it has been there for a long time or it is giving them the energy they personally lack. They are comfortable with the energy and think they need it. This is what happens in codependent relationships.

In light of all of this, it is clear that sometimes the best thing you can do for someone you care about is to not even think about them, especially if you have an opposing opinion about the course of action they are taking. When you worry about what someone is doing (such as their choice of boyfriend) or try to convince them that they are wrong, what you are essentially doing is questioning God or the God within them. You are preventing them from learning the life lessons they may really need to learn. You may be pulling them off their true path. Even though you have the best intentions, you may be committing some major spiritual no-noes, and in the end this may severely backfire on you.

This is not to say that you should not pray for people. Prayer can be extremely helpful if done properly. It's essential that you choose not only your words, but your thoughts and intentions behind your prayer wisely. Rather than praying for the specific effect you want for the person (or even what you are certain the person wants), pray instead that God or the universe will help the person on their spiritual path, whatever that is. Sometimes a spirit wants to have a particular unpleasant experience, even though their ego may be in total resistance. Sometimes a person is meant to become injured or even die, and the most loving thing you can possibly do is to allow this to happen with grace.

Your Energy versus Someone Else's Energy

Your spirit is made up purely of energy, while your body is made up of energy and matter corresponding to physical laws. The energy of your spirit and body is the part of you that survives after you die and that is busy while you are sleeping. It is the part of you that is engaged when you are meditating or using your psychic abilities.

Your energy is analogous to your DNA. Every living creature on the planet is made up of the same materials or stuff, but the way it is organized or coded makes it unique to you. It is for this reason that the energy that works best for you in your body is not that of your mother (unless you are a fetus), or your lover (unless you are in the middle of sexual intercourse!), or your guru, or even your favorite ascended master. *The best energy, or fuel, for your body is your own.* If you don't believe this, then take a look at the physical health of the many psychics, healers, and channelers who don't make a point of clearing out the foreign energies after completing their work. These people are usually overweight and suffer from a variety of physical and even emotional problems.

It amuses and disturbs me when people involved in the "New Age" movement declare, "I'll give you some energy" or "I got so much energy from being around those people!" Yes, sometimes when another person is happy, excited, and enthusiastic, you can absorb this energy and feel great yourself. But often you don't just get a single dose of foreign energy, but the establishment of a lasting link via an energetic cord, so that when your companion's jovial mood eventually sours (most people are not in a state of bliss twenty-four hours a day!), the nature of the energy you were so greedily sucking into your heart chakra won't seem so appetizing! Even worse, if you are feeding off someone else's energy, they may start to lose so much of their own that they feel depleted and exhausted. You may also inadvertently send over some of your own pain and grief through the energy cord you unintentionally created.

I have clairvoyantly observed the detrimental effects of foreign energies on hundreds of people. Sometimes these people are my clients, or readees, and sometimes these people are the unwitting recipients of the energy of my clients. This foreign energy can cause confusion, exhaustion, sadness, discomfort, pain, illness, and even death. It can keep people from loving themselves and others. It can keep them not only from achieving their dreams, but from even recognizing them.

As mentioned earlier, we are all energetically connected; if we were not, we would not be able to communicate and probably could not exist. So the exchange of energy is natural and desirable. What I am talking about here is when the amount of energy, or the force behind the energy exchange, is extreme or unbalanced. When performing readings, we always want to be aware of how we are exchanging energies with our clients in order to protect both parties.

Absorbing the Energy of Others

People who are particularly vulnerable to this type of extreme energy exchange are those who are "natural healers." These natural healers are people who care deeply about other people and do whatever they can to ease the suffering of others, sometimes to the detriment of their own well-being. These caring people often take on the professional roles of psychics, social workers, nurses, therapists, etc.

There are some very powerful spiritual healers, such as Native American shamans and East Indian yogis, who purposefully take on the disease or illness of another person in order to heal them. Sometimes these healers are then immediately able to release this illness from their own body, but not always. Sometimes these healers actually choose to suffer from someone else's illness on a long-term basis or even die from it because they have some spiritual agreement to absorb the karma of those they help. People who are natural healers (yourself, for example) also do the same thing, only unconsciously.

From my own personal experience as a healer by nature and study and profession, I have both consciously and unconsciously performed this method of healing. I can say with certainty that for myself and most people, taking on the suffering of your clients is not a prerequisite for being a good healer! Also, most of you have enough of your own karma to work through without the additional burden of anyone else's. So I don't advise trying this at home.

On a few occasions when my baby, Manny, was suffering from intense stomach pains and screaming out in agony, I prayed out of desperation that his pain would be transferred to me. Of course there were other healing techniques I could have employed, but they required more patience and rationality. My prayers were granted, and my son seemed to have immediate relief; however, I was then stuck with some hardcore pain that was so bad I almost wished that it would return to him! I was in so much pain I could barely care for Manny and feared I was going to have to call the paramedics. It was clear to me that if I chose to continue this type of healing, my profession would be short-lived and so would I. Fortunately, there are many other healing methods that are highly effective and do not require the healer to take on the suffering of clients. These are the techniques that will be focused on in this book.

Taking on Other People's Problems

A few years ago, I had a frightening experience with this type of unintentional "natural healing." I was leaving a party one Saturday night in Berkeley, California. I had not had any alcohol to drink. On the way to the car, we encountered a woman who appeared to be mentally ill. Her hair was a mess and she was wailing, "Someone help me! I can't find my home." I was mortified at her predicament and wanted to do something to help her, but my companion insisted that she was merely intoxicated and hurried me along.

Once in my car, I felt remorse about not assisting the poor woman, but I put in one of my favorite CDs and by the time I reached my apartment complex, I had forgotten her. I drove into the underground parking garage, parked my car, and entered the elevator. I exited onto the second floor and abruptly halted in confusion. I did not know which way to go and I could not remember my apartment number, even though I had lived in the same apartment for more than two years. I was completely disoriented; every door looked the same. I meandered from one door to the next, desperate for some sign that this was where I lived, becoming more and more confused and frightened. I wondered if I was having a stroke or if someone had slipped some LSD into my drink! Finally I let out a yelp of relief when I saw my companion (a fellow clairvoyant student) standing in the door of apartment number 212. I tearfully described my perplexing loss of memory and he laughed. "You were healing that woman. You took on her confusion. Just ground yourself and you will be fine."

"How do you know?" I implored.

He explained, "Don't you remember what she was muttering: 'Help me! I am lost. I can't find my home . . .' That's why you suddenly could not find yours!" Hmm, I hated to admit it, but he was right.

So how do you know if you are taking on the suffering of your clients, friends, family, and even street people? A common sign that you are taking on their problem as your own is if you are talking to one of them or thinking about them and suddenly you start to feel that their situation is hopeless, as if there is no solution. Another sign is when you feel a tremendous urgency to act immediately, or if you can't stop thinking about them and feel stressed by their situation. While this may fit your definition of "caring," any experienced social worker or therapist will also recognize this as a certain road to burnout.

On an emotional level, when you take on someone else's problem, then you can no longer really objectively help them, especially when this occurs during a reading or a healing. It's like attempting to save a drowning person when you are drowning yourself. Also, as already noted, you may be encroaching on another's spiritual path, which is presenting a difficult life lesson for the person to learn. When you take on someone else's energy or problem and try to solve it as your own, you are in a sense taking on some of their karma that they themselves need to work through.

This in no way means that you should not continue to help others or be supportive or care about them deeply. It is really just a matter of pulling back your energy, understanding that you are trying to solve a problem that is not truly your own, and getting some emotional distance so you can view their situation more objectively and effectively. Sometimes the simplest method of achieving this is to quietly state to yourself, "This is not my problem," even while you are in the process of healing them through doing a reading, spiritual healing, counseling session, making a donation, etc.

CHAPTER 4

MEI Pictures and Matching Pictures

Mental/Emotional Image (MEI) pictures are concentrated pockets of emotional energy and corresponding thoughts/ideas/beliefs that have accumulated in a certain location of our body. These pockets of energy are formed over time and are records of our experiences with corresponding feelings and thoughts about the experiences. They are frames of reference that motivate and control human perception; they dictate the manner in which people interpret and react to every aspect of life. Clairvoyants see this coagulated grouping of thoughtforms, emotions, and memories in the form of images or pictures, thus the term *Mental/Emotional Image picture.*

Some MEI pictures are born from an initial emotionally charged or traumatic experience. Oftentimes they were created centuries ago during a person's former incarnation (past life). This experience forms a core of energy that acts like a magnet for similar experiences and energies. Over time this collection of experiences can have a snowball effect. They can become extremely emotionally charged and have quite a strong influence on one's perceptions, attitude, and lifestyle. Some people believe that when we were initially created as spirits, we were essentially a "clean slate." We did not have any of these pictures. Over time we become polluted, clouded, and dimmed by the accumulation of these emotional and mental energies.

A core MEI picture is one that is developed early and over time attracts similar but less emotionally charged pictures. Many of our core MEI pictures were given to us by other people, early in our lives. They might have been handed over quite blatantly, as when a parent or teacher verbally tells us that we are defective in some way, or the picture could have been sent over energetically through telepathic thoughtforms.

As we move through everyday life, we are constantly being bombarded by other people's thoughtforms. Our self-esteem is very closely tied to how other people perceive us or how we think they perceive us, as well as the energy that they send (and that we accept). You may have noticed that when involved in certain intimate relationships, your self-esteem either rises or declines. This is largely because you are reading and to some extent buying in to the pictures that your significant other has of you, which may be totally unrelated to who you really are, but resonate with energy already in your aura.

MEI pictures can block our energy flow in a particular part of our body or energy field. They also create pockets of vulnerability. When a spirit or person wants something from us, they will usually plug into an MEI picture. During a clairvoyant reading/healing, it is helpful not only to uncover foreign energies in the chakras and aura, but also to look at what pictures these energies are attached to and then to describe these pictures. Otherwise, the foreign energy or similar energies may reattach themselves.

Not only do these pictures or pockets of energy attract similar experiences, they attract people into our lives who join us in playing out these experiences and who possess similar pictures, which are referred to as *matching pictures*. When someone has a matching picture with us, they have usually gone through similar life experiences. The people who are closest to us often have many matching pictures with us. Usually people who come to us for readings or healings have matching pictures with us, or one major core picture, which we are both working on at the time of the reading. Initially, this may be difficult to identify because their personalities and lives may seem quite different from our own.

In order to effect change in a person, these pictures need to be de-energized, illuminated, destroyed, or replaced. Just as accumulating these pictures is a natural process, so is discarding them. That is why we attract people in our lives with matching pictures. Every experience, event, person, etc., that we meet provides the opportunity to work through our MEI pictures so that these pictures need not control us. As already mentioned, oftentimes the energy from these experiences will glob onto the core pocket of energy to give it even more power. Just as frequently, these experiences or people will "light up" or activate the emotional energy from the picture so that we can reexperience it, release it, and move on.

Psychologists have observed for a long time that people exhibit patterns in their life that pertain to their experiences and relationships. You yourself have probably noticed how you tend to attract the same sort of love interest in your life or the same conflicts at work. When you send the intention out into the universe (through determination) that you plan to break this pattern and not repeat past mistakes, this sets a healing process in motion. The universe's response will be to send a person or experience into your life that will stimulate the core energies so you can eventually release this type of programming. In some cases you may encounter a string of unbelievably similar people within a frightfully short period of time, especially if you live in high-energy places like Sedona, Arizona, where I live, or when your determination to heal yourself is relentless.

I believe that when yogis or Buddhists talk about attaining "enlightenment" and "nonattachment," they are in a sense referring to eliminating these pictures. Since we can see these pictures during a clairvoyant reading, it is possible to work with them through clairvoyant healing by deenergizing the pictures so they have less power over our clients.

As healers, we do have the ability to actually remove a picture from the readee's energy field. But caution and discretion is advised in this area, since we may then be tampering with Mother Nature and our client's spiritual blueprint. Some spirits have worked very hard to accumulate their experiences and don't want some meddlesome psychic taking them away! Also, people ground through pictures in order to feel secure. If the MEI picture is ripped away from them too suddenly, the client may not be able to cope. What is more advisable is to identify these pictures and describe them to the client and let them know when they have "fallen into a picture" or are "stuck in a picture."

When someone is trapped inside an MEI picture, they are drowning inside a concept and emotion; they can't see the forest for the trees. This MEI picture will totally color their world. It is as if they had a paper bag over their head. Inside the bag are old snapshots of past situations and limited statements about life. The problem is not that they are trapped inside a paper bag, but that they don't know they are. The most helpful thing a psychic can do is remind the person that they are trapped within the confines of the MEI picture so they can calm down and become more of a neutral observer to their process. Oftentimes this reminder is all they need so they can begin to climb out of the picture where they can see things from a more balanced and realistic viewpoint, which will have a calming effect on their emotional state. They can then decide whether they wish to hold on to this picture or begin to establish a plan to work through the picture.

Sometimes a client will have been working on a picture for quite some time and is looking for the final catalyst to help them discard or "blow" the picture (a term used in clairvoyant training circles because you can visualize the picture exploding), which is the clairvoyant reading. However, some people are so deeply embedded in the MEI picture and controlled by it that if you try to make them aware of this fact, they will become very angry and accuse you of being insensitive.

When a psychic encounters a highly charged mental image picture and has a matching picture of their own, it may be difficult to read this picture or to talk about it. Imagine trying to read a book in the middle of a cyclone! The charge can be lessened by visually draining the emotional energy off the picture, while leaving the picture intact (see chapter 13). Since energy moves when it is observed, a psychic helps people to blow their pictures even when neither of them have an intellectual understanding or awareness of this process.

I make a point of getting at least a couple intensive readings a year from reliable clairvoyants in order to discover where I have fallen into a rut (picture) in my thinking and actions. Often a reading will set the stage for a paradigm shift, which makes room for a whole new set of experiences to enter into my life. Sometimes a client will come for a reading who may not be ready for lifetimes to work through certain pictures, but has been sent by God or the universe to the clairvoyant because the clairvoyant is ready to discard the matching picture. This is one of the main benefits of performing a reading and why it's a good idea for students to perform readings on a frequent and consistent basis. Reading helps move and release energy for both the readee and the reader.

Working Through MEI Pictures in Your Readings

The old adage "can't see the forest through the trees" can be applied aptly to MEI pictures: you don't see them when you are in the midst of them. During a clairvoyant reading, there are a few telltale signs you can watch for that will let you know when you have a matching MEI pictures with your readee. The more you have in common with your readee, the more matching pictures you have. Your readee might be so similar to you in terms of age, life experiences, issues, problems, and even appearance that there will be doubt that this person has been sent to you to help you work through your pictures.

When you encounter several people who could be your twin in a short period of time, you will know that you are getting close to working through a huge core picture, and your awe for the perfection of the universe and the divine order of things will really grow. Initially, you may be sent a readee who seems extremely different from you, but as your reading progresses, you will discover that you do share a similar issue and thus a matching picture.

Sometimes you will have nothing in common with the readee, but they might be very similar to a person in your life who was responsible for the formation of a picture, such as a parent or spouse. In this case, you may feel a strong aversion to reading this person, even before you begin the reading, and strong emotions during the reading (often anger or fear) will emerge.

As a clairvoyant reader, any time you discover that you are experiencing an emotion, it is helpful to acknowledge to yourself that you are experiencing the emotion, to get into the center of your head (see chapter 9), and then ask God or your higher self to help you understand why you are feeling this emotion. The answer will come when the time is right. In following these steps, you will become more of an observer to your emotional state and less of a victim to it. Other indicators that you have a matching picture with your client or are on the verge of "blowing" a core picture are when you are reading along and suddenly become highly emotional or can no longer access your clairvoyance.

MEI pictures affect clairvoyants not only during readings, but in their everyday lives. Any strong judgment or idea about how things should be or must be is really just an MEI picture. One way to tell that you are trapped in an MEI picture is when you are resisting a certain situation or convinced that there is only one way to deal with a situation, but that way is not working. We are most likely trapped in an MEI picture when we are in competition with God (for example, making statements such as "my life is not supposed to be like this"); when we are resisting the hand that God or the universe has dealt us (resisting is different than trying to make positive changes; there is no grace in resistance); or when we are certain of how things are supposed to be despite the fact they are not that way. These are the pictures that create our pain.

In addition to giving and receiving readings, watching movies can also help with the process of moving through and freeing ourselves of pictures that do not serve us. Just as with any experience in life, there is a spiritual reason why we see a particular movie at a particular time. Since movies consist of a string of millions of mental image pictures derived from the screenwriters, directors, and actors, they will certainly light up our own pictures. The more a person performs clairvoyant readings, the more adept they will become at moving though energy and pictures. I actually start to feel sluggish if I have stopped giving readings for a while, and often will start to watch a ridiculous number of movies until I resume a heavier reading schedule. Books can also have a similar cathartic effect. People who do not perform readings or watch movies are still naturally working through MEI pictures every time they converse with people or encounter new situations, only their process may be much slower and more painful if done unconsciously.

Conversely, there are many healers and psychics who get stuck in their pictures instead of working through them, and suffer more than the average person who is not doing any kind of energy work. These "sick" psychics and healers become drained and even traumatized because they don't know how recognize and work with their matching pictures and are not using the tools presented in this book or elsewhere for releasing energy and revitalizing their own energy source (see chapters 7–12).

Upon blowing or working through a core picture, there is going to be a period of adjustment, referred to as a growth period. During this period, all kinds of emotions, possibly conflicting ones, may arise, and it can feel very unsettling because you will have just discarded what you previously thought was you, but was really just a bunch of past time perceptions, ideas, and emotions. For a while you may find yourself hanging in midair, not knowing where you will land or even who you are. You may also experience grief for all the time you wasted being caught up in those silly pictures. Just remember to go easy on yourself; you were exactly where you needed to be when you were there, just as you are perfect as you are now.

CHAPTER 5

Clairvoyant Images

Clairvoyant images are essentially made up of the same stuff as dream images and visual pictures evoked through memory, imagination and visualization. Within our minds we have what my teachers called, for lack of a better term, "the picture-making apparatus or machine." This energetic apparatus seems to be located within the area of the sixth chakra, behind the physical forehead area. Many people refer to this as the third eye. Clairvoyant images are derived from the brain as well as from a universal source. They can be sent through both verbal and tele-pathic communication to other individuals or through visualization and prayer out into the universe where they can create and manifest physical representations (see chapter 12).

Clairvoyant and dream images can have both literal and symbolic connotations. For example, during several readings I have clearly seen the image of a person wearing a nurse's uniform. Sometimes I subse-quently discovered that my readee was actually employed as a nurse. At other times it was clear that my client did not work as a nurse, but possessed a nurse's caring and healing nature, which was symbolized by nurse's attire.

One of the most difficult aspects of performing a clairvoyant read-ing is knowing when an image is intended as literal or symbolic. Obvi-ously, if one misinterprets a symbolic image as a literal one, it will not only decrease the accuracy of the reading, but may cause the readee distress. For example, if you see an image of your readee stretched out in a coffin beneath a tombstone, this could literally mean that your readee is going to physically die. However, it may also symbolize dramatic change, as in a spiritual death.

There are several ways to deal with the problem of how to interpret a clairvoyant image. Oftentimes, along with a clairvoyant image you will receive a bonus from your intuition or knowingness (the psychic ability located in your seventh chakra), which gives you instant awareness of what it is you are looking at. Unfortunately this is not always the case, especially for beginning clairvoyant students. So first, I recommend that if you are confused as to whether an image should be interpreted symbolically or literally, you ask the image to show you another image that will provide more clarity. With patience and perseverance, your request will be granted more often than not.

During one reading, I saw the image of a heart that looked all black and that seemed to be struggling to continue beating. Unsure of the meaning of this image, I further probed the image by visualizing the weak heart and directing it to reveal more details. This time I saw an image of my client lying in a hospital bed with an IV in his arm, which told me I was looking at a literal image.

When further prompting of a questionable image fails to produce useful clues, you can tell your client, "I am seeing this image, but I don't know what it means." Of course discretion must be used when the literal interpretation points to something serious, like a death or severe illness or injury. It gets tricky when seeing information regarding the physical body because sometimes an illness may not yet be visual or noticeable to the readee but will already be having an effect on the energetic body. In the above-mentioned reading, I gently "tested the waters" with my client with the question, "Have you been experiencing any health problems lately?" My readee confirmed that he had recently had open-heart surgery, which helped me know that I was on the right track and further confirmed that the image did have a literal meaning.

During another reading on a female client, I again saw an image of a heart. It appeared to be bleeding and looked mutilated or crushed. This time further clairvoyant questioning of the image displayed pictures of an angry man jumping on her chest. Because it was unlikely that a man had literally been jumping on her heart, I was fairly certain I was dealing with symbolism. My intuition/knowingness and logical understanding of the effects of emotional trauma on the physical body told me that if my client did not release the pain that was associated with the man in the image, she could be vulnerable to a physical heart attack. As in most readings of this type, I described the symbolic images but also recommended that she follow up with a medical examination just in case the image also had a literal meaning. She later revealed that her husband of twenty-five years had betrayed her, and that she had undergone heart surgery a year before.

When training beginning clairvoyant students, I advise against asking the readee too many questions, since this pulls the students from their reading space and tempts them to rely on a source other than their own clairvoyance. Also, the readee may give an incorrect response (sometimes intentionally, sometimes inadvertently), which will confuse and negatively impact the certainty of the fledgling student. It also puts pressure on the readee to communicate and validate the student, which is not the readee's responsibility since they are there to receive.

When doing a clairvoyant reading, I suggest that you get out of your logical mind and resist the urge to interpret everything you see. If the clairvoyant image is not accompanied by a clear knowing, then simply describe the image precisely as you see it. Whenever I have been wrong about information in a reading, it was due to my logical interpretation and not to the image itself. Clairvoyant images are almost always pure and do not lie. There is always a reason a particular image is being generated. You don't always need to know the reason or the meaning for every image. You'll be surprised at how often your client knows exactly what is meant by the imagery you have described. Sometimes your client will not want you to know the meaning, and that is why you aren't getting the information.

Clairvoyant images are generated by the mind of the clairvoyant, by the mind of the person receiving the reading, or from a third party such as another spirit or one of the subjects of the reading. Clairvoyant images also come from what is sometimes referred to as the *universal mind* or the *collective unconscious* (a term coined by Carl Jung). Sometimes your readee will understand the meaning of the images you are looking at before you do because the images have been borrowed from their personal library rather than yours. Sometimes you won't be able to interpret an image because you are stuck inside an MEI picture (see chapter 4).

During a reading with a client named Sarah, I saw an image of a glowing golden heart that seemed to have been carefully placed in the back seat of a black limousine. I had absolutely no idea what this meant, and further probing did not help. I almost disregarded this image because it did not make sense to me, but fortunately I obeyed my intuition and communicated the vision to Sarah. She immediately burst into tears and explained that her father used to be a limousine driver and had given her a small golden locket in the shape of a heart a few days before he died. I felt that this image was generated by both her and her deceased father. The image really had no personal meaning for me.

During another reading, I was asked by a mother and daughter to explain the questionable death of young man who had been a close friend of the family. I immediately saw an image of a man lying on his side, his head casually propped up by one arm. He was smiling. Because it was uncommon for me to notice the position in which someone is lying during a reading, I suspected that this must be significant, although I had no idea why. I described the image, which prompted the mother to yank out her wallet and thrust a photograph into my hands. The photograph was of a young man lying in that exact position, with a huge grin on his face. I felt that this image was generated by either the man who had died or the women I was reading. These woman later revealed that they initially had doubts as to the authenticity of my reading abilities. Unbeknownst to me, I had participated in a demonstration that won their confidence so that they were able to trust the subsequent information I revealed regarding this man's mysterious death.

While I vehemently avoid the game of "prove it" or "test the psychic," I began making it a general practice at the beginning of a reading to ask my clairvoyance to give me a symbol related to the person in question so that my client and I would both know that I was tuned in to the correct person. This request has become so automatic that I no longer consciously have to voice or think about it; oftentimes the first image that comes to me in a reading is this telltale symbol.

After many years of doing readings, I have found that there is a direct correlation between the clarity of my images and the clairvoyant ability and permissiveness of my readee. When my clairvoyance is operating at full force, it is usually because my readee is naturally very open to their own clairvoyance. When I can't see anything, it is because this person does not have permission (their own or from others) to use their clairvoyance. When I see very amusing images, it is usually because my readee has a good sense of humor, just as dramatic images seem to come from dramatic clients. When I see images depicting one problem after another, it is usually because my readee is focused on problems. When I see lots of sexual images . . . well, you guessed it!

Usually, a symbol becomes a symbol because a person or entire culture had an experience with an object and then later the object was used to represent that experience. The swastika was used by the Nazi Germans, so now when most people encounter this symbol, they think of hatred and intolerance, although that was not its original meaning. As a child, I had an extreme fear of bugs, so when I see images of bugs surrounding a person, these bugs symbolize some kind of fear-producing agent in the readee's life (this has been confirmed on numerous occasions by my clients).

In the psychic realms, since there really is no time or space, the usual sequential process of symbolism can be reversed, so that the clairvoyant or readee encounters a seemingly meaningless and unfamiliar object during a reading and only later do they have a personal experience with this object that gives the object significance.

Clairvoyant images are almost like living entities. They have a life of their own, and they reveal themselves in mysterious ways. As a beginning clairvoyant student, it is easy to become frustrated with the mischievous elusiveness of these enigmas. I encourage you to treat these visions as your personal teacher or guru. At times your teacher will give you an immediate response and tell you exactly what you want to know in very straightforward terms. At other times they will send you blindfolded and stumbling into the forest so that you discover your answers through direct experience. Some of the most helpful traits a clairvoyant can have are patience, determination, and the ability to apply these simultaneously, with grace.

Library of Symbols

Over the years, I have built up a collection of symbolic images that help me pick up and interpret information more quickly and efficiently during a reading. I did not create them with my logical mind; rather they spontaneously and repeatedly appeared to me in my readings and later in dreams as well. On many occasions, these particular symbols appeared to other psychics when they were reading me. These particular symbols are shortcuts and signposts that provide information to me in a concise and easily identifiable manner. These images are animated; they move. They interact with other images to tell a particular story about the person I am reading. Their relationship to other images provides even more information than the image itself.

Clairvoyant symbols operate in the same way as symbols in real life. When you drive down the street, you will often see a stop sign. A stop sign is an easily identified and understood symbol that communicates the message that you need to stop. In order to fully understand its meaning, you need to look at its relationship to its location and to other cars and people, including yourself. A stop sign will always mean stop, but it may not be telling you to stop if it is positioned across the street or if it is turned away from you. In the same way, when a stop sign appears to me in a clairvoyant reading, I understand that someone is saying stop, but I need to look further to find out who is holding the stop sign, who is reading it, and why they are saying stop.

Some of the images I have accumulated in my personal clairvoyant library are those of a window, an apple, a tree, champagne glasses, a piano, a ceiling, a staircase, a mirror, a playground swing, a sun, and a stop sign. In chapter 16, I offer suggestions on how you can utilize some of these symbols to help you navigate your way through a reading. Over time, you as a clairvoyant will develop your own library of symbolic images. The more you work with them, the richer they will become and the more they will appear in your dreams and other aspects of your waking life.

PART 2

The Psychic Tools

CHAPTER 6

Introduction to the Psychic Tools

The psychic tools are visualization techniques that can be utilized throughout a psychic reading as well as in your daily life. When performed in solitude, they also form a simple yet powerful method of meditation. These clairvoyant tools can help you prepare to do readings and healings on other people by strengthening your visualization abilities. They will protect and energize you, help you maintain boundaries, aid in the release of foreign or unwanted energies, help you be in present time, facilitate a sense of calmness and neutrality, and strengthen the communication between you and your innermost self. In other words, these are self-healing techniques. They are also methods that can later be used in the healing of others. In the following chapters, I will explain the purpose and value of each tool and then provide a step-by-step description of how to use each one.

When you are visualizing something, you are not "just using your imagination," a popular expression that implies you are merely playing around with some mental processes that go no further than your mind. As I already described in previous chapters, your thoughts consist of energy. This energy can be propelled outward into the universe to elicit a response. Likewise, when you form a mental image in your mind, you are actually organizing energy into a powerful form that may influence other energies in yourself (mind, spirit, and body) and in other people. Therefore, when you are visualizing or utilizing the "psychic tools," you will actually be manipulating, moving, and changing energy. Sometimes this will be accompanied by an obvious corresponding physical sensation or emotional response. For example, when you ground, you may feel pain pumping out of your foot; when you call back your energy, you may feel a tingling or pulsating sensation in your head.

Other people can also feel the effects of your visualizations. At the beginning of the reading, while my client is sitting across from me, I prepare for the reading by running through my repertoire of psychic tools. On several occasions, my more sensitive clients (usually other professional psychics who are unaware of these tools, but are in desperate need of them) have suspiciously asked, "What are you doing to me? I can feel all kind of things happening with my energy." Surprised, I assured them, "I was not doing anything to you. I was totally focused on myself. In fact, for a few moments there I was not even conscious of you being in the room. I was grounding myself and running my earth and cosmic energies. Your body was just matching my own."

Beware of Expectations

In addition to reaping the benefits of the psychic tools that will be presented in subsequent chapters, sometimes it is the corresponding physical sensations that propel the novice clairvoyant from a state of faith to one of certainty. However, I must caution that the most certain road to failure and frustration is the one laden with expectations.

You will experience the psychic tools in your own unique way. Some of you will be blown away by your first visualization attempt and others will not feel a single thing. Some of you will find using the psychic tools to be fun, easy, and gratifying, while others will initially be frustrated and may call it quits before realizing the benefits. Some of you who have already been using similar techniques for years will appreciate the reminder that there are many paths to the same kingdom, while others will think that their techniques are superior and feel irritated by my suggestions. The important thing is to do what works for you. Sometimes, before you know what works, you need to have faith and experiment a bit. Some miracles occur instantaneously, while others take time and perseverance.

CHAPTER 7

Psychic Tool 1—Grounding

Webster's Vest Pocket Dictionary defines grounding as "a conductor that makes electrical connection with the earth or a framework." For animate and inanimate physical objects, grounding is achieved through the law of gravity. Gravity is defined in the same dictionary as "attraction of bodies towards the center of the earth." Without gravity, we would be plummeted into space and would not be able to exist on earth. We would be unstable, like a feather caught in a cyclone.

To some extent, our physical bodies are always grounded or connected to the earth (even when flying in an airplane, we are still connected to the earth's atmosphere by the gravitational pull, therefore we can walk down the aisle of the plane without floating away). But what about our energetic or spiritual bodies? Some people are more grounded than others, and our grounding, our connection with the earth, can change drastically from minute to minute. Oftentimes, when a person is experiencing stress, nervousness, pain, or extreme emotions, their spiritual body becomes ungrounded. When a person is ungrounded, even though their physical body is still attached to the earth, the rest of their energy may be all over the place. It might be soaring above their head, searching for a kinder and gentler abode; or it might be racing through whatever unfortunate person happens to be in their path.

People who lose things frequently, who become hysterical or "hyper," who are spacey, who have trouble following directions, or who are not conscious of what they are doing or feeling are often ungrounded (don't feel bad, most of those adjectives describe myself as well!). When you are ungrounded, you are much more vulnerable to becoming the effect of whatever or whoever is around you, and other people may find it difficult or annoying to be in your presence.

For example, if you are ungrounded and visit a friend who is also ungrounded and in a lousy mood, within minutes your original cheerful disposition may be replaced by your friend's grouchiness. Or if you are ungrounded and driving, not only might you become lost, you might also become as irritable as all the other drivers who are in a hurry, even though you have plenty of time to reach your destination (road rage would probably not occur if everyone were well grounded!). In the same respect, if you are ungrounded during a psychic reading, you will be more likely to match whatever negative energies are in the room.

The grounding of our spirit and even our physical body can be strengthened through the use of a grounding cord. This energetic vehicle will harness your energy so that you can focus and remain calm and strong even in the face of adversity.

Picture a thousand-year-old redwood tree with enormous roots going a half mile or more deep into the earth. Do you think a strong gust of wind or an overly enthusiastic lumberjack could knock over this tree? Not likely! Could this wind capsize a ship secured into the depths of the ocean by a rope as thick as a man and an iron anchor as large as the Empire State Building? Probably not! In the same way, if your body and spirit are connected into the earth by a strong energetic cord (achieved through visualization), then when your boss unexpectedly reprimands or fires you, when a mugger jumps out at you from the bushes, or when the person you are clairvoyantly reading suddenly leaps from their chair and starts barking like a dog, you will be able to retain your calm composure and respond rather than react. If this does not seem likely, then you are probably just not used to being grounded!

In addition to securing you to the earth and harnessing your energy, grounding is a very powerful and effective means of releasing negative energy or energy that is no longer serving you, as in the case of pain, anxiety, stress, unwanted thoughts, etc. Gravity not only pulls you toward the earth, but also everything in and around you. So your grounding cord can ground out everything and everyone that is in your body or energetic field that no longer serves you. Any worries, any emotion, any thoughts, any image, any pain, any problem, or anyone else's energy can be immediately released through your connection to the earth.

A grounding cord can be visualized as any object. A strong rope, a column of light, a string of flowers or stars, a waterfall, a tree, an extension of your legs, a hollow pipe, a hearty string of pearls, or a fluffy pink boa (for formal occasions!) are just a few possibilities. The grounding cord should be plugged into your first chakra (spinning energy center), located at the base of your spine. It extends and connects you to the center of the planet. In the realm of spirit, there is no time or space, so your grounding cord can instantaneously reach the center of the earth, and of course it can pass through whatever happens to be beneath you. You can ground anywhere, even from an airplane. However, grounding outside, with your feet touching the earth, is often the easiest.

While you can ground from any part of your body, I suggest grounding from your first chakra because this is the energy center that actually regulates the functioning of your lower body and its connection to the physical world. It is important to realize that even though this is where the connection point is located, you can easily release energy from any point of your body or energetic field, even from the top of your head. Just imagine whatever you wish to release within yourself dislodging itself effortlessly from wherever it is located, and immediately passing through your first chakra (as if that were a drain) and falling down your grounding cord until it is released into the center of the earth. Thanks to the gravitational pull of the earth, you don't really need to exert any effort. Just let gravity suck whatever you wish to release (you don't need to know what that is) down your cord.

Once whatever you are releasing reaches the center of the earth (which is scalding hot), it dissipates and returns to its original source, so you are not polluting or hurting the earth in any way. When you release another person from your energy field, you are actually freeing their energy so it can be returned to them. You are not hurting them in any way. You may experience feelings of guilt or fear when you imagine a loved one falling down your grounding cord. These feelings have to do with breaking your former agreement to heal, carry, support, and feed that person your energy, and with that person's resistance to detaching from your field. If you do feel guilty when you release someone down your cord, then ask yourself what color might represent that feeling and visualize the color releasing down your cord as well. Also remember that a person has no more right to be in your field than they do to touch your physical body or enter your home without your permission.

The following example will illustrate how to release a person from your energy field with the use of your grounding cord. Let's say that you keep thinking about your boss, who is worried about meeting some deadlines. You realize that you can't stop thinking about your boss because his energy is inside your head. Imagine that there are some trap doors at the bottom of your head. Then visualize your boss and his energy (ask yourself what color represents your boss' energy or assign it a color, and see that color releasing so that next time you see that color, you will know whose energy it is) falling through these doors and being sucked into your grounding cord, where he continues to fall until he reaches the center of the earth. Then see his image exploding or dissipating. If you become worried that you are hurting or irritating your boss by sending him into the fires of the earth, then visualize a color that represents the worried feeling and send it down your cord as well. Then imagine that his energy is being cleansed in the hot earth, and in your imagination watch it as it returns to his body, which you can postulate is growing happier and healthier as it fills up with his own essence.

Once you have grounded your body, it is important to make sure that your aura, or the energy field surrounding your body, is tucked into your grounding cord so that you can release whatever stubborn foreign energy may be trapped inside. This is easily accomplished by willfully tucking or inserting the entire circumference of your aura into your cord below your feet. Remember that your aura surrounds your entire body, including your head and feet. Even though the bottom of your aura is what is tucked into the cord, anything lodged in the top of your aura will be sucked downward by the gravitational pull. This is done through your imagination and intent. The more clearly you can visualize this, the more effective it will be.

You can practice grounding anytime, anywhere. I recommend practicing grounding when you are alone in meditation so you can really focus, as well as in public places so you can experience the difference. I suggest playing around with your grounding in a variety of situations, such as when dealing with a stressful family event, when attending a staff meeting, when running or doing aerobic exercise, when you are lost, and even when you are intoxicated!

When performing grounding the first few times, you may want to do it alone in a quiet place so you can feel free to release any emotions that may come up. Some people like to ground themselves in their car. While it is very helpful to be grounded when driving, you should be cautious because visualizing any of your psychic tools does take some concentration that will pull your attention away from anything else you are doing at that moment, which obviously can be dangerous when driving. Also, sometimes grounding may cause you to feel sleepy due to the various energies you are releasing, and this could cause further problems when driving

Grounding can be done when you are standing or sitting. In order to prepare yourself to perform clairvoyant readings, I suggest that you ground yourself while sitting in a chair, versus the floor, since you will usually read other people from a chair and what you do in your meditation space will create an automatic response in your reading space.

Some yogic postures and dance practices naturally ground a person, while others have the opposite effect. It is always good to ground yourself when beginning and ending any activity. If you engage in any type of spiritual/psychic practice that facilitates the release of your spirit or traveling of your energetic bodies, I highly advise that you ground yourself and call your energy back to your body at the completion of the session. Otherwise you may have a difficult time driving home or functioning in your daily life.

When you visualize your grounding or any other psychic tool, it is helpful to see it in as much detail as possible. With your grounding cord, you should occasionally check the connection points to make sure it is secure (one end connected to your first chakra, the other at the center of the earth). Sometimes you will have to willfully create the details of your cord, while at other times your cord will show itself to you in a form that appears spontaneously, without your conscious manipulation. When this happens, you are apt to be surprised and even impressed with the imagery that came from somewhere other than your logical mind. The important thing is to really see the cord in your imagination rather than just intellectually postulate that it is there. This attention to detail demands some discipline, but the results will be more fruitful.

If at any time you notice that your grounding cord has changed in a way you do not desire, or you feel uncomfortable with its appearance, or it appears damaged, or you see the image of someone you know in it, then it is a good idea to destroy this grounding cord and create a new one, preferably one that is in some way slightly different from the last. The reason for this is because your grounding may get polluted with the energies you have been trying to release, or may become the target of energies that wish to influence or control you. When you change your cord, those energies have a harder time locating you again.

If you are having difficulty visualizing a certain part of your cord, or you find it very difficult to concentrate when you attempt to create one, you are probably being affected by some foreign energy. This is similar to what happens with a clogged vacuum cleaner, a malfunctioning garbage disposal, the rusty pipes connected to your kitchen sink, or even your own intestines.

Destroying Your Grounding Cord

If there is foreign energy affecting your grounding, there is an easy solution: get rid of it! All you need to do is will that energy to go down your cord, or destroy it along with the cord and continue to create and destroy new ones until you are no longer experiencing the difficulty.

Destroying your grounding cord is very simple to do. Just imagine that you are rolling it up into a little ball, and then see that ball exploding or dissipating into nothingness. (If you are having any difficulties with destroying, read chapter 12.) There are also preventative measures you can take against attack of your grounding by postulating and imagining that your cord is impenetrable. You can even give it a protective shield similar to the one that protects the Starship Enterprise on *Star Trek*! Even if you have complete faith in the cleanliness of your grounding, it is still helpful to occasionally destroy and recreate it (even though it may seem easier to just keep the old one—sure, you'd also save time if you never took a bath or changed your clothes!).

Just like your energy and your mind, your grounding cord can easily get stuck in past time. The type, size, and nature of your grounding cord will change from day to day or even minute to minute. Sometimes a thin and light cord is sufficient, while during stressful times a super heavy-duty cord is in order.

One way to make sure that your cord is in present time is to create a new one in your imagination and write the date and time on it. You can also write your name on it with the same color as the clothes you are presently wearing. Then postulate that you are bringing your grounding cord into present time, in sync with where your body currently is, which is, and can only ever be, in the present. If you take a vacation, move to a new apartment, spend the night with a friend, etc., you should make sure that your grounding cord is connected to the earth below your present location and not where you were previously located. Jet lag and culture shock could be minimized and even prevented if most people understood the concept of grounding in present time.

Grounding Yourself

The following exercise can be performed in a number of ways. I suggest that you read the exercise through a few times and then attempt it. If you have difficulty recalling each step, you can attempt the exercise as you read along. Another effective method would be to dictate the words into a tape recorder and then play it back. You could also practice with a friend, taking turns reading the exercise to each other.

After performing this grounding exercise a few times, it will become natural, and you can then play around with creating your own grounding methods and individualized grounding cord. Give yourself at least ten minutes to perform the following exercise. The more time you spend grounding, the greater the benefits.

Close your eyes, sit in a chair with your feet touching the ground, and relax. Imagine that there is a very heavy and strong rope, weighing hundreds of tons, sitting under your chair. Picture this rope and all the details. Examine the fibers. How thick are they? In what way do they twist? What is the color of the rope? Is the rope consistent all the way down in terms of shape, color, and size? How long it is? How thick is it? Does the thickness change from top to bottom? Smell the rope. Taste it (oops, you may need to pull out some of the prickly fibers from your tongue!). Notice that the rope is hollow inside, and this hollow is lined with very strong and slippery metal. See both ends of the rope and notice if the rope is frayed at all or if there is a neat knot on each end. You are free to change anything about the rope that makes you doubt its strength or makes you uncomfortable.

Now, physically, pantomime picking up part of the rope. As you reach down under your chair, see yourself picking up one end.

Next, bring the end of the rope up to your first chakra, at the base of your spine. With your left hand (remember, you are holding the rope in your right hand), feel the base of your spine. See your first chakra at the base of your spine spinning like a washing machine.

Now you are going to insert one end of the rope into this spinning center. The knot on the rope is bigger than the chakra, so once it is in there, it will not fall out. See it in there. Tug on it. If it comes out, make the knot bigger, then try again until it is secure. You can always use some hearty glue to stick it in there and hold it in place, glue that cannot fail unless you wish it to come loose.

Now reach under your chair again and take hold of the other end of the rope. Also under your chair is a very heavy, very large cement brick. Loop the rope around the brick. Now, at the count of three, you are going to drop this rope into the earth. It is the kind of rope that can expand as long as it wants, even millions of miles. There are no time or spatial limitations when dealing with energy and your imagination, so it only takes a a millisecond to reach the center of the planet. This rope can penetrate any kind of physical matter, so even if you are at the top of a twenty-story apartment building or flying in an airplane, you will be able to ground.

Now see the rope in the center of the planet. What does the center of the planet look like? Is there molten lava? What color is it? If you are having any difficulty, you can even draw a circle around the brick and write "center of the planet" with your magic crayon. You may try tugging on the rope to see what happens to the brick. If it rises up a bit, you may want to secure it more firmly into the center of the planet. Congratulations, you have formed your grounding cord!

Now just watch this cord for a few minutes. Look at it from the top to the bottom. Notice how your body feels. Now that your cord is secure, it is time to release out of it. Since the gravity of the earth is naturally sucking all the foreign/negative energies out of you, your aura, and your cord, you don't have to exert any effort. Just relax and watch to see what is being released. If you feel yourself making an effort, then release this down your cord. If you are becoming distracted by thoughts about other people, your work, or various problems in your life, know this is the energy that you are releasing. Visualize these distractions in the form of an image or symbol and see them falling down your cord into the center of the planet.

At this time, it may be a good idea to ground your aura. Imagine that the part of your aura around your feet is melting into your grounding cord (which in this exercise is in the form of a rope). You may need to first expand the circumference of your rope so that all of your aura can be tucked into the rope. Now postulate that all foreign energies in your aura, even from the very top of it, are effortlessly falling down through your grounding cord into the center of the planet. When you are finished, you can thank your cord for its good work and then see the cord exploding into a million pieces. Once it is fully destroyed, create a new grounding cord. Introduce yourself to this new cord and ask it to keep you secure and help you release, throughout your day.

Now that you have released all the unwanted energies, it's important to fill yourself up with your own energy, which you will learn how to do in the next chapter.

Grounding Your Surroundings

Once you have mastered the concept of grounding yourself, it is important to ground your surroundings. Otherwise, the gravitational pull of your powerful grounding cord will inadvertently suck up whatever energies surround you, and these energies may overwhelm you. This is similar to what happens when you are vacuuming the floor and the nearby rug gets sucked into the vacuum cleaner as well, making it difficult to clean the portion of the floor you were concerned with. Sometimes the rug may even damage or break the vacuum cleaner. If your grounding cord sucks up all the energies in the room, then you will likely experience those energies, which would defeat the purpose of your grounding. The solution here is to give your surroundings (that is, the room you are sitting in) a grounding cord of their own. This will help cleanse the room, strengthen the power of your own grounding cord, and allow your cord to work just for you.

Visualize the room you are occupying. Imagine that you are drawing a column of golden light in each corner of the room. It is a column or pillar, much like in the Greek Coliseum or outside the typical white house. It is very wide and sturdy even though it is made of light. Each column runs from the ceiling of the room (it could extend upward to the roof) down to the floor. Once it reaches the floor it continues to extend below the floor, past the foundation of the house, down through the mud and rocks and water until it reaches into the center of the earth. Once you have at least one column in each corner of the room (some rooms have more then four corners so you could do a column for the other corner, but this is not essential), then make a column that is twice as thick in the center of the room, extending this one downward to the center of the earth. Next, connect each column in the corners to the one in the center of the room with lines of golden light. By the time you are finished, you will have what looks like a may pole.

Now you can command all the energy in the room that is not in alignment with you and your goals to leave the room through these columns of light. Imagine that the earth is effortlessly pulling down deep into its center the energy from people, spirits, or other entities; extraneous emotional energy; any energy that is getting in the way of your serenity, happiness, ability to accomplish your tasks, etc. As the energy releases, you can look to see what colors are falling down the columns, or you can just know that they are being released. As you do this, be aware of any physical sensations you may be feeling.

Once you have grounded the room, it's time to own it. Imagine that you are writing your name, in a color of your choice, across at least four of the walls. See your picture hanging on the wall as well.

Once you have finished grounding and owning the room, you can go on to ground your entire house, office, etc. You can repeat this procedure for each room, or you can imagine that the entire building is surrounded by a golden ball of light. Imagine that the ball of light has an absolutely enormous grounding cord that secures it firmly into the center of the planet. Imagine all extraneous energy releasing down through this grounding cord. Next, you can go on to ground the entire street, then the neighborhood, city, state, country, or even the universe!

Benefits of Grounding and Owning the Room

Grounding and owning the room not only protects you and keeps your own grounding cord intact, it actually allows you to heal a room. When I conduct house healings, 95 percent of my technique is the one just described. Once you have grounded a room or house, you will find that it is either much easier to be in it, to keep it clean and organized, or to move away from it if that is what is in your best interest.

Grounding a room or building can be done while you are in it or from a remote location. When you ground and own a location, you are actually making it safe for yourself. If you ground a location before a job interview, a party, a confrontative meeting, a court proceeding, or even a visit to the grocery store, it is much more likely that you will arrive at your location feeling comfortable and that things will either work out in your favor or they will at least flow in a much more pleasant and peaceful manner.

Grounding a Lost Object

You can use the technique of grounding to help find any lost object or person. All you need to do is ground yourself first, and then ground the object with a grounding cord of the same color. Visualize and feel yourself being happy as you find the object, and then start wandering aimlessly around the location where you believe you lost it. If the object is somewhere else, you may suddenly feel inspired to go to that location, or the object will turn up sometime in the near future.

This process doesn't have anything to do with thinking or clairvoyant reading. I have greater success with grounding an object as opposed to clairvoyantly reading the location of the object, because my logical mind usually gets in the way with thoughts about where the object should logically be. Personally, I have a 99 percent success rate with finding lost objects through the use of grounding. However, I do know other psychics who are quite adept at finding objects clairvoyantly, so I encourage you to try finding them through reading as well as through grounding.

Grounding an object seems to work in a few different ways. For objects that are hidden right under your nose, grounding the object removes whatever energy may be concealing the object from you, while grounding yourself removes the energy from your aura that is blocking you from seeing the object. This process also helps remove blockages from your memory. Grounding yourself and the object with a grounding cord of the same color creates a magnetic attraction on the physical plane between these two cords that helps you find the object. Since thoughts and emotions create reality, visualizing yourself finding the object while feeling happy naturally draws the lost object to you.

CHAPTER 8

Psychic Tool 2—Self-Energizing Technique

As discussed in chapter 3, your energy has the ability to leave your body and aura and travel anywhere. Oftentimes it is hanging out in places like your workplace, in any project you have been focused on, in your spouse's aura, or even in your computer! Most people have a large amount of energy in the future or the past, which makes it difficult to appreciate and make the most of the present moment. Since your energy is where your thoughts are, if you are worrying about where you should live in six months or about a rude comment your coworker made several weeks ago, then your energy is out of present time and plugged into the source of your worries.

The most extreme example of a spirit's energy being separated from the body is in death. When a person is sick or has organ failure, it is usually because their own energy is not running through that part of their body, either because their energy is somewhere else, or because someone else's energy is in that part, obstructing the flow.

Our energy often goes to our relationships and the people we are in relationship with. When this happens, it is harder to think and act for ourselves, to focus on ourselves or creative projects, and to maintain our emotional, mental, and physical health. When our energy is engaged in an unhappy or abusive relationship with a negative thinking or behaving person, we are particularly vulnerable to illness and exhaustion. However, even if we have a perfect relationship, when too much of our energy is going to that relationship or person, we can still become unbalanced. Anytime a person suffers from an addiction, whether to a substance, to their job, or to another person, they are experiencing a problem with their own energy flow. One way to solve this problem is by using techniques that aid you in calling back your own energy.

If you spend most of your time thinking about your lover, spouse, child, friend, or whoever, you are most likely giving them too much of their energy, or their energy is occupying too much of your energetic field. Anytime you decide you don't want to think about someone or something anymore but can't stop yourself from having obsessive thoughts, then this is a sure sign that you need to call back your energy. Calling back your energy will not only help stop unwanted thoughts, it will also decrease confusion and increase your ability to communicate with your inner voice. It will also help you feel more alive, peppy, motivated, and enthusiastic about your life.

Just be aware that other people can very strongly feel when you are extracting your energy from them, or when you are shifting it away from a project that they are invested in as well, and you are likely to get a strong reaction from those people. In the case of calling your energy back from your boyfriend, you could get any number of reactions. He may suddenly begin to feel insecure and call you to find out why it's been three full hours since you last talked! Or he may welcome his newfound sense of space and autonomy, which will make him feel so happy and appreciative of you that he buys you a gift or even proposes. On the other hand, he may finally have enough distance from you that he can do what he has been unable to do for months—break up with you! (Oops, did I say something wrong?) The only sure thing will be that he and the universe will notice your shift in energy and respond in an appropriate manner for your ultimate good. However, your ultimate good is not always what you desire in the moment. You may or may not be emotionally ready for the response you get when you call back your energy.

People who are involved in creative projects such as artists, writers, filmmakers, etc., will really benefit from the tool of calling back their energy because part of the creative process has to do with leaving one's body and entering into the project at hand.

While I first began writing this book, I spent about four hours a day typing ferociously at the computer, unaware of anything besides the words pouring out on the page, and not even really aware that I was moving my hands over the keyboard. This worked well during the writing process, but once I was finished for the day, it was very annoying because I found I could think of nothing else. Not only was I losing sleep, but I was walking around like a zombie, totally absorbed in my book. Several times a day my son's father would ask me if I was all right and even my baby would be looking at me quizzically, like "Where are you, Mommy?" The problem was that so much of my energy was merged with this book. Oftentimes the only way I could rectify the situation was by calling back my energy during a meditation session.

I have found that oftentimes the creative process requires us to leave our bodies and go elsewhere so that we can be free to explore new avenues and be totally immersed in our projects. This is fine until it is necessary to come back down to earth and accomplish the more mundane tasks of life, like driving to work or paying our bills. Then we need to have a way to get more fully back into our bodies and into the present moment.

The psychic tool of calling back your energy will help tremendously with this necessity. During a clairvoyant reading or healing, it is particularly important to call your energy back both during the reading and upon completion of it because it is so easy for your energy to enter the other person's energetic field as you are wandering around in there.

One of the difficulties I have had as a psychic is that during particularly challenging readings I will sometimes go too deeply into a person because I will be trying so hard to look at the source of their difficulty, while they are not really open to knowing it. So rather than back off, I go deeper and deeper until I find the answer. When this happens, essentially what I am doing is merging my energy with theirs, and by the end of the reading not only do I feel depleted, but I may not be able to stop thinking about the person (a sure sign that this has happened is when I start having nightmares about the person!). The only way I have found to rectify this situation is to consciously call my energy back when I notice that I am doing or have done this.

During a clairvoyant reading, you will be releasing lots of energy as you read, particularly when you use a grounding cord. If you don't fill yourself up throughout the reading, you will not only become exhausted, but you will be more vulnerable to bringing in undesirable foreign energies. Anytime you use the powerful release tool of grounding, it's important that you call back your own energy. As my teachers used to say, "Nature abhors a vacuum." If you don't fill yourself up with your own energy after you have grounded, then something else will (possibly the energy you just released!). There's a pleasant thought!

Calling Back Your Energy

Visualize a big golden shimmering sun. Its rays are molten hot and so bright that you must squint when you look at it. See it levitating a few inches above your head. Now pretend that you are taking a magic marker and writing your name in the middle of this sun. Just beneath your name, see a strong shiny magnet. This is one of the most powerful magnets in the world, but the only thing that it will attract is your own energy. Now you are ready to call back your energy.

Postulate that wherever your energy is, no matter how far away, within a few moments at the most it is going to return to you in your golden sun. Call back your energy from your relationships, from your job, from your goals, your projects, your family, your pets, your possessions, your past, and your future. All of this energy is going to collect up inside your golden sun first, where it can be cleansed and revitalized. Know that any foreign energy that is attached to your energy will not be able to withstand the heat of your golden sun. See the sun getting bigger and bigger until it is ready to burst.

Now using your physical fingers, touch the top of your head. Pretend you are poking a hole in your crown chakra, or the top of your head. Now physically take your finger and poke a hole in the bottom of your golden sun. (Note that by physically going through these actions, you are helping your spirit and imagination to more fully accept and integrate these actions.) Once you have done this, you can relax your hands.

Now imagine that all of your revitalized energy that has collected up in your golden sun is effortlessly pouring from the bottom of the sun into the top of your head. It instantaneously falls to the tip of your toes and fills up your feet, ankles, calves, thighs, torso, chest, shoulders, and neck. It spills into your arms and hands, filling them up until your energy flows through and out of the little spinning chakras in your hands and into your aura. Your own energy continues to fill up your neck, face, and head, spilling back out of the hole in the top of your head and into your aura.

Know that your body and aura are getting filled so full with your own energy, your own life force, that the energy overflows from your eyes, mouth, ears, and nose. It continues to fill up your organs, such as your heart and lungs, and you even see it flow through your veins and cells. See the energy flow through your chakras so strongly that it causes them to spin. See a little bit of your energy as it runs down your grounding cord, strengthening it and helping you own it. Once you are certain that you have completely filled up your entire body and being, imagine that you are sealing off the hole that you created in the top of your head. Thank your golden sun for working for you and then visualize it floating off into the atmosphere until it's time to call upon it again.

CHAPTER 9

Psychic Tool 3—Neutrality

A psychic's best friend is her neutrality. A psychic's worst enemy is her emotional response as well as expectations and attachment to outcome. When you are neutral, you are calm and collected. You are like a conscientious captain, navigating his ship safely through stormy seas, which may require changing the ship's original course. When you are caught up in the whirlwind of your emotions and expectations, you are like a desperate captain who is so intent on reaching the desired destination that he forces his ship into the eye of the storm, becoming lost at sea and causing his crew to declare mutiny. During a clairvoyant reading, the psychic must navigate her way through emotions and energies as tumultuous as any hurricane and address problems of tidal-wave proportion. If you don't know how to swim well, you are likely to sink, no matter how clearly you can see images or pick up extrasensory information.

Many of your clients will be in pain, in fear, in doubt, and in trouble. Many people who come to you for a reading are not just coming for a reading. They are coming to be healed, to have all their pain eliminated, all their problems solved, all their worries banished—instantaneously. If they don't leave the reading feeling better (even though you just gave them important or even life-saving information, but information they did not want to hear), there is one person they will blame . . . YOU.

Some people will ask a question, but will then do everything possible to block you from seeing the true answer. Some will demand that you tell them everything while revealing nothing, greedily guarding their secrets with every ounce of their being, erecting fortresses around their quivering souls faster than you can burrow through their walls of defense. Some will lie. Some people will worship you, some will lust after you, some will compete with you, and still others will hate you, being unable to be okay with themselves until they have turned you to mush. On very rare occasions a client could actually become violent.

In your readings you will see people who are hapless victims of insidious abuse and who are molesters of children. You will read thieves, liars, drug addicts, and adulterers. People's problems will range from being unable to find their favorite toothbrush, to losing custody of their children, to losing their own mind. Some people will be hysterical, and some will be speaking in tongues. Some will be suicidal, some will be dying, and some will seem already dead. During a reading you will find that people are unwilling or unable to make the changes that you know are necessary for growth. You will trace the path they are now on as it meanders into their bleak future and you will see loneliness, despair, and death. Sounds like fun, huh?

Actually, this may sound crazy, but some of the most fun, exciting, interesting, and inspiring readings I have done included many of these elements. When you are reading from neutrality, it is like watching a scary movie or an emotional drama. You will view all kinds of interesting life experiences, to which you ordinarily would have no access, in the safety and comfort of your own mind. You can be totally absorbed in what you are watching, and even experience a variety of emotions (without becoming the emotion). You might have some level of expectation or hope for the end of the movie, but know that there is nothing you can do to change the characters or to rewrite the script. You may go home pondering the moral of the story or recalling some climactic moment, but you likely will not lose any sleep over them.

On the other hand, if you lost your neutrality during the reading, it will be a lot more difficult to deal with these challenges. You will have a hard time maintaining your focus, and you will be inclined to give advice based on your own limited information rather than wait for the infinite wisdom of your clairvoyance to reveal itself. If you lose your neutrality, you may lose your temper and lose your ability to communicate effectively and honestly. So, with all of that said, how does one accomplish neutrality?

Reading from the Center of Your Head

Just as your spirit is free to leave your body and travel anywhere, it can travel anywhere within your body as well. While some of your energy is distributed throughout your entire body at all times, there is a part of you as a spirit that tends to center itself in a specific place. Many men (but certainly not all) are either located in their second chakra (sexual center) or in the analytical part of their brain. Many healers and therapists tend to be in their heart chakra.

The location of your spirit naturally changes throughout the day, from situation to situation. When you are playing with your children, you might be in your heart chakra. When you are arguing with your spouse about finances, you might be in your third chakra. When you are having sex (good sex), you will be in your second chakra. When doing a clairvoyant reading, oftentimes your energy will naturally go to your sixth chakra (corresponding to the third eye), since this is where your clairvoyant abilities lie. However, as the reading continues, you will be vulnerable to matching whatever chakra your client is operating from, or falling into your own matching pictures.

When you read from a chakra other than your sixth chakra, the reading will tend to take on the energy of that chakra. Since your lower chakras have more to do with emotions, you will read through the filters of these feelings and be more vulnerable to their influence. When you remain in your sixth chakra, or the center of your head, you can maintain a certain degree of neutrality there that you cannot maintain in the lower chakras. (Note that being in the center of the head is not the same as being in your analytic mind, whose location is also in the head.)

Many psychics perform readings because they are natural healers. They care about people and want to help them. Unfortunately the majority of psychics out there aren't aware of the difference between the center of their head and their fourth chakra. This is fine until they encounter a difficult person to read and then lose their ability to objectively see information and communicate it, or they weaken their own system by taking in too much of the readee's energy because of their emotional involvement.

I always know that I have dropped down to my heart chakra during a reading when I begin to cry or feel so hopeless or angry that I can barely remain in my seat. Sometimes I become so wrapped up in saving the person that several minutes will pass before I realize I have stopped reading and am just spewing advice that is not helping anyone. Eventually I realize that I have lost my neutrality and within a minute of performing the neutrality technique described in the next section, I'm back on track, providing clairvoyant information that contains far more wisdom than my logical mind or my heart are able to provide.

Obviously, it is not necessary or desirable to be in the center of your head, or sixth chakra, all the time. Some of the greatest joys in life are when you feel intense love in your heart chakra, when you have a sexual experience in your second chakra, or when your spirit flies off into daydream land somewhere high above your seventh chakra. There is a proper time and place for objectivity just as there is for reckless abandon. You must remain objective during a clairvoyant reading. Your effectiveness and well-being depend on your ability to do so.

Neutrality Technique

First, sit down in a comfortable position and close your eyes. Bring your attention inward. Take your physical hand and place a finger on your third eye, which is slightly above and directly between your eyebrows, and press gently with your finger. Now postulate that you are bringing your awareness and your spirit about two inches from your finger, in the center of your head. Once you are there, take a step or two back. Ask yourself where you just came from. Did it seem like you were down lower and now you are higher, or were you above your head and now you are in a lower position? You may or may not be able to discern your previous location at first, and that is fine. I suggest that you do this merely for your own awareness of where you tend to center yourself.

Now that you are in the center of your head, imagine that you are looking out of your third eye, as if it were a window in your forehead, right where your finger is touching the skin. (You can keep your finger there or remove it at any time during the exercise. If at any point you are no longer certain that you are in the center of your head, bring your finger back to your forehead and repeat the procedure just de-scribed.) Pretend that you can actually look out this window and that you are looking at what is really in the room. For a second you can open your physical eyes to remind yourself what the room looks like, then close your eyes and pretend that you are seeing what you just saw with your eyes. Since the window of your third eye is slightly above your physical eyes, you may want to imagine what the room looks like from a slightly elevated position. Now call any of your energy from your lower body or chakras, as well as any of your energy that may be floating above your head, and tell it to come to that point in the center of your head, a couple inches behind your third eye.

Now we are going to create a special place for you in the center of your head. See it as a single room. Put a comfortable chair or sofa in the center of that room with your imagination. See the color of the up-holstery. Sit down in the chair and notice how it feels. Is it soft like a pillow or hard like metal? Imagine that you are taking a magic marker or some paint and then paint your name on the four walls of the room. As you do this, know that you are owning this room, which is a repre-sentation of the center of your head.

Next, give this room, the center of your head, a grounding cord. You can ground this room in the same way that you would actually ground a room in a house (see chapter 7). Put columns of golden light in each corner and connect these to a large column in the center. Then command any foreign energies that may want to keep you out of the center of your head, or that have been occupying that space, to go down your grounding cord. Watch this energy as it leaves the center of your head. Notice how this feels on a physical level.

As a final step, visualize yourself sitting in the chair in the center of your head. Then stand up and run around this chair. With your imaginary hands, touch all the walls, the floor, and the ceiling of this room in the center of your head. Dress up in your favorite dance costume and celebrate being in the center of your head by dancing the silliest dance you can think of. Congratulations, you have just claimed the home of your neutrality!

CHAPTER 10

Psychic Tool 4—
Running Your Earth and Cosmic Energies

Your physical body is in a state of health when your energy is flowing through it. When the flow of energy has completely stopped, you will be dead. When the flow is sluggish, you will feel sluggish and your immune system will be compromised. When energy is stuck or has ceased to flow in a specific area of the body or energetic counterpart (i.e., in the chakras or aura), you will often experience pain, numbness, or disease in that location.

When energy is flowing through your body, it not only reflects a state of health, it also protects the body from invasion by foreign energies and entities. Most people have either learned or intuitively discovered that a good way to protect the body from harm or evil is to visualize light around the body. What they don't realize is that this light should be flowing. After all, a moving target is much harder to shoot than a stationary one. If you don't want someone to find you or glob on to you, then moving often or quickly will be your best strategy. Think of the vitality and power generated by Niagara Falls or the rapids of the gushing Colorado River compared to the stagnancy of the stale, flea-infested, and oftentimes putrid waters of the Great Salt Lake in Utah or the lethargic swamp lands of the South teeming with all kinds of mischievous varmints.

There are many ways to increase the energy flow through your body and aura. Acupuncture, massage, physical exercise, energetic healing, dancing, singing, painting, and even showering increase the flow of energy and therefore relieve pain and discomfort.

Exercise is one of the easiest and most natural ways of increasing the flow of energy in the body. When you are engaged in aerobic exercise, such as jogging, walking briskly, rollerblading, playing basketball, etc., you are obviously moving your body, which causes your energy to move within your body. When you are sedentary for a long time, the energy in your body slows down. Breathing also circulates energy through the body. The ancient art of yoga uses exercise and breathing to consciously propel energy throughout the body to attain optimal health, peace, and even euphoria. Another easy way to circulate energy throughout the body is through visualization.

During a clairvoyant reading, your body remains sedentary. Because your attention is so focused on whatever it is you are clairvoyantly viewing, your breathing and autonomic nervous system will often significantly diminish to match that of a person in a deep state of sleep. While it is helpful to remind yourself to breathe whenever possible, it is not really practical or possible to perform structured breathing exercises at the same time that you are clairvoyantly reading another person. And I have yet to see anyone jog around the room at the same time that they were doing a clairvoyant reading.

Earth and Cosmic Energies

Both your body and the earth consist of the same energy, called *earth* energy. When you are outside in nature, you naturally run more earth energy than when you are inside a building made out of synthetic materials. I began to see the value of running earth energy when I moved to Sedona, Arizona. The difference between a person who has spent a few hours trekking through the meandering canyons of Oak Creek or climbing the stunning red rocks compared to someone who has just flown in from a city like New Jersey and has been away from nature for months, if not years, is phenomenal. Those who had spent even a couple hours outdoors had vibrant auras, spinning chakras, and appeared far healthier and more attractive. Oftentimes I would feel the tingling of earth energy in my feet as soon as a person who had recently been hiking entered my office. This would remind me of the importance of taking some time out from my readings to go take a walk, since I was looking more like a depleted city dweller than a resident of one of the most beautiful natural spots on earth.

Earth energy enters the body through the feet chakras. It is a somewhat heavy or coarse energy, but can be adjusted to your own comfort level through visualization and intent. While earth energy can run through any area of your body, your upper body and chakras are more delicate and do not need as heavy a dose as your lower body and chakras. Your upper chakras are better designed for the processing of what are commonly referred to as *cosmic* energies, energy gained from the air and from the source of your spirit.

In acupuncture, the earth and cosmic energies are referred to as the *yin* and *yang*, and much attention is paid to the balancing of these energies for the relief of pain and disorders such as arthritis, carpal tunnel syndrome, diabetes, epilepsy, paralysis, etc. In his enthralling book *Autobiography of a Yogi*, Paramhansa Yogananda attributes cosmic energy to the acquisition of miraculous powers. Yogananda describes his meetings with two women from India who never ate. He explains that one of these women, Giri Bala, did not eat any food for over fifty-six years, yet she remained in a state of maximum health. At the age of twelve, she had pleaded with God to help her control her insatiable appetite for food. Her prayers were answered in a vision where a guru appeared and taught her a secret yoga technique that allowed her to recharge her body with cosmic energy from the ether, sun, and air. (Yogananda, p. 536). Her case was rigorously investigated by several reputable Indian scientists and found to be authentic.

The other woman, Therese Newman, had not consumed any food or drink in over twelve years. Upon praying to Saint Teresa in 1923, she was miraculously healed of blindness and paralysis. Soon after, every Friday, she would fall into a deep trance in which she would relive the crucifixion of Christ. The stigmata (sacred bleeding wounds of Christ) would appear on her head, breast, hands, and feet, and blood would pour from her eyes. She stopped eating soon after her healing, knowing that she would be sustained by the grace of God and the cosmic energies of the universe. Her case was authenticated by the Catholic Church, who oversaw the rest of her life and monitored her activities and associations. (Yogananda, p. 537).

I must admit that although I frequently run my cosmic energies, I still have an enormous appetite for edible food and am not yet ready to totally replace my passion for chocolate chip cookies and french fries with a diet of cosmic ether! However, in the several years that I have used visualization to consciously replenish my cosmic energies (sometimes accompanied by exercise and breathing), I have been able to eliminate pain within my own body and other people's bodies and to revitalize myself when feeling tired and stressed. I have also observed many students and classmates undergo remarkable changes in their mental, emotional, and physical health as the cosmic and earth energies helped release generations of programming, MEI pictures, and foreign energies.

During a clairvoyant reading, the simplest and most effective way to make sure that energy is circulating adequately throughout your body is through visualization. The following techniques will teach you how to tune in to your cosmic and earth energies and circulate these throughout your body and energetic fields. These techniques can be used during a clairvoyant reading as well as during any other activity, whether you are simply sitting in meditation, working at your desk, or running a marathon.

Running Your Earth Energy

Find a comfortable chair to sit in. Close your eyes and turn inward. Destroy your current grounding cord and create a new one. Let your attention drop down to your feet. Imagine that you can see your little feet chakras spinning around. Postulate that they are going to open up as wide as possible. Notice how this feels. Now close them down as far as possible. Repeat these steps several times and then postulate that you are opening your feet chakras up to 80 percent.

Now visualize a spot deep in the earth directly beneath you where the energy of the earth lies waiting for your call. Find the cleanest spot, where there are no toxins or chemicals. See a color for this earth energy and bring it up through the ground, through the grass or floorboards, and up into your feet chakras. Let the earth energy circulate through your feet chakras, cleaning them out. Imagine that your feet chakras look like miniature washing machines where you can see into the circular doors. The earth energy is washing out foreign, stuck energy from your feet chakras.

After a few moments, let the earth energy effortlessly rise up your legs, running through the bones, muscles, skin, and veins of your ankles and calves up to your knees, where they circulate through and cleanse your little spinning knee chakras. After a few moments the earth energy will rise up through every cell of your thighs, buttocks, and genitals until it reaches your first chakra (root chakra), located at the base of your spine, or at the opening of your cervix if you are a woman. Let the powerful flow of earth energy circulate through your root chakra until that chakra is spinning and glowing brightly. Then watch as gravity sucks 80 percent of the earth energy back down your grounding cord and into the center of the planet. Take the other 20 percent of earth energy that is flowing freely through your first chakra and bring this up through your body. As it rises, let it circulate through each of your major chakras as well as through your muscles, bones, and skin, until it rises up and out of your crown chakra, spilling out into your aura. Let the earth energy fall to the bottom of your aura around your feet and rise up again until it reaches the top of your aura.

Continue to watch this energy pattern for several minutes. You can visualize your body as it is sitting there and watch the circulation process. In addition to using your visualization, notice how the flow of energy feels throughout your body. Do you feel any peculiar or unexpected bodily sensations?

If you are having trouble with this exercise, you may need to adjust the flow in terms of the strength or amount of energy coming in. Play around with these. If that still doesn't help, then try finding another spot within the earth and adjust the color of the earth energy (avoid very dark or muddy colors or colors you dislike) and see if that makes a difference.

I recommend practicing this technique as a meditation exercise in itself for at least twenty minutes a day for a week before running your cosmic energy. If possible, keep a journal and record your experiences related to the exercise. Record any unusual occurrences that begin to happen in your body or in your life. This will help you realize the benefits of running earth energy as opposed to the benefits of running cosmic energy.

Integrating Your Cosmic Energy with Your Earth Energy

Check in with your grounding cord and create a new one if necessary. Run your earth energy for a few minutes, as directed in the last section. Next, visualize a point way up in the sky. This point will be what we call the *cosmos*, where cosmic energy comes from. You can think of and visualize the cosmos as being above the sun or way out in the universe, or see it as a place in heaven, somewhere over the rainbow, or even located in the hands of God. I like to think of my cosmic energy as coming from whatever source created me.

Next, imagine that there is a bright golden energy effortlessly pouring from the sky. This energy is totally neutral; it contains no foreign energy. See it fall or pull it down into the top of your head, or crown chakra. See it spinning around your crown chakra, cleansing and activating that chakra and all of its abilities. After a few moments, watch as it pours down the back of your head through two channels on either side of the sixth chakra. These channels run all the way down your back along the spine. Watch as the spinning of the sixth chakra causes the cosmic energies to flow down through all of your upper chakras. Watch as the cosmic energy flows down through the vertebrae of the neck, all the way down the spine. The cosmic energy races down the back channels until it lands in the first chakra, where the earth energy is already circulating. Watch as 20 percent of your cosmic energy continues to flow downward through your legs, out the feet, down into the center of the planet, as well as down your grounding cord.

Next, bring your attention back up to your spinning root chakra. Watch as the cosmic energy joins with the earth energy. See these two colors and watch them intermingle until they form a new color. Then take this new color (which will be a combination of 80 percent cosmic energy and 20 percent earth energy) and watch as it flows up the trunk of your body, out the top of your head. These channels run alongside the front of your major chakras. Watch as the energy flows freely through every muscle, bone, and vein of the front of your body and anywhere it has not yet had a chance to flow.

When the mixture of energy reaches your throat chakra, watch as some of it breaks off and travels to each shoulder and down each arm, racing to your hand chakras, where it circulates around and around until the chakras become full and the mixture of earth and cosmic energies overflows out into the aura surrounding your hands. See the rest of the energy mixture as it flows up through your face and head and fountains out of your crown chakra, spilling into your aura. Watch as your entire aura from the bottom of your feet to the top of your head swells with this radiant energy. Watch this pattern of energy flow for at least ten minutes a day for a week as a meditation, and notice what thoughts, feelings, and sensations occur.

Helpful Tips

When running your earth and cosmic energies, there are a few important factors to keep in mind. The first is that you don't have to do any work or put any effort into making the energy flow; you are merely inviting it in, directing it, and watching it flow. If you find yourself making any effort, then choose a color for that effort and watch it release down your grounding cord.

Also, understand that this energy is neutral. As long as you call the energy from a fresh, clean source, it will be clean. Proclaim that no other energies can interfere or combine with your earth and cosmic energies without your conscious permission, and this will be so.

Keep in mind that running your earth and cosmic energies is not just a visualization exercise. The energy flow is causing all kinds of changes to occur in your body, and as we have discussed in other chapters, sometimes when you release pain or emotions, you will feel these as they release. So if you feel any unpleasant sensation, know that this is temporary and not due to the earth and cosmic energies themselves, but rather to whatever materials the earth and cosmic energies are helping you release. This is a very powerful exercise, and therefore it is best to perform it in a safe, comfortable, and private environment for a while before attempting to do it when you are driving your vehicle or interacting with a lot of people in a professional setting.

The pattern of energy flow described here is one that seems to work, but it doesn't have to be set in stone. If you are having difficulty with it, I suggest that for a few weeks on a regular basis you continue to follow the pattern, because difficulty with it could indicate places where you have energy blockages or MEI pictures. However, I do encourage you to experiment with running your earth and cosmic energies however you see fit. Some people prefer less structure, and in that case they may choose to let the energy flow more freely.

CHAPTER 11

Psychic Tool 5—
Creating and Maintaining Boundaries

Often when I am performing a psychic reading, my readee will be so interested in what I am saying that she will expand her aura until it encompasses me. This if more likely to happen if my readee closes her eyes and falls into a deep state of relaxation. When my client's aura intermingles with my own, or vice versa (it is much easier to blame everyone else for encroaching upon your space than it is to acknowledge that you are invading theirs!), this not only feels uncomfortable to my body, but makes it more difficult to clairvoyantly read the client.

If you try to look at an object by putting it right up to your nose, you will not be able to see it clearly or see the whole thing, because it is too close. This concept also applies to psychically viewing a person's aura. This is why I usually have at least a few feet of physical distance between me and my readee, even though my eyes are closed. Sometimes I find it helpful to ask the readee to sit back in her chair and call her aura closer to her body. However, this request sometimes confuses or invalidates the readee. Therefore I often opt to take matters into my own "psychic hands" by visualizing an object at the end of my aura and postulating that my client's energy is receding to the opposite side of this separation object.

A separation object is valuable because it helps you create an energetic boundary between yourself and others, and in turn helps strengthen psychological boundaries, which may be weak (a separation object is a necessity for people who struggle with issues of codependency). A separation object reminds your body and your energy what is yours and what is not yours. It also serves as a method of protection. However, I prefer to refer to this tool as a separation object rather than a protection object because when your focus is on protection, you may inadvertently attract that which you are trying to avoid (through your resistance).

This technique can come in handy in everyday life, as I discovered one afternoon several years ago when I attended a fascinating lecture on crop circles given by the pioneering and inexhaustible researcher Colin Andrews. The lecture hall was packed and I took the only remaining chair. A woman with a child strolled into the room, and a generous man gave her his seat and walked to the back of the room, where I was seated. The lights were dimmed as Andrews began his slide show of the exquisitely complex crop circles. I have no idea how much time had passed until suddenly I was overwhelmed by a heavy wave of exhaustion.

"Oh my gosh, what is wrong with me?!" I wondered. A minute before I had been feeling great, but now I felt that if I did not lie down, I would pass out. Thankfully, I became aware of the gentleman who had earlier relinquished his seat. He was standing next to me only a couple feet away. I tore my eyes from the slides to glance at him and noticed that he was uncomfortably shifting his weight from foot to foot. "Hmm," I wondered. "Could I be matching this man's state of exhaustion? After all, he has been standing all this time."

I quickly imagined that there was a bright red daisy circulating around the edge of my aura. I visualized his energy as a bluish color leaving my aura and returning to his body. I then called back my own energy to my body. As I did this, the man looked at me as if on some level he knew I was doing something, and then walked to the other side of the room.

I instantaneously felt better and returned my attention to the lecture. However, about twenty minutes later I again felt that same wave of exhaustion. "Maybe I was mistaken," I said to myself. "Maybe I am just getting sick and it had nothing to do with that guy." The lecture ended and as I stood up to leave, I stumbled into the same man who at some point, without my knowledge, had inconspicuously taken a position right behind me. I extracted myself from the room, rechecked my separation object, and once again felt like my normal self.

A separation object can be visualized as any object: a flower, a tree, a fence, a mirror, a hundred dollar bill (to remind you of your abundance), etc. It is helpful to use the same type of object over a period of time, because you can take a clairvoyant look at the object from time to time to see if it has changed due to the energy it may have absorbed or been affected by. As with a grounding cord, you should frequently destroy the separation object and create a new one to make sure it is working for you in present time.

Also, different situations may call for different sizes, strengths, and qualities of an object. If I encounter a hostile person who is actually wishing me harm, I will sometimes imagine a mirror or a fan that is flinging back whatever energy is coming at me. At other times I will visualize a giant heart with a smiley face on it to remind myself (and maybe that hostile person) that love is stronger than hatred. I might even visualize something really funny or ridiculous to change the negative vibrations around me, since amusement is a much higher vibration than anger or fear.

Your separation object should be at the edge of your aura. If it is only at the edge of your body, or somewhere within your aura, then whatever you need separation from will still have access to your aura and will affect you as if it were in your body. You can visualize a single object that rotates around your aura, or you can use several objects. Beginning students who have less trust in their separation object tend to want to create more of them, to cover every inch of their aura. However, one object will work just fine.

You can postulate that even though the object is located at a single spot on the edge of your aura, it has the ability to protect your entire aura and body. You can see the separation object as being stationary or as orbiting around your aura, since moving energy is more powerful than stagnant energy, as mentioned earlier. You can use your other tools, such as running energy and grounding, in conjunction with your separation object to further increase its effectiveness.

A separation object is a highly effective tool, so you have to be careful not to create such a strong fortress around yourself that you become invisible or isolated. This is usually not a problem until you have been practicing the technique for a long period of time.

CHAPTER 12

Psychic Tool 6—Creating and Destroying

The process of clairvoyant reading and healing requires you to be able to create certain images and then destroy them. You must be able to consciously create a reading screen and a viewing receptacle in order to have a place where your clairvoyant information can present itself. You must then be able to destroy these images so they don't have a negative impact on your health, and so new information will have a place to display itself.

The techniques presented in this chapter and book, when practiced over time, will dramatically increase your ability to create visual images and destroy them. Your ability to create and destroy visualizations may be directly related to your ability to create and destroy many other things in your life, and it will be important for you to be aware of this when you find yourself struggling with a certain technique. When you create and destroy an object in your mind, you are moving energy and impacting everything around you.

There are many people who have no inkling of their tremendous creative potential. You hear them say, "I don't have a creative bone in my body." These very people have jobs, children, houses, and bank accounts. Who created these things in their lives, if they did not? Our lives are a continual cycle of creation and destruction. From birth to death, from preschool to high school graduation, from marriage to divorce, from beginning a new job to resigning from it, from purchasing a new dress to donating it to a used clothing store, from earning a nice fat paycheck to spending every penny of it, these are our creations and destructions.

During every moment of our lives, we are creating and we are destroying. When I am thirsty, I go to the kitchen and pour a glass of milk, and I have just created a glass of milk. Of course I did not make the glass or milk the cow, but ultimately I formed an idea of a desire in my mind and took the necessary actions to create a glass of milk for myself. I then consume the glass of milk. The milk that I consume no longer exists. Essentially, I have destroyed the milk.

I get in my car and see I am low on gas. I know I need more gas. I have a mental image picture in my mind of what I will do to get more gas. I drive to the gas station and fill my car up with gas. I did not drill in the ground for the gas, and I did not haul it over to the gas station, but I did drive there and pump the gas into my car. Essentially, my thoughtforms helped me create the gasoline that I desired for my car. I then drive my car for a week, and suddenly the car has consumed the gas. The gas I had created is no longer there. The gas has been destroyed. I have destroyed it.

I believe that everyone has equal abilities when it comes to creating and destroying. However, people differ drastically in terms of their issues and MEI pictures surrounding these two activities. There are all kinds of emotions and thoughtforms that affect a person's ability to create or destroy. Some people feel guilty when they create something for themselves, or even think about creating something, while others feel guilty when they release or destroy something, such as a relationship with a romantic partner, a job, etc.

Many people have a lack of understanding of how the physical laws of creation work. Others have fears, insecurities, anxieties, family programming, and mental blocks that get in their way. Actually, most people don't have a problem creating (although they'd tell you otherwise), it's just that they are too busy creating other things that don't allow time or space for their new creations.

One reason it's important to meditate before performing a clairvoyant reading is that when your head is so full of thoughts and any number of foreign energies, there is no place for the clairvoyant information to go where you could possibly distinguish it from the rest of the traffic in there. Once you make the decision to only focus on the clairvoyant information, or certain visual images, then you will have to find a way to get rid of or destroy all the other thoughtforms in your head. This is done through meditation and practice of the psychic tools presented in chapters 6–12. If you have trouble letting go of all the garbage in your head, you may also have trouble letting go of all the garbage in other areas of your body and life, or vice versa.

As we have discussed in other chapters, clairvoyant reading and healing speeds up the process in which thoughtforms, emotions, and foreign energies become stimulated and are then released, both for the person giving the reading/healing and the one receiving it. Anyone who embarks on a path of clairvoyant reading and healing needs to be comfortable with this process of release and destruction.

Release and destruction involve change. If you cannot tolerate change in your own life, then you will have a problem with destroying. If you have a problem with destroying, then you and your life are going to become overwhelmed with your creations to the point that you become ill, can no longer create what it is you really want, and eventually have some kind of breakdown, which will cause you to have to make changes in your life anyway. If you cannot tolerate change in your own life, then seeing it or initiating it in your readee's or healee's life is going to be too painful for you. During your readings, you will therefore block yourself from seeing images that have to do with change and will be unable to effectively communicate messages regarding change. You will only be able to read people who are as stuck as you are!

Now, after reading the preceding paragraph, you may be thinking, "Well, I don't like change, and I don't feel particularly creative, and I know I hate to let go of anything, whether a possession or a relationship. So maybe I'd better stop reading this book and let go of any further silly

ideas I might have about learning how to do clairvoyant readings."
Well, stop that thought immediately! Sure, doing clairvoyant readings
is going to speed up the release and transformation process, which will
force you to deal with your resistance to destroying on a more intense
level. But eventually you are going to have to deal with these things
anyway if you hope to achieve your dreams and have a truly fulfilling
life. It's up to you whether you want to do it now or thirty years from
now.

If your life is not going the way you want it to, or things are working out just fine but you are constantly plagued with anxiety and the
fear that at any moment your life might change, then you have a problem with creating and destroying, and the only way you are going to
learn how to cope with your life and find more peace and happiness is
to deal with these gifts that God gave you more effectively and gracefully. Clairvoyant reading and/or practicing the techniques presented in
this chapter and book will help empower you to consciously create and
destroy so that you can become a better reader, a better healer, and at
the very least a more peaceful and confident human being.

If you have a strong interest in doing clairvoyant readings, then you
are meant to do them. Don't ever let your fear of not being good
enough stop you from learning what it takes to become good enough!

The "D" Word

One day I casually mentioned to a close friend that I was writing a
chapter on the subject of creating and destroying. He emphatically insisted, "I wouldn't use the word *destroy* if I were you. That's too
strong a word. It might make people uncomfortable."

I responded, "What's wrong with that? Destruction is a part of
everyday life and if it makes people uncomfortable, then isn't it better
to help them learn how to become comfortable with it than to just not
bring it up? I know a lot of things I say in this book are going to make
my readers uncomfortable and that is okay, because the purpose of this
book is to provide techniques, tools, and methods for coping with

whatever makes them uncomfortable. Maybe they weren't brave or strong enough to face these topics in the past because they didn't know that there were solutions. This book is about solutions."

I became aware of the importance of the ability to destroy after doing several readings in which my readees asked me to look at why they were having problems with creating and manifesting in their lives. One of my very first readings involved a woman named Sarah. Sarah was longing to create a new relationship. She had not dated anyone for three years, since her divorce, and she was feeling very lonely and frustrated. When I put up a viewing receptacle and asked it to show me some information regarding who her next boyfriend would be, I immediately saw an image of her opening her closet door and being buried under an avalanche of clothing, boxes, and miscellaneous junk. She thought this was funny and admitted that this was pretty much what happened whenever she opened her closet doors. (I will explain how to create a viewing receptacle in the next chapter.)

"But what does that have to do with a relationship?" Sarah asked. I didn't have the foggiest idea, so I asked that image to show me another image. The next image I had was of furniture. I saw a big green sofa that looked very comfortable, but was very worn and old. I asked this image what it meant, and I saw a man reclining on the sofa. He had a bald spot and a big tummy. He was watching a wrestling match on TV. I hesitantly described this man to her, thinking this was probably not the kind of boyfriend she would want to hear about! However, I was relieved when she said, "That perfectly describes my ex-husband, and our sofa. He gave me all the furniture when we divorced." I continued the reading, trying to ignore all these elements, since I was only interested in learning about her future boyfriend.

I destroyed the images and viewing receptacles that I was looking at and created a new viewing receptacle in the form of a rose. I saw a faint image of a man holding a bouquet of flowers, knocking on the front door. When my readee opened the door, a flood of water pushed him down the hallway. I focused on the water and saw images of kids, furniture, and, once again, the readee's husband. He started to strangle the guy with the flowers, who then ran down the stairs and out of the apartment building.

The whole story was becoming clear. Sarah was having trouble creating a relationship not because there were no interested men around, but because there was no room in her house or her life for a new relationship. She had been divorced for three years, but her husband's energy was so present that he might as well have been sitting on the sofa in the middle of her living room right then. I intuitively realized that the very first thing Sarah needed to do was physically clear out her closets, which could symbolize the areas in her life where she was unconsciously holding on to the past. Next, she needed to get rid of her sofa and any other furniture that her former husband had been grounded into. Most importantly, she needed to release her husband's energy, which occupied several areas of her body.

Sarah at first adamantly refused to get rid of the sofa, citing all kinds of reasons why this was impossible. When I suggested that perhaps she was not ready to let go of her husband's energy, she admitted that she was still having a hard time with the divorce and talked to her ex-husband frequently. She had thought that if she found another man, it would be easier to let go of the past, but was beginning to realize that the opposite was true. She also told me that every time she attempted to throw something away, she would become confused as to whether to put it in the garbage, give it to charity, etc., and then she would just stuff it away in the closet.

While I was looking to see what might help Sarah with all of this, I saw an image of her looking in front of the mirror, examining her rear end, with a frown on her face. It seemed like her inability to let go of things, or in a sense to destroy them, was also making it difficult for her to let go of excess weight on her body, which made her feel less attractive and therefore made her less attractive to potential suitors. (Most people I know who are overweight have problems with destroying in terms of letting go of unhealthy relationships from the past and letting go of possessions. Some of them actually eat more than they need because there is an unconscious fear that they might not be able to create more food when they need it in the future.)

In order for Sarah to create a new relationship, she needed to bring her agreement with her husband into present time. They had gone through a legal divorce, but not an energetic one. Spiritually she had not been ready to break off the relationship, so she didn't. When I asked her if she'd like me to help her with this, she said, "No, I'm not ready to let go." I told her that this was okay, and that the important thing was that she realized this. Eventually she would need to either physically reunite with her ex-husband or energetically break their agreement. Until she did so, it was unlikely that she would create a relationship with another man.

To close the reading, I clairvoyantly looked for one action she could take that would not overwhelm her. I saw her having a party where her friends came over and helped her clean out her closets. They would not have the same attachments and resistances to getting rid of things, and they looked like they were having fun. She thought this was a great idea and knew exactly who she'd ask for help.

The elements of this session repeated themselves time and time again in reading after reading, and taught me about why we must be able to let go of things in order to create our present dreams and desires. They also showed me how resistant people are to change. I learned that doing something as simple as cleaning your house, or donating a box of old clothes, can be an enormous first step to clearing out all kinds of other stubborn energies in your life. I learned how to monitor where I am in my own life by paying attention to when my home, car, purse, or wallet becomes disorganized and overflowing with items I haven't used in months or even years. I now know that if my outer life is messy, my inner life is even messier!

The Importance of Faith

We all want to feel secure, to know that if we leave a relationship or job, if we sell a house or a car, that there will be an even better one right there for us so we won't have to feel any anxiety, loneliness, stress, or uncertainty. How many times have you said to yourself, "I can't leave my job until I find another one," or "I can't let this relationship go (even though my boyfriend broke up with me two months ago) because what if I never meet anyone as handsome or funny or compatible?"

The truth is, many times (but not all) you won't create what you ultimately crave in your heart until you make a leap of faith and destroy what is no longer serving you so that something that will serve you can move in. Life actually may work this way because you are meant to learn about having faith—faith in God, faith in your ability to create, and faith in your ability to handle any situation for a temporary period of time. If you have no faith, if you can't deal with uncertainty or loneliness or even poverty, then you will always be a prisoner to what seem to be your needs but are really your desires. You can always handle so much more than you think you can. You are so much more powerful than you could ever imagine!

The good news is that when you jump into life, perhaps blindfolded but with both feet first, you usually don't have to deal with the things you fear the most for too long, because life does want to reward you for putting your dreams over your fears.

Creating and Destroying Simple Images

The following technique will help you exercise your visualization muscle and will help you practice creating and destroying images. It will also act as a powerful meditation in which all other thoughts in your mind will dissipate. Because it requires you to be so active, you will be less likely to be distracted by extraneous thoughts. If you find that you do get distracted or get very sleepy, as soon as you notice that you have gotten off track, go back to the last number or letter you were working on before you lost awareness of it.

Begin by giving yourself a grounding cord (see chapter 7). Imagine that you are standing in front of a blackboard, holding a bright red piece of chalk in your right hand. Draw the number one on the blackboard. Once you are finished, study the number to see how it looks. Is it a straight line or kind of wiggly? How big is it? It is very bright on the blackboard or kind of faint? Now imagine that you are holding an eraser in your hand and watch as your hand completely erases the number one. Check your grounding cord and invite any energy that has been stimulated to release down this cord, into the center of the planet.

Next, repeat this exercise by going through all the numbers until you reach number twenty. Then repeat this exercise by going though all the letters of the alphabet.

Creating and Destroying Objects

When you visualize an object in your imagination, you are actually creating the object on an energetic level. This object will actually possess properties that can have an effect on the physical plane. When you imagine that you are destroying the object, you are actually moving and changing the molecules that make up this energy form. When you create and destroy an object, an energy force is set in motion that affects all other energies surrounding it. Therefore, you can utilize this process to move and release unwanted energies.

Creating and destroying objects is a simple yet extremely powerful healing method. Practicing this tool on a frequent basis not only will keep your energy moving, but will also help you exercise your visualization and concentration muscles. I recommend that you try creating and destroying objects when meditating and reading, as well as when you are at work, walking your dog, swimming, watching movies, etc. Practice this technique for varying periods of time and notice how you feel after you have been creating and destroying objects for several minutes as opposed to a few seconds.

This technique has become such an ingrained practice for me that often I will realize that I am in the process of creating and destroying an object (usually a rose because that was the only object my clairvoyant school utilized) without willfully attempting to do so. I will discover that there is actually a negative energy near me that needed to be cleared out or dealt with. My subconscious somehow sensed this and went to work way before my much slower conscious mind became aware of the situation or could respond.

In order to create and destroy objects, you will first need to learn how to create a reading screen. This is described in detail in the next chapter, so I recommend that you read chapter 13 now and then come back and read the rest of this chapter.

The first step in creating and destroying objects is to quickly create a red flower on your reading screen. See all of its petals, its stem, and its leaves, and then destroy it. Next, create a blue flower, observe it, and then destroy it. Now create a yellow flower, observe it, and destroy it. Next, create a black flower, observe it, and destroy it. See how quickly and for how many minutes you can continue to create and destroy these flowers.

Then try another category of objects. In your imagination, visualize a car. See the color, the shape, and the size of the car, observe the interior and the exterior, and then destroy it. You can explode it, erase it, see it crash and blow up in flames, watch it melt away, or simply watch as it disappears. Next, create an airplane. Observe it and then destroy it. Do the same with a boat, a train, a bicycle, of a pair of roller skates.

Next, check in with your grounding cord to make sure it is connected into your first chakra as well as the center of the planet. Create an image of a person who, to your knowledge, does not exist. Observe that person's features. Then destroy that image of the person. Next, create an image of a person you used to know but haven't seen in years. Observe the person's features, and then destroy that image. Know that you are not destroying them, but that this process may remove any of their energy from your body and aura.

As a final step, visualize a person who is currently in your life, someone you love. Observe their features, their clothes, the look on their face. Then destroy this image. Again, remember that you are not hurting them or doing anything malicious. You are merely moving energy associated with their image. They may actually feel this energy movement or spontaneously think of you as you do this exercise. Don't be surprised if they call you or come over for a visit soon after you create and destroy an image of them.

Cleaning Your Reading Screen

The following techniques can be used to clear off any stuck or foreign energies from your reading screen that may be getting in the way of your clairvoyance. They can also be used very effectively to clear off your chakras, a particular body part, or an area of your aura, and to practice your creating/destroying skills.

On the upperhand left corner of your reading screen, visualize a little red footprint. Observe the footprint, and then destroy it. Directly next to it, create another footprint in a different color. Observe the footprint, and then destroy it. Moving from left to right, continue creating footprints as if you were walking across your reading screen. When you get to the far right side of the screen, go back to the far left side, immediately under the row that you just walked, and continue to create and destroy these colored footprints. Continue the exercise until you have created and destroyed a footprint on every part of the screen. You can substitute any image for the footprint, such as a hand, a flower, a sun, or the moon. Every time you create and destroy the footprint, you are releasing energy from your screen that may be hindering your clairvoyance.

Another way to clean off your reading screen is to imagine that you are plugging the cord of a vacuum cleaner in to an outlet on the side of your reading screen. Change the vacuum cleaner bag and destroy the old one before turning on the vacuum, and then proceed to vacuum every square inch of your reading screen. When you are finished, destroy the vacuum cleaner.

Manifesting a Desire

Through use of visualization and clairvoyance, anyone can learn to create and manifest their desires, dreams, and wishes, no matter how big or small these are. With all the literature published on the subject, most people have at least heard of, if not directly experimented with, the concept that thought creates one's physical reality. There are so many great books currently available that teach people the universal laws governing manifestation through thought that it would be redundant (as well as impractical given how much other information needs to be covered) to go into much detail here. In addition to using the clairvoyant technique for manifestation that I am about to describe, I also recommend the following books on the subject: *The Power of Your Subconscious Mind* by Joseph Murphy, *Your Heart's Desire* by Sonia Choquette, *You'll See It When You Believe It* by Wayne Dyer, *Your Life: Why It Is the Way It Is, and What You Can Do About It* by Bruce McArthur, *Creative Visualization* and *Living in the Light* by Shakti Gawain, and any book by Marianne Williamson.

Begin by giving yourself a grounding cord. Then create a reading screen (see chapter 13). On the viewing or reading screen, create an image of a crystal lotus flower. Notice the number of petals, how open the bud is, how long the stem is, etc., and then ground the stem into the center of the planet. Then visualize yourself standing inside the lotus, receiving your desire. See yourself at the moment when you realize that you have been granted this desire. See yourself looking jubilant, ecstatic. You are so excited that you are jumping up and down, with tears pouring forth from your eyes, and you fall to your knees in gratitude, thanking everyone from God to your mother who brought you into this wonderful life where your dreams would be realized as they are now.

Next, look for a color of any energy that might be blocking you or has been trying to block you from having this desire in your life. This energy could belong to you or to someone else. Once you see this color, you can either conduct a mini reading on it, or help the color release down the stem of the lotus into the center of the planet.

Now choose a brilliant color that represents your desire and let it circulate through the lotus. See it grow bigger and bigger until it expands outside the lotus and outside your reading screen, until it is filling up your entire body and aura and filling up the entire room, then the neighborhood, then the entire city, state, country, and universe. As you do this, continue to feel gratitude and happiness for achieving your goal.

As a final step, imagine that you are cutting the lotus from the ground, and watch it float off into the universe to begin creating for you. Or you can hand it up to an image of God that you have created. See it floating into God's hands and see God blessing this creation. You can also imagine that you are planting the lotus in a lovely garden. Every few days you can check on the lotus to see if it is growing or if it is in need of attention. Water it with love and excitement, using the color of the desire's energy whenever you take a peek at it.

PART 3

Clairvoyant Reading

CHAPTER 13

Learning to Read Yourself

In this chapter, you will learn the clairvoyant reading techniques that are the foundation of this book. These simple techniques can be learned by almost anyone for the purpose of accessing information. You can use them when reading yourself or other people, animals, energies, etc. This particular chapter provides exercises for reading and healing yourself. In the following chapter, you will learn how to apply these techniques during readings on other people.

As a beginning clairvoyant student, it is best to perform the following exercises when you are alone. If you are indoors, it is essential to secure yourself in a room where no one else is present or will be coming in. If you are outside, then find an area where you are the least likely to be disturbed.

The ideal time to practice these techniques is when no one else will be in the house. As you practice your psychic tools and perform clairvoyant readings, your energy will change and whoever is around will unconsciously sense this and become very curious about what you are doing. Therefore, they will likely come up with a very good excuse to disturb you, whether that means knocking on your door or energetically joining you, which may make it more difficult for you to concentrate. Unplugging the phone is also essential, since this is usually the time when your relatives will call. If you feel you are being distracted by other people, then invite their energy to go into a glass bubble, look to see what color their energy might look like, and visualize the bubble floating back to them.

Make sure you turn off any music within hearing distance and especially the television set. Music may be relaxing for some forms of meditation, but it can be very distracting when reading. If you clairvoyantly read in a room (or house) where a television set is turned on, you will likely start picking up images from the television, which will interfere with the images of the energies you are intending to read.

Informing the Universe of Your Intention to Read

The time you spend doing a clairvoyant reading is unique from the rest of your day. You are accessing a part of yourself that has different intentions, concerns, energies, and relationships. Therefore it is helpful to make it clear to your body, mind, and spirit that you are embarking on a special project that requires a shift. This can be done by establishing a routine that you go through prior to every reading. As part of this routine, and to help your body make this transition, it is helpful to put your body into a position that will give it the signal that it is time to perform a reading (the same is true for meditation or even writing). Designate a room, a part of a room, or a chair that is intended only for clairvoyant reading. At the very least, find a cushion to place on your chair, or a cozy blanket to drape over your shoulders, or some warm slippers for your feet that you will use only when you read.

Sit in the same position every time you read. I recommend sitting upright with your feet on the floor since this will facilitate your grounding and make it easier to stay awake (since we always or usually sleep in a reclining position, our bodies are programmed to fall asleep when placed in a reclining position). This is also the position you will be most likely to sit in when reading another person. Placing your hands on your lap with your palms facing upward will facilitate the flow of your energy and will also serve as a cue in future reading sessions that you are intending to perform a reading. Close your eyes and keep them closed until you are finished with your session and ready to shift back into your other daily activities.

Whatever you do to set yourself up for a reading, it is important to do it in a way that is as nurturing as possible, as with meditation. This is your special time to go inward, to shower yourself with the personal attention, respect, and love that you deserve and need in order to lead a happy, stable life. When you give to yourself in this way, you send a message out into the universe that you are worthy and open to receiving respect and love in general, and you will begin to attract other people who reflect these qualities back to you (see chapter 22).

Accessing your clairvoyance will be easier if you meditate beforehand. If you have followed the steps given thus far in this chapter, you will find that you are now in an ideal situation/position for meditation as well as for clairvoyant reading. Meditation helps you focus and empties out the extraneous thoughts cluttering your mind. It also helps you relax your body. Clairvoyant reading can be done anywhere, at any time, regardless of how you have prepared yourself. Reading in itself is a type of meditation, since it requires complete concentration and focus. If you read for fifteen minutes or longer, you will discover that your consciousness and brain waves have shifted. However, it is much easier and safer to access your psychic abilities when your mind is clear. If you begin to read without first meditating, you will find that the first several minutes (if not longer) of your reading time will be spent releasing those pesky thoughtforms that have nothing to do with the reading, particularly if you are new to psychic reading.

To prepare yourself for a reading, I recommend that you take about twenty minutes to run through the psychic tools presented in chapters 6–12 before attempting to access your clairvoyance. If you have other meditation styles or techniques that you prefer, then meditate in any way you'd like and complete the last five or ten minutes of your meditation with a run-through of the psychic tools. The psychic tools are not only meant to protect and heal you during your clairvoyant reading, they are also warm-up exercises for utilizing your visualization/ clairvoyance. Once you feel grounded, centered, energized, and protected (using the psychic tools or whatever methods you'd like), you are ready to begin reading.

Prayer

Beginning your reading/meditation with a prayer will help you set the energy of your session and connect with the source of your energy and information, and will serve as a further cue to let your spirit know that it is time to access your clairvoyance. It will also serve as protection. Any prayer that you like will work. Some people prefer a structured prayer, while others may say a mantra or some simple words of gratitude. I usually start a reading with words of gratitude regarding the reading, such as this: "Thank you, God, for the gift of my clairvoyance. Thank you for helping bring forth the most helpful information at this time. I thank you for your protection, your wisdom, and your assistance as well as the assistance of the universe and all of my guides."

The energy of gratitude is one of the highest forms of energy that exists. Within gratitude there is joy, acceptance, love, and forgiveness. When you pray by expressing your gratitude, either for what has already occurred or for what you hope to manifest, you are bringing these healing energies into your reading space as well as into your life. Structured prayers such as the Lord's Prayer are beneficial to recite when dealing with negative energies, because they are highly energized by the masses of people who have recited them throughout history.

The words of your prayer are, for the most part, insignificant compared to the zeal with which you pray. Whether you are making up your own words or reciting a well-known prayer, your prayers will be much more effective if you are focused and aware of every single word, and you say each word not just with your mouth or brain but with every ounce of your being. This is true whether you pray to God, to Jesus Christ, to Muhammad, to your Creator (whoever that is), to the universe, or to a particular saint, ascended master, spirit, etc.

Clairvoyant Reading Technique

The preliminary steps just described are highly recommended to help you prepare to access your clairvoyance. However, the following three steps are the meat and potatoes of a clairvoyant reading: creating a reading screen, creating a viewing receptacle, and calling energy into your viewing receptacle. If you perform nothing else in this book except the following three fundamental steps, you at the very least will know how to access your clairvoyance.

Creating a Reading Screen

If you are going to access psychic information through clairvoyance, you must have a place where this information can be displayed. Just like you need a television screen in order to watch a television program, or a monitor in order to view information on your computer, you will need a reading screen in order to view your clairvoyant images. From the center of the inside of your head, with your eyes closed, image that you are looking out through your third eye (located at the middle of your forehead, in between and slightly above your physical eyes) at a screen that is placed a few inches out from your forehead. Notice or decide what this screen looks like. It can be the size of a small television screen or as big as a movie screen in an extravagant theater. Notice if the screen has a border and what that border looks like. Notice if the border or the sides of the screen are straight or bent or symmetrical to each other. Notice or decide on the color for the border of your screen as well as for the inside of the screen. Notice if there is anything that you would consider unusual about this screen.

Whenever you create an image, such as your reading screen, it is a good idea to ask your mind to first just notice what it looks like before attempting to consciously create it. After a reasonable period of time, if you don't get an impression of how it looks, then make a decision to design it a certain way. Sometimes your screen or another object you are attempting to visualize already exists, and the way it appears has to do with the type of energies that are affecting it and you. If you don't like what you see, then simply imagine that you are grounding out the part that you don't like, or imagine that the entire screen is being destroyed, and then consciously decide how you would like to recreate your screen. Next, observe the appearance of this new screen. Patiently continue watching this screen for a minute or two to see if any aspect of it changes. Any change that does occur (without your conscious manipulation) will be a result of the energy that is affecting it.

Grounding Your Reading Screen

You can release any mischievous energy from your reading screen (including energy that might be getting in the way of you focusing or visualizing your screen) by giving your reading screen a grounding cord. In chapter 7 you learned how to create a grounding cord by connecting your body to the center of the earth. In the same way, for the same reasons, you can give your reading screen its own grounding cord. Just imagine that you are connecting your screen with a column of energy into the center of the planet. You can imagine that the grounding cord for your screen looks like anything, such as a strong metal pole, an anchor, a tree trunk, etc. Once your reading screen is secured into the center of the planet, invite whatever foreign energy that might be affecting it or blocking it from your vision to be released from the screen's grounding cord. Watch or imagine that a particular color is effortlessly being sucked down the cord by the gravitational pull of the planet and imagine it being absorbed into the earth. Now look at your reading screen again and notice if it has changed.

Creating a Viewing Receptacle

Once you have created a reading screen where you can focus your attention, you then need to create a viewing receptacle that you can place on the screen. Within this receptacle will appear the energy/information that you wish to read in the form of color and images. A reading screen is like a dining room table. You sit yourself down at the table and on it you place a receptacle, like a bowl, which will hold your soup. If you poured your soup directly onto the table, your soup would spill all over. It would not only be difficult to eat your soup, but there would be a big mess that would require a lot of effort to clean up. A viewing receptacle placed on your screen is like a disposable bowl placed on a table. It contains the energy and information so it that it can be digested as easily as it can be disposed of. The viewing receptacle not only receives information/energy in the form of images and colors, but will be directly affected by energy so that its appearance will be altered. You will read the energy initially by watching to see how the receptacle is affected.

The viewing receptacle can be visualized as any neutral object, such as a bubble, balloon, or flower. Most of the clairvoyant training programs throughout the country suggest using the image of a rose as the receptacle. A rose is a good image to work with because it can be visualized in a very simple manner, such as in outline form, or in all of the complexity of a real rose with its numerous petals, leaves, and thorns. Roses come in all different colors, shapes, and sizes, they can be open or closed in a variety of positions, and they can be destroyed easily by plucking away their petals. Also, because a rose has a stem that grows from the ground, it has its own naturally built-in grounding cord. The image of the rose was always used as the viewing receptacle in my own clairvoyant training and is therefore the one I am most comfortable with. I will use the word *rose* interchangeably with the term *viewing receptacle* throughout this book.

Since a rose can be visually complex, it is helpful to place a real living rose or a picture of a rose in front of you and closely observe it before trying to visualize one. Over time it will become easier to create this image in your imagination. If you feel that the image of a rose is too complex, I suggest just starting off with the image of a glass soap bubble and gradually working your way up to that of a rose.

Grounding Your Viewing Receptacle

Visualize or imagine that you are looking at your reading screen. Now imagine that you are placing a clear, *neutral* crystal rose onto your reading screen. This rose is transparent, so you can see inside it. The rose is neutral—it has no charge or meaning at this point. It is a blank canvas. Notice how it looks. See the size and the shape. You have just created a viewing receptacle! If you are having difficulty visualizing the rose or whatever image you are using, then give the receptacle a grounding cord. Connect the stem of your rose into the center of the planet, and postulate that the gravity of the earth is effortlessly sucking up any energies that may be interfering with your visualization.

If you notice that your receptacle is doing something unusual or taking on a life of its own, don't be alarmed! Your rose is being affected by some kind of energy and you are already performing a reading by seeing the effects of this energy! Whenever something unusual happens with an image that you are visualizing, there is a reason for it, and it's up to you to use your clairvoyance to explore the reason for that behavior. If it wasn't important for you to see, you wouldn't notice it!

Calling Energy into Your Viewing Receptacle

The purpose of performing a reading is to gain access to information from a source other than our logical mind. In order to do this, we need to have a question or a goal in mind that will then direct the information into our viewing receptacle. This question or goal can be very simple or very complex; it can concern yourself or someone else. For example, you might wonder what your creative energy looks like. You might wonder why you are feeling sad. You might wonder if your psychic protection is working for you. You might wonder whether or not you should marry your fiancé. You might want to know why your boss is mad at you, why you procrastinate, what the pain in your stomach is trying to tell you, what energies are affecting your third chakra, whether you are going to get the job you applied for, etc.

The answer to whatever question you ask will come in the form of energy. A clairvoyant reading is as simple as inviting this energy into your viewing receptacle and then asking your viewing receptacle to show you the answer in the form of colors and images. Here are three methods for doing this. I recommend that you do all three exercises, although this is not essential.

Exercise 1

On your reading screen, create an image of a neutral clear glass rose. Study the shape of the rose and the petals. Next, imagine that the rose you have created is traveling to the outermost layer of your aura. Take a few moments to see what happens to your rose. Did the appearance of your rose change? If you notice anything unusual or different about the rose, ask whatever change has occurred in the rose to give you another color, image, or message about the meaning of what you are looking at in the rose. Then destroy this rose by imagining that is it exploding into a million pieces.

Exercise 2

On your reading screen, with your imagination, create an image of a rose. See the color, shape, and size. Study this rose for a few moments. Now postulate that the stem of the rose is a grounding cord. Ground the rose deeply into the center of the planet. Postulate that the rose represents yourself and that the stem/grounding cord is going to release any foreign energies that you are now ready to release. Watch the rose and its grounding cord and notice if anything changes about the rose. You can end the exercise as soon as you see a change occur, or you can continue with a more in-depth reading by investigating the meaning of these changes. Further investigation involves asking the rose more questions and then waiting for further changes in the rose or for images to appear. Remember to destroy the rose when you are finished. You can see it exploding, or imagine that you are erasing it with a colorful eraser, or pretend that it's dissolving in a brilliant fire.

Exercise 3

On your reading screen, create another image of a neutral transparent rose made of glass. Postulate that the rose represents something in your life that you would like to create, such as a job, a lover, money, happiness, etc. Before consciously manipulating the rose in any way, just watch the clear rose and notice what happens to it. Does the color change? How open is the rose? What is its posture like (standing erect or wilting)? Is there a particular color coming into the rose? How many petals are there? Are there leaves or thorns on the stem? After watching the rose for a few minutes, you will most likely notice something happening that you did not intend to happen. You will probably be curious about at least one aspect of the rose. So continue with your reading by asking the rose to tell you the meaning of that aspect.

For example, let's say your rose turns purple and pink, there are only a few petals on the bud, and the whole flower is drooping to the left. There are so many aspects to explore! In this example you could first ask the purple to tell you what it represents. Once you pose a question to it, just relax and watch. You should not be trying to figure anything out because this process has nothing to do with your logical mind. Just wait and literally see what happens. (For many clairvoyants, students and experts alike, the hardest part of reading is being patient and letting go of the need to control.)

Next, you can ground the stem of the rose into the center of the planet and watch these aspects to see if they remain constant or if they change or leave the rose. Since this rose represents something you would like to create in your life, you can play around with it in a variety of ways. You can imagine that you are giving the rose to God and then watch the rose to see what happens. Or you can imagine that you are showing the rose to a particular person in your life (like your spouse or your mother) and again watch the rose to see what happens to it. When you are completely finished with this exercise and satisfied that your rose represents only you and the vibration you would like to create it in (for example, enthusiasm versus fear), then imagine that you are sending it off to God or the universe to help with your creation.

Troubleshooting

I am not a visually oriented person. I am having trouble visualizing my screen and my viewing receptacle. What can I do?

For some people, visualization takes practice. Start with a simple visualization exercise, focusing on just one aspect of a simple object. For example, hold a piece of fruit in your hand, like an apple. Study it for a few minutes and then close your eyes and imagine that you are looking at the same apple. Some people become overwhelmed by their expectations of how their visualizations or clairvoyant images are supposed to look. Sometimes I can visualize an object as vividly as if I were seeing it with my physical eyes, while at other times, I can just see enough of an object to know it is there. If all you can muster up is the outline of an object, then that is completely acceptable. If you are unable to do even that, then just postulate that you are visualizing the object.

When I call the energy I want to see into my viewing receptacle, nothing happens. All I see is black.

Congratulations! You are seeing something . . . black! There is a reason for everything you see and everything you don't see! If you draw a blank or just blackness, there are a couple things you can do. First, be patient. Continue to watch the black (or nothingness) for a few minutes and see what happens. Then ask the black (or nothingness) to show you an image of what it represents and continue to observe. If nothing happens, then try grounding your reading screen and the viewing receptacle to release any energy that is blocking the information. The best advice I can give is to be patient and calmly relentless in your intent to get an answer!

I have been known to sit for half an hour in total silence in front of a client until the elusive information to an important question finally appeared (the client is usually more willing to let the question go than I am!). Anytime information is not easily accessible, there is a reason for it and that reason may be what is blocking you or your readee or both from being where you would like to be in your life. Pursuing the answer, no matter how much work it takes on your part, is what will make your readings effective and valuable. There are plenty of capable but lazy psychics out there who will give up immediately if the information is not made available. This serves no one, especially the psychic. When information you are seeking resides in your or your readee's unconscious mind, when there have been years, if not decades, of psychological defense mechanisms and other energies repressing this information, you will find that it is much harder to see. Sometimes you may not be ready emotionally or psychologically to deal with the answer that comes to you. If this is the case, you will probably get distracted, fall asleep, or naturally give up (which may be what is supposed to happen; our defense mechanisms are there to help us, even through they block us at the same time).

Another reason you may not get a response when posing a question to your viewing receptacle is that you may be asking the wrong question. Early in my clairvoyant training, I read a client who asked the question, "Should I marry my fiancé?" I put up a clear glass image of a rose on my reading screen and posed the same question to the rose. I got absolutely no response. After about fifteen minutes of trying all of the above suggestions, the answer finally came to me, which was that in the realm of spirit, there is no should or should not! There was no answer to that particular question. I reframed the question to the rose and asked, "Would my client be fulfilled and happy in her life if she married her fiancé?" The response was immediate—an image of her crying. I have had this same experience so many times that without a doubt I can advise that you should never use "should" in your questions!

Whenever I attempt to do the exercises in this chapter, I fall asleep.

There are a few reasons why you might fall asleep during clairvoyant reading and meditation. The most obvious reason is that you are tired! I used to pride myself on the number of hours I could sit in meditation on a daily basis, being totally alert and focused. That was until the birth of my bouncing baby boy, when I became a single mother who worked three different jobs (not including writing this book) and went to filmmaking school full-time. Now I am lucky if I can meditate in an upright position for two minutes before falling asleep.

If at all possible, try getting a good night's sleep and then change your routine. Try practicing your clairvoyant exercises earlier in the day, after you have had a chance to digest your food but before you are hungry again. Drinking one small cup of coffee or black tea before attempting these exercises might help as well (not that I want to advocate the use of caffeine; I have seen the negative impact of too much caffeine on the throat and the fifth chakra in several readings).

You might also try reading in a different location. If possible, avoid reading and meditating in a place where you usually sleep, whether that is in your bedroom or on the sofa in front of the TV, since your body is programmed to sleep in these situations. Make sure to practice these exercises in an upright position; reclining or lying down will cause most people to fall asleep. Experiment with reading and meditating after you have engaged in some physical exercise. Physical exercise naturally gets your energy flowing and might help you focus, although it could have the opposite effect on some people.

When I read myself, I don't know if I am getting accurate information or if I am being biased by what I want to see.

Reading objectively is a challenge and one reason why I personally find it much easier to read people I don't know than myself. If you are having this problem, try the following exercise.

Visualize a rose and postulate that this rose will contain the accurate and unbiased answer or information to your question. Then create another rose and postulate that it contains the energy of the answer you would like to hear. Ask the first rose to show you a color, and then ask the second rose to do the same. Notice whether the colors are the same or different. Ask each color to show you what it represents.

For example, let's say you have just met a good-looking guy and you are hoping he will ask you out. Waiting to see if he does is, of course, too agonizing, so you decide to do a little clairvoyant reading for yourself. When you pose this question to your viewing receptacle/rose, you see an image of him calling you on the telephone, but you are not sure if you are just making this up. So you destroy that rose and create two new ones. The first rose, which represents the true answer, is blue. The second rose, representing your desires, is green. When you ask the blue to show you what it means, you see the good-looking guy sitting in an office buried in papers; he seems stressed out. When you ask the green to show you what it means, you see the two of you smooching! The fact that the two colors and images are different probably indicates that your exact desire may not manifest. However, now you have a better idea of why he has not called. It's not that you are unworthy of his attention, but that he is distracted by his work.

This exercise will help you explore your biases, but will not eliminate them. As long as you realize when reading yourself that you are not neutral and that your information could be heavily biased, you will not get into trouble. (The problem of personal bias is significantly reduced when you know nothing about the person you are reading.) Over time, you will be better able to distinguish between psychic information that is coming from your ego versus information that is coming from a higher source. Don't let the fear of confusing the two get in the way of practicing and enjoying your readings.

I enjoy reading other people, but when I try to use my clairvoyance on myself, I get too distracted and give up before getting any results.

It is a lot harder for most people to read themselves than it is for them to read other people. When reading yourself, you are susceptible to the same distractions that make it difficult for so many people to meditate (or even get to the point of attempting to meditate). It is very easy to get lost in all the energy in the form of thoughts that are swimming around in your mind and aura. Foreign energies can easily distract you. One solution is to use a tape recorder. As you do the exercises in this chapter, give a detailed account of everything you are doing, seeing, and experiencing. Another solution is to do the exercises with a partner who can verbally guide you with questions and listen to your responses.

It is in no way mandatory that you first read yourself before reading other people, and if you are having too much difficulty reading yourself, or it's not fun, then by all means move on to reading someone else, which will be covered in the following chapter. When you read another person, you have no choice but to focus on that person's energy. The moment your thoughts wander, you will no longer be reading the person (who is sitting there, excitedly waiting for your communication), and you will momentarily realize this and come back to the reading (which is not usually the case when you are reading yourself).

Many people think that they can only read another person once they have perfected their clairvoyance. That is the one of biggest mistakes you can make! The only way to develop your clairvoyant abilities, or any ability, is to practice and to take risks. The more you practice, the more you will realize what you can do. As long as you begin by reading receptive, supportive people who understand that you are just learning, you will be fine! (I don't recommend accepting money for readings until you are confident and have a number of readings under your belt—see chapter 23).

There is value both in reading yourself and in reading others. Continue to try both of these experiences and over time you will find that they get easier. Many of the difficulties you run into when you are first beginning to develop your clairvoyance will soon become obsolete as you grow and heal yourself through reading and using your psychic tools. Who you are now is not who you will be later. The path of clairvoyance is a path of growth, and there is richness and meaning in every difficulty you encounter in your meditation and readings and everyday life. This book would not exist if it were not for the challenges I have faced during my own readings.

CHAPTER 14

How to Read Another Person

In this chapter, you will learn everything you need to know in order to effectively perform a clairvoyant reading on another person.

Communicating Expectations

Expectations for the reading should be discussed before both parties agree to participate in the reading and preferably before the client arrives for the reading. These expectations include the length of the reading, whether compensation is expected, the general format of the reading, whether the future will be addressed, and whether the client will have an opportunity to ask questions. Most people feel some level of anxiety prior to a reading because they don't know what to expect or whether their expectations will be met. If they have no idea how much you will charge them or whether there will be an opportunity for them to ask you a pressing question, then their attention will be focused on their anxieties and on the future. Since as a reader your attention will tend to go to where the readee's attention is, you will have a harder time concentrating in the present moment, which is where your clairvoyant images are located. You will also sense your readee's anxiety, which will decrease your enjoyment of the reading.

Discussing expectations is an ethically sound practice, particularly when financial compensation is involved. The more you are in integrity, the less energy you will expend. Communicating expectations minimizes future ethical dilemmas and arguments, and decreases the possibility of disappointment and resentment for both parties. Most importantly, when both parties understand the expectations upfront, they can make the most conscious and informed decision about whether or not to proceed with the reading.

That being said, once expectations have been communicated, they should not be set in stone, because after all, you can never know (even if you are psychic) how either of you will feel once the reading has begun. The readee may be really happy with the reading and request that the time of the reading be extended. You may agree to look at the future, but when the time comes you may only receive information about the present. The format of the reading could change depending on the particular issues of your client.

At any point, either you or your readee may decide that the reading is not going well and chose to terminate it. Of course, if this happens, the agreed-upon compensation may need to be reconsidered. As a reader you are never obligated to complete a reading or give a reading, and one of your most challenging but rewarding lessons will occur when you are faced with the dilemma of whether or not to prematurely end a reading if something about it does not seem conducive to your well-being. The more money you stand to make from a reading, the more difficult this dilemma will be. For more discussion on this issue, see chapter 23.

Location

Prior to the reading, you will need to find the right location for the reading. Ideally this location will be a quiet one with minimal distractions, where you can feel safe sitting across from a stranger. That being said, the truth of the matter is that you can do a clairvoyant reading anytime, anywhere. I have performed readings on crowded airplanes, at raucous parties, in moving vehicles, on mountaintops in the rain, in an agent's office at the Federal Bureau of Investigation, and at psychic fairs where I and thirty other psychics were doing readings so close to each other that the hairs on our arms were touching. A reading can be performed under any circumstances. However, for the purposes of learning how to do readings and feeling grounded and comfortable, ideally you will want to make arrangements so that you and your readee can sit in two comfortable upright chairs, in a well-grounded, peaceful environment. As you become more experienced, you will want to practice reading in more distracting and uncomfortable places so you can realize that you too can read under any circumstance.

Timekeeping

During a reading, it is helpful to have a clock or timer nearby so you know when your time is up. Some people are fine with the sound of a timer, though personally I find it too jolting. I prefer to have a large clock placed on the wall behind my readee at my eye level, so I can effortlessly open my eyes and glance at the clock without breaking my concentration. Oftentimes I have an inner alarm clock that tells me when we are nearing the end of the reading. You may have experienced a similar phenomenon when waking up on the morning of an important event. You may set your alarm clock, but then find that you wake up a couple minutes before the clock is supposed to go off. This is because there is a part of you that is awake and aware of everything going on around you at all times.

However, when you first begin doing readings, you will have greater difficulty judging the passage of time and will be more inclined to get drawn into reading longer than you intended by the desires of your overzealous readee ("Please, just one more quick question!") and by your own compulsion to heal every problem your readee has ever had! A clock or timer will not only help you judge the passage of time, but you may actually need to show it to your readee in order to bring them back to "reality" and help them understand that the reading is really over.

Pre-Reading Meditation

I recommend meditating for at least twenty minutes before embarking on a reading. This meditation should include psychic tools such as grounding yourself and the room, centering yourself, running your energy, creating and destroying objects, clearing your chakras, etc. Meditation will help flush out all the rambling thoughts of the day so information of a more subtle nature can be grasped. If you don't spend some time meditating or working on your tools prior to the reading, the first several minutes of the reading will be more of a struggle and the clairvoyant information may not initially be as vivid or accessible. You will also be less vulnerable to negative energies at the onset of the reading if you take the time to secure yourself to the earth and have your energy running before your readee enters the room.

Setting an Intention

At the start of a reading, it is also a good practice to pick one or two things that you are going to work on or intend to accomplish during the reading for yourself. This could be anything from postulating that you are going to work on your grounding tools to kicking out a former girlfriend's (or boyfriend's) energy from your aura. Setting an intention will serve to remind you that you are equally as important as your readee and that reading is a healing and personal growth process for you as a reader. Also, when you are using your clairvoyant abilities, you are accessing the spiritual realms where time and space and physical limits do not exist. It is here where intentions, dreams, and wishes can manifest much more quickly and with less effort (see chapter 12).

Setting Boundaries

You will often sense the readee's energy coming toward you before you actually attempt to tune in to that person. This might happen before the readee arrives or as soon as they enter the door. You will know this is happening if you spontaneously think about them or if you begin to pick up clairvoyant information before you have officially "tuned in" to them. Sometimes you may feel nervous and therefore be drawn to take a peek at the readee before you start. Some readers will actually do a reading before the readee arrives so they feel less pressure during the reading, a practice I discourage. A reading is not a performance and it does not need to appear flawless.

I personally set strong limits for myself (and for my students) in that I am only allowed to read that person when they are in front of me and when I have officially begun the reading. If I find myself thinking about the readee before or after the reading, then I know there is an energy exchange going on that could become messy very quickly. It is for this reason that I generally do not ask the readee what their questions are before I officially am ready to start the reading, and once the reading is over, I cease to discuss their issues. Otherwise the reading could continue on a telepathic level for days, years, or even an entire lifetime!

It's important to understand that if a woman approaches you on a Saturday and schedules a reading for the following Tuesday, you could potentially end up reading her for the next seventy-two hours if you aren't careful. Your aura could become merged with hers and then you will begin to feel and live all of her pain, problems, anxieties, etc., without even being aware that this is happening. The way to avoid this is first to make the commitment to yourself that you will not permit an energetic connection to form until you consciously will this connection to form, and then to establish a routine that lets your body and spirit know when the reading is beginning and when it is ending. Using your psychic tools on a regular basis will also help you with this.

Don't Allow Anyone in the Room Except the Readee

Invariably, a client will arrive for a reading and they or their companion, whether it be their husband, mother, or friend, will ask if it's all right if the companion stays in the room. Ninety-nine percent of the time I say no, unless the readee is a child (see chapter 19). There are a few reasons for this. First of all, the energy of the readee's companion could easily interfere with the reading and you may inadvertently start reading that person without being aware of this. Furthermore, clairvoyant readings tend to be very personal, and you don't want to be inhibited in any way from sharing information of a personal nature.

On many occasions when I had to put my foot down and asked the readee's companion to wait outside or return in an hour, it actually turned out that the readee had questions about their relationship with that person and never would have felt comfortable asking or talking about those issues in the companion's presence. Sometimes clients just don't know how to speak up and set boundaries for themselves, so you will need to do this for them. Remember, during a reading you are in control.

Most clients understand when you explain that another person's presence will interfere with your reading, and they really appreciate that you are trying to give them the best experience possible. Occasionally the readee will explain that they are in an intimate relationship with their companion and are working on similar goals and this is why they want to both be present for the reading. In that case, you can ask them if they are seeking a relationship reading and read them as a couple, as discussed in chapter 18.

Reading Routine

I have fallen into a particular routine that assists me in maintaining boundaries. This routine also helps keep the various steps of the reading organized and signals my subconscious as to when the actual reading is going to begin.

Begin by greeting your readee. Introduce yourself. Show your readee where to sit. I like to read directly across from my readee, with a few feet of space in between us so our auras are not totally enmeshed, but close enough so we can speak on intimate terms and hear each other well. Both parties should be sitting upright in comfortable chairs or sofas.

Eliminate distracting sounds and music. Whether the readee comes to you or you go to them, it is important for you to take control of the environment before the reading begins. If you cannot assert yourself enough to ask to rearrange some furniture or turn down the music, energetically you won't be able to assert yourself enough to get past the readee's resistances or to keep the readee out of your energy field. Music or noise from a television set often will pull you out of your body and out of the reading.

Next, explain to your readee what a clairvoyant reading entails. This is what I usually say to new clients: "So what I will be doing today is a clairvoyant reading, where I will be looking at different images that come up. Some of these will be symbolic, while others will have literal interpretations. As I talk, some things will make sense while other things may not make any sense at all. Eventually things will become clear."

Highlighting the General Order of Activities

Next, I explain that I will first go into a light trance and ground myself. This trance is nothing deeper than a relaxed state of awareness. I mention that I will now close my eyes and have them closed for the entire reading. I let the readee know that this will take a few minutes and I won't charge them for this time.

I then explain that after I go into my trance, I will ask my readee to state their name a few times in order to tune in to their vibration, and that throughout the reading I may ask them to restate their name if I feel I need to strengthen or reestablish my connection with them.

I explain that after I am tuned in to their vibration, the readee will have an opportunity to ask questions or discuss their issues, or at that point we will discuss the format of the reading.

Next, I reassure the readee that I will walk them through the process and that there is nothing they need to do now except to keep their feet flat on the floor (to keep them grounded) and to remain in an alert state of consciousness with their eyes open. Many clients automatically match me as I go into a trance, and then I have more difficulty reading them, so I do what I can to keep them awake. However, some people just cannot help but close their eyes, and to force them to keep their eyes open would make them too uncomfortable. For these people, I just gently remind them from time to time to come back to their body, and I ask them to repeat their name more often than those people who naturally stay alert.

Running Through Your Psychic Tools in the Presence of the Readee

When I first began doing readings, I felt awkward taking the time to run through my psychic tools while sitting across from another person. I felt self-conscious, as if they were staring at me, judging my appearance, my clothes, and the way my eyes fluttered. I felt like they were thinking about the money they were paying for every second I sat there in self-absorbed silence. Over time I realized that yes, some people were doing these things. But many others were sitting there worrying about their own behavior and appearance, while the majority were very happy to give me whatever time I needed to get ready to give them the best reading of their life.

Years later I still take a few minutes at the start of every single reading to run through my psychic tools (I do this even if I already sat in meditation for an hour before their arrival—something I'd like to do all the time but don't!), and I'm at the point now where I really couldn't care less about what anyone is doing or thinking during that time. In fact, lots of times I completely forget that there is anyone sitting less than two feet away and staring at me. I am only reminded of their presence when they sneeze or move their chair.

Taking this time for yourself in the presence of the readee is vital to your well-being and it serves your readee in a number of ways. Even if you just spent two hours meditating before they arrived, it's necessary to check your psychic tools to make sure they are still working in the presence of your readee. Your readee's energy will have an effect on your grounding cord, your ability to stay in the center of your head, and on your tools such as running your earth and cosmic energies. So you want to double-check that these are still working for you after your readee has arrived.

Furthermore, meditating in the presence of your readee makes the statement to yourself and to your readee that you are important and that you have a right to take care of yourself at all times. As you take care of yourself in the presence and under the scrutiny of another person, you are modeling this behavior for your readee. Some readers start picking up information about their readee during this time. As mentioned earlier, I try to push away this information until I have made sure that I have sufficiently prepared and cared for myself.

Running through your psychic tools at the start of every reading will also serve as a signal to your body and your psychic faculties that you are about to begin a clairvoyant reading, so that when you actually attempt to access the clairvoyant information, it will flow more easily. I tend to not officially start the time for the reading until after I have gone into a trance and run through my tools, although some people feel strongly that this is time spent on the reading and they should be compensated for it.

Furthermore, during a reading, you should periodically take short breaks from reading to run through your psychic tools to make sure you are still reading from a grounded place of neutrality, releasing whatever needs to be released, and energizing yourself. This again is good modeling behavior. In professional readings, I tend to worry that my readee will feel cheated from their time, but I know that taking these breaks makes me a better and clearer reader, and people usually appreciate this.

Redistributing Your Energy

As part of your pre-reading meditation, you will want to redistribute your energy from your lower three chakras to your upper chakras. As you go through your everyday life, there are lots of times when it is necessary and desirable to have your energy running though your lower chakras, particularly when you need to use your body for physical activity. However, during a reading, your body really doesn't have to do anything beyond maintaining its minimal automatic functions. Instead, your psychic and cognitive abilities will be needed in full force, and therefore the chakras that house these abilities will be in greater need of your energy. By redistributing your energy from your lower chakras to your upper chakras, you will call forth the inherent spiritual abilities of the fifth, sixth, and seventh chakras, while inhibiting the energies of survival, control, and emotion that are associated with the lower chakras and that are less conducive to clairvoyant reading. Energy can be redistributed through a simple visualization of opening and closing your chakras and moving your energy upward or downward.

Begin by creating a reading screen in front of your sixth chakra, or third eye, located slightly above and between your eyebrows, in the center of your head. Then visualize your first chakra, which is located at the base of your spine. You can imagine that it looks like the lens of a camera that opens and closes. Look to see how open it is. Is it open 100 percent, 75 percent, 50 percent, or is it totally closed? If you are having trouble determining how open it is, you can visualize that there is a gauge or a meter with numbers on it, and then ask the percentage of how open it is to appear on the gauge.

Now it is time to close your first chakra down so that it is only about half open. On your reading screen, imagine that the opening of your first chakra is getting smaller and smaller until it is only half open. You can give your gauge a grounding cord and imagine that any foreign energy in your first chakra is effortlessly falling down the cord into the center of the planet. Look at your gauge and watch as the arrow goes to 50 percent. As you close down your first chakra, notice how it feels. Are you experiencing any bodily sensations? Do you feel any emotions or pain being released? Do you feel more relaxed or nervous? Realize that as you close down your first chakra, your own vital energy is naturally rising up to your higher chakras.

Next, create a clear glass rose on your reading screen that represents your own energy in your first chakra. Look to see what color it is. Now watch that color as it rises up your chakras until it gets to your crown chakra. Once the color reaches your crown chakra, imagine that your crown chakra is opening up like a lotus, and visualize it growing brighter and brighter.

You can then repeat this process with your second and third chakras. Again, start off imagining that these chakras are growing smaller and smaller, so that any excess energy is squeezed outward and upward to your third eye (sixth chakra) and crown chakra (seventh chakra). See these spinning energy centers expand and grow brighter as you remind yourself that you are now activiating the energy in these higher chakras, which will further stimulate your clairvoyance and make it easier to remain centered, balanced, and calm.

Turning Down Your Analyzer

One of the most challenging things about doing clairvoyant readings is that you need your analytical mind to at least lead you to the doorway of your clairvoyance in terms of helping you formulate questions that will elicit a clairvoyant response. However, once you have posed a question with the use of your logical/analytical mind, you must abandon that part of yourself momentarily so that extrasensory information can come to you.

Consciously turning down your analytical/logical mind is a very simple but effective technique that can remarkably decrease the thoughts and general noise level of your mind. It will bring you into a deeper state of relaxation where you can enjoy the flow of your clairvoyant images rather than resist or doubt or question them. While you will still have access to your logical faculties, these will no longer dominate your intuitive processes.

First say hello to your reading screen. Check to see if it has any holes or is dusty. Give it a grounding cord and release any energy that has accumulated on it. If you don't like how it looks, then destroy it and create a new one. On your screen, place a big, old-fashioned gauge with a big arrow. This represents your analytical mind. Postulate that whatever you do to this gauge will actually affect the part of your brain that generates your analytical thoughts.

First look to see at what number your analytical mind is currently set. Next, give this gauge a really big grounding cord and ground it firmly into the center of the planet. Now very slowly start to move the arrow on the gauge down by five degrees. As you do this, look for the color of energy that can now be released from this gauge into the center of the planet. When you turn down your analytical mind, you are releasing extraneous energy that you do not need. So this exercise is giving you a healing at the same time that it's helping prepare you to use your clairvoyance.

Notice how you are feeling. Let any emotions or fears that come up be released down your own grounding cord. You may want to increase the size of your grounding cord. Now slowly continue to move the gauge down further and further until it is at the 10 percent mark. You really only need 10 percent of your analytical mind to be operating at this point. Continue to release any fearful thoughts that suggest you may lose control or not be able to think anymore. Send these thoughts and emotions down your grounding cord. The nature of your logical mind is that it wants to be in control of every aspect of your life, even when its presence will only interfere with your goals.

Turning Up Your Clairvoyance

This is a warm-up exercise that will help you begin to flex your visualization "muscles" and stimulate/clear your sixth chakra. It also serves as a signal to your mind that you are preparing to enter into an altered state of consciousness, in much the same way that a hypnotic suggestion works.

Begin by visualizing your reading screen. Imagine that there is a big eye on it. This is your third eye, which corresponds to your sixth chakra and your clairvoyance. Notice how big the eye is and how open it is. Notice all of its details. What color(s) is it? Does it have eyelashes? Is there makeup on the lids? Is it clear or is it bloodshot? Is it an alert eye or is it a sleepy eye? Is it a happy eye or is it crying? Give your third eye a grounding cord and ask any foreign energies to release out of it.

Drain out any energy that may be getting in the way of your clairvoyance. This energy could be in the form of atheism, competition, self-doubt, past-life or childhood trauma, etc.

While atheism and competition are not necessarily bad things in everyday life, when they are in your clairvoyant "space," they are deadly. Imagine that you are sitting quietly, trying your hardest to concentrate, to notice the most delicate of changes occurring behind your fluttering eyelids, completely unsure of yourself and what you are about to experience. Or maybe you are a more experienced psychic, brimming with confidence and excitement about this grand opportunity to do another reading, but then someone approaches you, perhaps a stranger, but most likely someone you adore: a parent, your wife, a client, etc. They snuggle up close, slide up on your lap, fling their arms around your neck, snuggle up against your ear, stare passionately into your eyes and holler at the top of their lungs: "Who do you think you are, you stupid idiot? Why would you of all people be able to do this? You will never be good enough. You won't see a thing. You don't have what it takes!" (This is competition.) Or: "There is no such thing as this psychic crap, you imbecile! You've never seen any of this before, so why do you think you could now? It's not real. None of it is real!" (Atheism, skepticism.) While this is a silly scenario, do you think this might just have a wee bit of an impact on your concentration, confidence level, or enthusiasm for doing a reading?

Now imagine that this charming individual is not physically present, but their energy, their thoughtforms, their emotions are. They might as well be right in your face because their energy is going to have the same impact as if they were there, only it will work you over on an unconscious level. So you won't see it coming and you won't know why it is you just got distracted, why you are so frustrated, or why it is you fell asleep or got up from that chair and decided it was time to wash the dishes. All you'll know is that suddenly the last thing you want to do is the very thing you most wanted to do five minutes ago: experience your clairvoyance. This is why we do exercises like this one, and so many of the others throughout this book.

Getting back to the exercise, you have just drained any foreign energies from your third eye on your reading screen. Next, see a color for the energy as it drains out and then look at the eye to see if any of its attributes have changed. If your third eye does not look very open, then you can imagine that it is opening as wide as you can possibly open it. See this third eye getting bigger and bigger until it fills up your entire reading screen and still it grows bigger and bigger.

If you'd like, you can connect your third eye up to God by visualizing God as a golden ball of light and seeing a cord connecting the eye to the ball of light, and then filling up your eye with God's light. Talk to your third eye and tell it that you are going to need its help in a big way. Thank it in advance for working for you. Promise it that you will do everything you can to honor whatever it wants to show you by trusting that its images are relevant to the reading and by sharing the images with the readee.

If you'd like, you can also put up a gauge that represents your clairvoyance and visualize that the arrow on the gauge us going up to 100 percent open. Then pick a color that represents your own enthusiasm and amusement. Fill your third eye with this color. To increase the energy of fun and amusement in your readings, dress up your eye in a funny way. Give it long, curly, silly eyelashes or see it doing funny tricks with its eyebrow. Remember, laughter and amusement are the highest vibration of energy, and problems, worries, doubts, etc., cannot exist in the energy of amusement. Sometimes you need to make an extra effort to create amusement when you are not feeling particularly amused, but remember, laughter is infectious.

The Psychic Is In: Preparing to Read

This next technique is also optional but can be quite useful. When I first began reading out of a metaphysical bookstore in Sedona, I often had very little time to meditate or prepare myself before beginning a reading. I was still settling into the idea of charging money for readings and was nervous about the responsibility that seemed to go with that. I found it necessary to come up with a visualization tool that would help me get into my clairvoyant reading space quickly and confidently, and here is the technique I developed.

First, imagine you are entering a room. It looks just like the room where you are going to do your reading. However, under the rug or the floor boards is a trap door. You open up the trap door and see a staircase. You follow the staircase down several flights until you reach a door with the sign "Clairvoyant Reading Chamber." You open the door and see a coat rack. You take off your coat and your hat in preparation to read. You then put on a special hat that says "Clairvoyance." You find some slippers. These are your favorite clairvoyant reading slippers, which you wear only when doing readings. Next, imagine that you sit down in your favorite clairvoyant reading chair. You might even take a swig out of a glass bottle that is labeled "Clairvoyant Reading Potion." This potion enhances your abilities. Yum, it's so delicious! You are now ready to begin your readings.

This exercise is very simple. You can make the décor of the clairvoyant reading chamber as basic or as elaborate as you'd like. Often, if I only have a minute or less before I'm supposed to start my reading, I will just visualize that I am entering the room, hanging up my coat, and putting on my clairvoyant reading hat. This serves as a sign to my unconscious that I am ready to begin the reading.

Saying a Prayer

I cannot teach you how to pray in words.
God listens not to your words save when He Himself utters them
through your lips.
And I cannot teach you the prayer of the seas and the forests and the
mountains.
But you who are born of the mountains and the forests and the seas
can find their prayer in your heart.

—Kahlil Gibran, The Prophet, 1923

I always say a prayer before doing a reading. I say it out loud so that I, my readee, and any other being in the room can hear the prayer. Prayer helps set the intention of the reading and it sends a clear message to any spirits, entities, or negative influences in the room or around any of the participants that any interference on their part will not be tolerated. It's like a mission statement, a declaration, a contract. Physicists will tell you that nature abhors a vacuum. Space is not empty. It is filled by whatever is closest to it and strongest. If you have competing sounds in a room, the loudest sound will be heard the most. The strongest smell will be experienced, and the brightest light will outshine the weaker lights and overpower the darkness.

It's the same with energy and prayer. If you sit down for a reading, or at work, or when getting into bed, and state: "I now bring peace here," or "Please, God, bring peace here," then you strengthen this intention, this desire, by focusing on a symbol that represents this intention, such as a peace symbol, a dove, Jesus, a star of David, or your favorite soothing color. You are invoking peace to be there with you in that space, and anything that is not peace will not be able to exist in that same space.

So prayer serves as an invitation for some energies to participate and for others to excuse themselves immediately. The readee needs to know what energies you are invoking or dismissing since some of those energies are a part of them. Many clients understand the power of prayer and will be grateful, if not relieved, that you are making a point to pray during their reading. Of course there are some people who are uncomfortable with prayer because they don't understand what it is or have negative connotations associated with it (for example, they think that only fanatics pray).

As a clairvoyant reader, you are also a spiritual teacher and you can demonstrate to these people that prayer in this instance really has nothing to do with religion or fanaticism, but is more about evoking a desired outcome of energy, such as peace, love, joy, etc. When I pray, I do mention the word God; however, when I first started out as a clairvoyant reader I referred to God as "the Supreme Being" or as "the universe." I used to be a lot more concerned about offending people than

I am now. I feel that if anyone is offended by the mention of the word God, that is their problem, not mine. Even if someone is an atheist, they should still be able to appreciate that God symbolizes something positive and helpful.

Visualization for Prayer

During a prayer, I will visualize a color that represents God. For me, this is usually a bright sparkly golden color. I will imagine that I am encompassing myself and the readee inside this color so that we are totally immersed in it. Since this is the color and energy of God, we are inside God and protected by the attributes we feel God possesses. This bubble not only helps us maintain a connection with God, it also keeps out any energies that are antithetical to the qualities normally ascribed to God. It reminds us that the reading is taking place between me, as a reader, and the readee, and that no one else with or without a body is invited to participate unless otherwise noted. At this time it is also helpful to ground the room again, which you should have done when you first reviewed your tools at the start of the reading (see chapter 7).

Tuning In to the Readee

In the last chapter, you learned how to clairvoyantly read yourself. In terms of the basic clairvoyant reading technique, the only difference between reading yourself and someone else is that when reading someone else, it is first necessary to tune in to that person's frequency, vibration, spirit, energy, etc., in order to establish a direct line of communication.

This is similar to what happens when you want to talk to someone on the telephone. There are millions of people out there connected into the same telephone system. In order to speak to a particular person, you need to dial their personal phone number. In the same way, if you desire to talk to a particular person face to face, you need to take steps to initiate the conversation. First, one of you will have to approach the other and get that person's attention, either through verbal communication, such as yelling, "Hey, how's it going?" or through nonverbal communication, such as touching the person's shoulder and looking into their eyes. Once this happens, you are communicating.

In the same manner, if you desire to perform a clairvoyant reading on a particular person, you must do something to establish a connection with that person. The first step is very simple; it requires you to merely have the intention to read that person. The next step is tuning in to that person's individual vibration as a spirit. Oftentimes clients will have lots of different people and energies around them. If you proceed with the basic reading technique without first tuning in to your specific client, you may end up reading the wrong person!

Next, create a new reading screen (see chapter 13). Set your crown chakra to a neutral gold color. You can do this by visualizing your crown chakra as a spinning disk or as an open golden lotus flower.

Then create a viewing receptacle/rose out in front of your reading screen. Create and destroy a couple of these, and then ask your readee to say their name. Ask the readee to say the name they were born with three times, and then their current name three times, and then any other names they have gone by, such as nicknames or names from previous marriages. While the readee says these names, invite their energy to come into the viewing receptacle. Then look for a color that represents their energy.

Once you see a color, take that receptacle and put it over your crown chakra, and ask your crown chakra to match that color. Once your crown chakra has matched the readee's color, adjust the color of your crown chakra so it becomes a bit darker or lighter than that of the readee. This is to remind yourself that you are separate from your readee.

Troubleshooting

I see different colors with the readee's different names.
The reason I ask clients to say every name they have ever gone by is because people identify with certain names. Names contain so much energy and hold a lot of information. Often I have found that when a

person says their birth name, it is a very different color and vibration than their married name. If you find that different colors are coming up with each name, you can go with the name they are currently using or whichever name they like the best, since this name will be more in present time. You will sometimes need to use your intuition to determine whether a color is really the appropriate one. If all else fails, have them repeat their first name several times and go with the color of their first name. You could also combine two colors and match your crown chakra to both of these. Most of the time, however, you can just use the first color that comes to you when the readee says all their names.

I am not clearly seeing a color.

Create and destroy a few roses and then ask the readee to repeat all their names. Really listen to the sound of their voice. Ask the vibration you hear to go into your newly created viewing receptacle/rose. Postulate that it is the readee's higher self or a part of their very soul that is going into that receptacle. If you still do not get a color, then just postulate that you are matching your crown chakra to theirs.

I clearly see a color, but then it changes and I see another color.

If you see one color, but then it changes to another color, I recommend putting a grounding cord on your viewing receptacle and postulating that you are grounding out any foreign energies. Look at the colors coming out of the rose and look at the color remaining in the rose. Whatever color remains in the viewing receptacle/rose is the correct color to use. If there is still more than one color, choose the one that appears the most vibrant, or combine the two to make a third color, or swirl the two together. As the reading progresses, you can repeat the tuning in process and you will most likely discover that one of the colors has clearly become the dominant one. This is because as you clairvoyantly read a person, you tune in to that person's spirit/energy and their spirit will naturally move in closer to their body. The more present the readee's spirit is in their body, the easier it will be to see the color at which their spirit is vibrating.

I don't like the color I see and feel a strong resistance to matching that color to my crown chakra.

There are a few reasons you may feel resistance to a particular color. One might be because you have matching pictures with the readee that keep you in resistance to the energy that the color represents. Try creating and destroying some roses around your crown chakra. Postulate that you are clearing any of your own matching pictures. Have the readee repeat their name and try matching your crown chakra to this color, whether it is the original color or a new color.

Another reason you may resist matching your crown chakra to your readee's is because the color represents a very low vibration (such as judgment, pain, or anger) that your body does not want to match. If the color looks and feels very unattractive to you, put it into a rose, ground the rose, and see if the color changes. The color may not really represent your readee's spirit, but rather foreign energy affecting your readee. If all else fails, put up a rose that represents your readee's next step, i.e., the next higher vibration they are really seeking to move into. Match your crown chakra to this vibration rather than the one your readee is currently in.

My body becomes very uncomfortable as I tune in to the readee.

It's important to frequently check in with your body to make sure you are running your own energy rather than your readee's energy. It's common for a clairvoyant reader to totally match their body to that of their client or other readers in the room. If your body goes into pain or discomfort, it could mean that you are releasing matching pictures, but it could also mean that you matched your body to the level of pain and discomfort that the readee feels.

If you are reading a person of the opposite sex and you match the energy in your body to theirs, you could be adversely affected. You may feel overly sluggish or nervous, bored, angry, etc. The point of the tuning in process is merely to match a part of your crown chakra to the readee's vibration; it doesn't at all mean matching the energy of your body to theirs. Revisiting your psychic tools of creating a protection/separation rose and running your earth and cosmic energies, as well as imagining that you are bringing your own energy back into your body while the readee is bringing in their own energy (see these as two different colors), will help you separate your respective energies. You may also need to open your eyes for a moment and physically look at the difference between your body and your readee's body to prove to yourself that they are not the same.

Sending Your Readee a Hello

Once you are tuned in to your readee, send them a visual "hello." This hello can be any welcoming, friendly object, such as a bouquet of flowers or a balloon with a smiley face on it. In your imagination, postulate that this object will go to wherever the readee's spirit is, and then watch to see where the object lands. You can aim for their crown chakra and see if it goes there or somewhere else. See if they accept your hello, give you one back, return yours unopened, etc. If they don't accept it, you can try again or ask another viewing receptacle to show you the reason for this rejection. If they still don't accept your hello, there is a good chance there will be resistance to accepting your communication during the reading as well.

If you become aware of the resistance, it might help to talk to your readee about it in gentle terms. You could say that you notice some energy around them that does not want them to make changes and that might try to block them from hearing what you are going to say. Sometimes merely talking about resistance or interfering energy causes that energy to release. You can help your readee release this resistance by giving them a grounding cord and watching to see whether the energy releases. Once it releases, send them another hello and see what happens this time. If you still don't get a warm response, nothing is lost. The purpose of this exercise is not to change your readee to make them like you more, but rather to first acknowledge their spirit, and second to understand how open the readee is to you and your communication. Being aware of a readee's resistance will prevent you from falling into the deadly trap of blaming yourself for a difficult reading.

Listening to the Readee's Questions

Some readers prefer to have their clients state any questions or issues they would like addressed prior to the commencement of the tuning in process. However, I have found it useful to tune in first and then have the readee voice their questions, because as they ask their questions, I actually use their voice as another means to connect with their individual blueprint. This makes it easier to read the client rather than any other energies in the room. Furthermore, as the readee states their questions, I imagine that their question is not just going to me, but is really a call to God and the universe and their higher self to provide the readee with answers. These answers may come through me in the form of clairvoyant images that I can share with the readee, or the answers could be delivered directly to the readee via their own insights and experiences. This process of focusing intently on my readee's voice helps me concentrate and at the same time brings me into a deeper state of relaxation.

Should the Readee Ask Questions at the Start of the Reading?

The answer to this question is complex. All of the clairvoyant training schools in the United States offer student readings to the public. These readings are structured readings that follow a particular template or format (see chapter 16) and often run anywhere from one-and-a-half to two hours. Some schools do not permit the readees to ask questions until the last ten or fifteen minutes of the reading. There are a few reasons for this.

First, for the purpose of clairvoyant training, it is often helpful for a student to have no information or predetermined notions about the readee and to have no restrictions about what they can or can't see or talk about. A readee's question acts as a focal point, drawing the readers attention to this one point, which could eliminate countless other points. New students can easily get stuck in answering a readee's question when that question may not really be what the readee is truly longing or needing to know. Clairvoyants see all kinds of things, including spirits and energy blockages, that many people are not conscious of, but that may be playing an enormous role in a person's life. A clairvoyant student will be more likely to spontaneously see and talk about these energies if they are not limited by questions. More experienced readers are often aware of this problem and can allow readers to ask questions while keeping an open mind and allowing themselves to access and talk about information that may not have anything to do with a readee's question.

Often in my readings, when a client asks a question that seems rather shallow or unrelated to herself (for example, "Will my great niece finish college?") I will quickly attempt to answer the question ("Yes, I see a tall girl with red hair wearing a graduation hat and drinking champagne"), but then I will silently pose this question to myself: "Why is my client asking this seemingly unimportant question?"

The answer I get might be in the form of images that show my readee stealing her niece's graduation hat when she is looking in the other direction, and then trying to take some steps, but then her feet get all twisted up. When I ask this image to show me what it means, maybe then I'll get another image, this one of a man dressed in an army uniform towering above her, handing her a mop. The readee might then affirm that her father was in the army and he didn't feel girls needed to go to school.

I may then become aware of the depression this woman has been feeling. I'll see her standing in front of a mirror and her clothes are too tight. She looks so exhausted that she can barely walk. I will talk to her then about how she has been stifling her need to learn, to experience life, how she has ignored her desire to go to school or to get a more challenging job. She may think that the reason she doesn't make any changes is because of her depression, but it's actually her father's energy and programming that she bought forty years ago that told her to forget those dreams and remain a housewife. Her depression is just a symptom of ignoring her inner voice. So, as this example illustrates, this readee's question about her niece actually turns out to be the starting point that will let me get to the real issues. Her question in this case is almost a symbol, a key that I can use to help illuminate the real question.

A beginning clairvoyant student who is not yet adept at working with questions might just answer the question about the niece, saying, "Yes, she will graduate," and go no further. Another student might attempt to look at the niece's future but instead pick up information about the readee's unhappiness and desire to go to school herself (because this is really what her spirit needs to know). This is fine. I'd much prefer that a reader get to the real issues. However, if a reader has a particular question swimming around in their head, they may become confused and discouraged to the point that they cannot seem to get a direct answer to the question. Some of the staff at one of the clairvoyant schools I attended would not even permit the question about the niece to be addressed. Instead they would tell the readee, "This reading is for you, so ask us a question about yourself, one that really matters." This would sometimes alienate and invalidate the readee, who would not understand what was wrong with this question.

Some clients need to get warmed up and form a bond of trust with a reader before they feel comfortable discussing personal issues, and so by asking seemingly unimportant questions or questions about people other than themselves, they can determine whether or not you are truly psychic and whether they can feel safe with you. Many people will hide their true questions in more benign questions. I feel that it really is not the readee's responsibility to ask the right question (although it helps!), but rather it is the clairvoyant who needs to learn how to work with the readee's question (or lack of questions) so that the readee will receive the communication they really need to know. This is similar to the relationship between a psychotherapist and a patient. The patient may come in with initial complaints, issues, or problems, but it is really up to the therapist to decipher and redefine the true issues. If patients could do this themselves all the time, they would not be in need of professional help. The same could be said of the relationship between a clairvoyant reader and the readee.

I know that some of my clairvoyant teachers would disagree with the above statements. One of my teachers, who is very brilliant and successful and one of the most talented healers I know, has every

readee fill out a questionnaire about themselves that includes information about their family background, current activities, and present issues and concerns. This questionnaire lets clients know that if they
want the best answers, they are responsible for making sure they ask
the right questions. This helps my teacher get right to the heart of the
client's issues without wasting time having to use his clairvoyance to
uncover facts that the readee is already aware of. This makes things a
lot easier on himself. He's not at all interested or willing to play the
game of "prove it." At the same time, I know that despite what he
says, he will still get to the true issues of a client even if they don't ask
the right questions. He is really only interested in working with clairvoyant students or people who are aware of their spirituality and are
truly working on themselves, and if they don't want to fill out the questionnaire, he has no interest in reading them.

This approach is certainly a valid one. However, as I already explained, for the purposes of clairvoyant development and neutrality, I
believe that beginning students should have as little information as possible about their client so they can prove to themselves (and themselves
only) that whatever information they are receiving is coming from their
clairvoyance rather than from their logical mind. After you've been
reading for thirty years (actually a lot less), you can use any approach
you like!

Most people do have some questions and they may feel frustrated
with the reading if they are never given the opportunity to ask them. If
clients are told upfront that they can ask questions later in the reading,
they will relax, knowing that eventually they will get the answers they
are looking for. Often, most of their questions will be answered during
the course of the reading, so by the time they are given the opportunity
to ask questions, they may not have any more. If you are using a predetermined template, it is always a good idea to at least give the readee
the option to ask one or two questions at the end of the reading.

Some clairvoyant training schools that offer student readings permit readees to ask questions only at the end of the reading, while others let them ask questions at the beginning. Personally, I have found

that the readings where I ask my questions upfront feel more satisfying to me as a readee in that I immediately feel relieved and confident that my concerns are going to be addressed. It also seems, with this format, that readers tend to focus on topics that are of more interest to me. However, the overall quality of a reading does not seem to vary greatly with either approach. In professional readings, many times a readee will not have any questions or will want to wait to see what you come up with before asking their questions. For the sake of your training, the more people you can read, the more opportunities you will have to experiment with your own format and ordering of events, and you will find what works best for you.

You Are a Detective

It's important to understand that clairvoyance works by giving you clues in the form of images. Every time you see a clue, you must ask this clue to show you another clue. Don't expect the entire answer to be revealed in a single thoughtform. You may occasionally get thoughts or auditory messages and that's great, but even so, you will always want to back up any nonvisual information with further clairvoyant investigation. Images rarely lie, while auditory messages are less reliable because they may come from a source other than yourself or the readee (clairvoyant images can occasionally come from other beings, but this happens far less frequently—see chapter 24). Also know that you are often not going to know the meaning of your images. The moment you realize you are trying to interpret the images with your logical thoughts, stop, turn down your analyzer, create and destroy a few roses on your reading screen, and tell yourself that you are just going to look for further visual clues.

As we discussed in previous chapters, there will be many times when you will never know what your clairvoyant images mean because they are symbols that have significance for your readee only, and perhaps your readee doesn't wish for you to know the details of their life. That's okay, because it's not your business to know everything about the person you are reading. The important thing is to wait for an image to appear or for a change to happen with your viewing receptacle/rose, and to communicate exactly what you are looking at. This is your job and you don't have to do anything beyond this.

Also keep in mind you are not responsible for what you see. When you get into making interpretations with your logical mind, then you become responsible because these interpretations may or may not be accurate. After performing a few readings, you will be better able to determine when your knowingness is giving you revealing insights and when your logical mind is drawing conclusions. Leave it up to your readees to draw their own logical conclusions. If you feel they have no idea what you are seeing or talking about, ask the mysterious image to explain itself with another image. There will be plenty of images that never really make sense, and that is all right. It is human nature to want to understand everything. As a clairvoyant, your job is not to have all the answers, but rather to sit back, observe, and describe the images on your reading screen.

Reading with a Question or Issue in Mind

The basic clairvoyant reading technique is the same whether you are performing a structured reading answering questions or merely looking to see what comes up for the readee. In chapter 16, you will learn some common formats or templates for structured readings. For the purposes of this chapter, I will illustrate how to perform a less structured reading.

Let's assume that you are already tuned in to your readee and have sent them a spiritual hello. It is time to begin the actual reading. Your readee says she is wondering about which direction to go in her life, and whether changing careers would be a good idea. These two questions are related and I suggest focusing on the most specific question first, since it may reveal information about the more general question as well.

On your reading screen, create a clear crystal image of a rose. This rose will reveal the answer to the question about the readee's career. Take a deep breath, relax your body, and just watch the rose to see what happens to it. Look to see if there is a color coming into it. If you see a color or even sense one slightly, ask this color to show you a picture or an image. Then take another deep long breath and patiently watch the rose. You can also watch to see if the rose changes in any way. Does it open or close, shrink or get really big? Does it move, disappear, or grow brighter? Does a petal appear or disappear? Do you see more than one color in the rose? Any change, image, or minute detail you suddenly notice is the springboard for more explicit information.

When you notice one or more changes, pick one of these and make the decision to investigate it further. There are two ways to perform further investigation. The first is to just watch the clue of most interest (for example, the opening of the rose) and keep watching it to see what it does next. This is fine to do if the rose is active and changes and images seem to be appearing effortlessly.

The second method is to destroy this rose by imagining that it is exploding into a trillion pieces. Create a new rose and tell it to show you the meaning of the opening of the rose you just destroyed. Every time you destroy an object and create a new one, you are exercising your visualization muscles as well as moving energy. You are increasing your clairvoyant abilities while increasing the flow of clairvoyant energy. Any time you start to feel stuck, like you are having trouble seeing or are feeling frustrated or incompetent, destroy whatever you are looking at and create a new rose that will provide images to reveal either what you are seeing or what you are having difficulty seeing.

If you patiently watch your rose and nothing appears or you see only black, know that this nothing is really something. Destroy the rose, create a new one that represents the nothingness or blackness, and ask it to show you an image that will illuminate the situation. Continue to do this until you see something. Know that the moment you see any change to your rose, you have just used your clairvoyance! When this occurs, you can never again say or even think that you are not clairvoyant!

After you are satisfied with the information you see and communicate regarding the readee's career, put the images you have been looking at into a receptacle and blow it up. Now create a new receptacle that will reveal the sought-after information regarding the readee's path in life. Most likely you already touched upon some of these issues when discussing the readee's career, since a person's career has to do with the larger picture of their life, but you can still look at this specifically to see what else comes up. You might also choose to use part of the "life path reading template" taught in chapter 16 of this book as a guide to help you with this particular issue.

Knowingness

Sometimes information will come in on a knowing level or auditory level. It will just snap into your head, like "this person is a nurse," and it will be so clear that you will feel compelled to talk about it. When this happens, I do encourage you to talk about it. You can let your readee know how the information came in. This is not your clairvoyance but rather an ability in your crown chakra called *knowingness*. It is instantaneous information. Some people are more adept at this than others. I had a good friend in my clairvoyant training program who often received instant bursts of information as the readee was saying their name. The information was very straightforward and turned out to be quite accurate. My friend was more comfortable receiving information through his crown chakra than through his sixth chakra. Personally, I like to back up information delivered in the form of thoughts by asking for confirmation in the form of a clairvoyant image. Then I can be sure that it's not just my logical mind generating thoughts, or spirits giving inaccurate information, which can happen.

Communicating the Image to Your Readee

Some readers prefer to watch their viewing receptacle/rose and see the images for a while before talking about them, while others will talk about everything they see the moment they see it. I have found that students who take the latter approach tend to progress faster, because they don't have time to analyze every single thing and judge whether or not it is worthy to talk about. They censor themselves less and therefore allow the information to flow. You will find that as you talk about whatever you are seeing, more and more images will appear.

What I discovered was that the more I talked, the more images I saw. I even feared that if I didn't talk, the images wouldn't come. By talking uncensored in a stream of consciousness about every single detail, the clairvoyant information does flow more easily. After eight years of reading, I still prefer to talk simultaneously as I read, and I encourage you do to do the same, no matter how insignificant or silly your images seem to be.

The only time I censor myself is if I think my words might have a very strong impact on the readee's life. If they ask me when someone in their family is going to die or if their husband is having an affair, I will watch my images and double-check them by asking for more images to confirm the first image before revealing the information (see chapter 21).

Overcoming Blocks to Communication

Energy can interfere with your readings both by making it more difficult to access visual information or by preventing you from communicating this information to the readee. As a beginning clairvoyant student, there were plenty of times when I stopped myself from sharing valuable information. Since I was reading alongside other students, a variety of thoughts inhibiting my communication would come up. I might not say something because I felt like it wasn't my turn to speak, or that I was talking too much and the other students were getting irritated with me. Sometimes I would worry that I was saying the wrong thing, or that what I might say would upset the readee.

As a clairvoyant reader, there will be plenty of times when you will struggle with similar concerns. The important thing is to be aware of when you are seeing something but not sharing it. The moment you become aware of this, you should ask yourself why. If it is because you are afraid you are wrong or are nervous about your readee's response, I encourage you to use your psychic tools. Create and destroy some roses in front of your fifth chakra. Check to see which chakra or part of your body you are in. Reground yourself and postulate that you are getting rid of the energy that doesn't want you to communicate to your readee. Then make yourself talk about what you are seeing. If you are seeing something, there is a reason for it. Don't ever forget this.

Furthermore, every time you talk about something that you are afraid to talk about, you will become a stronger reader and a stronger person and the energies in the room that made you hesitate will have less of a hold on you. After a few years of reading, there will be very few times when you will hesitate to talk about anything you are seeing. Until then, there of course will be times when you will fail to communicate what you are seeing, and that is all right because inevitably you will later find out that you were 100 percent correct. If this happens, don't kick yourself too hard, but instead resolve to speak up in the future.

Avoid Getting Validation from the Readee

During a reading, you must not fall into the trap of trying to get validation from your clients. I cannot overemphasize this! There are several reasons why seeking validation through confirmation from your readee can be problematic.

First and foremost, your readee is not there to make you feel good. It's not fair to put that burden on them. You are there to give to them, not the other way around. You will benefit from the reading by using your tools, blowing your matching pictures, exploring, discovering, and learning—not by getting warm fuzzies from your readee.

Secondly, the feedback of your readee is often not accurate. Many people don't initially know what you are talking about. They may say, "No, you are wrong, that's not how it is," when in fact you are right on. For example, during one reading I was seeing images of the readee in which she was getting thinner and thinner. I saw her pushing away food and even vomiting into a toilet. When I said to the woman, "It appears that you have an eating disorder," she vehemently denied this. I let these images go and went on to answer one of her questions. But within a few minutes, the same images were appearing again. So once again I suggested that she was suffering from an "eating disorder," and this time she became irate. I was reading with several other student readers and I could sense that they were feeling uncomfortable and wondering why I did not just shut up, but I could not. I had enough experience under my belt to know that if these unwelcome images were continuing to intrude upon my reading screen, then there had to be a reason for this; they had to hold some significance. Suddenly after my third attempt to discuss the subject, the woman blurted out, "I don't have an eating disorder, I have a digestive disorder!"

During another reading, I clairvoyantly saw the readee wearing a white uniform and carrying a tray of medical instruments. I told her, "It looks like you are some kind of doctor's assistant." She immediately snapped, "No I'm not, you are wrong," which threw me off and shook my confidence. It wasn't until an hour later that she said, "You know, I think there was something to that image you saw, because I am actually a dental assistant." Had she not said this, I might have wondered for the rest of my life why I saw that image, except for the fact that I had already been reading long enough to know that the only reason I would be seeing images that clearly was if there was something to them. Both these examples also demonstrate the importance of describing images without drawing logical conclusions. Leave that up to your readee.

Your readees will actually respect you more if you don't seek out their confirmation because it will be clear that you are really picking up your own information rather than manipulating them into revealing things about themselves. In a reading, you tell your readees about themselves, not the other way around. Of course every person is different. Some people will be so excited when you "get something right" that they will share with you exactly what's happening in their life and how you just described it so beautifully. But a lot of other people will remain silent, which is fine. I know that validation feels great, but there are some serious drawbacks to becoming dependent on it. When I train my students, I demand the utmost discipline, including the following rules.

1. Never open your eyes during a reading, and don't look at your readee once the reading has begun. Opening your eyes will pull you out of your trance. You will become less grounded, and be pulled from a neutral reading space to a healing space. Some people have a hard time with this because they like to feel connected on a deep emotional level with people. Neutrality is key to performing an accurate reading, and the level of neutrality and accuracy decreases in direct proportion to the amount of time a reader spends looking at the readee.

2. Never ask your readee for confirmation (this is a hard one). For example, don't ask, "Do you do this kind of work?" or "Is it true that your boyfriend hits you?"

3. Keep your questions to a minimum regarding the readee's life.

4. Read with other clairvoyants whenever possible (see chapter 17).

Troubleshooting

I get images that make no sense to me, and when I ask for clarification, I continue to get more images that don't make sense.

There is a reason this is happening, and it does not have anything to do with your clairvoyant ability. More likely, it has to do either with your readee or with your own matching pictures—probably both. This is not a problem. Just keep talking about what you are seeing. It may make perfect sense to your readee. Sometimes your readee may not want you to know what you are seeing, though it makes perfect sense to them. Sometimes there are other energies that don't want you to see because this would mean that your readee would kick them out.

One thing you can do if you keep asking for more meaning but still get nowhere is to ask your readee if they know what you are talking about. If they say no (be aware that people sometimes deny it when they do know, or they don't understand until later what you were talking about), then you can pose the question to your viewing receptacle: "What is it that is blocking me from understanding my images?" However, most of the time the readee will say, "Yes, I know exactly what you are talking about." In this case, I advise against blurting out, "Then please tell me, because I don't have the foggiest idea what I'm talking about." Instead, be satisfied (to the best of your ability) that you are on the right track and continue reading with certainty and confidence.

What should I do if the readee tells me I am wrong?

Let's say you have just given the readee some clairvoyant information of a detailed nature and the readee blurts out, "No, you are wrong." You can handle this a few different ways. One is to revisit whatever you just told the readee. Put up a rose for whatever they said you were wrong about, and ask the colors and images to appear that will either help you confirm the earlier information or help you understand why there is this discrepancy. Perhaps this second set of images and the way you communicate will help the readee understand what you were saying in a different way.

I have done a surprisingly large number of relationship readings for women where I saw that the woman's partner was mistreating her or abusing her in some way. During some of these readings, when I saw an image of the man hitting the woman, the woman insisted that I was wrong. Sometimes I destroyed the roses I was reading, recreated new ones, and again watched to see how they were interacting. Again I would see some similar images, but I might get a detail that would shed light on what I was talking about. In one of these cases where a women adamantly denied that her boyfriend was ever violent toward her, my reexamination of their relationship led to images of a purse, and the man was emptying out the contents. The woman then blurted out that her boyfriend had gone into her purse against her will because he was looking for signs that she was having an affair. A layer of her defenses suddenly came down. When I saw another violent image later of her boyfriend pulling her hair, she admitted that he had done this. Since I had gotten three different images that confirmed the initial one, I was very confident that I was right about the abuse. It was just a matter of having sufficient patience and perseverance to break through her denial.

I am not saying that you (or I) will never be wrong about things. You could misinterpret your images or occasionally let your own biases taint your reading. What I am saying is that there could be other explanations, and it's important to explore what those are before discounting the information you've received and doubting your own clairvoyance.

Empowerment versus Problem Solving

As mentioned in other chapters, as a clairvoyant reader, your line of inner questioning will often determine the clairvoyant answers you receive. If you are looking for problems in a person's life, you will find them, just as if you are looking for what is working in their life, you will find this as well. As a clairvoyant, you can decide to read from either a space of problem solving or a space of validation. Reading from validation does not mean that you disregard the difficult issues of a person's life, but rather that you look for what empowers the person. In a similar manner, you have the choice of whether to verbally communicate about the images you are seeing in a positive, optimistic manner or in a negative, pessimistic way.

A problem is only a problem if someone labels it so. Some readees, just like some readers, are totally focused on their problems. If you start to find yourself thinking, "Wow, this poor person! What a mess her life is!" or you become overwhelmed that you can't help them, then you can be sure of two things. First, you have lost your neutrality. You need to get back into the center of your head, reground yourself, and create and destroy some viewing receptacles in front of your fourth (heart) chakra. Secondly, realize that you are in a problem-solving space. Create a rose and fill it up with the energy of problems, and then move this receptacle as far away as possible before destroying it. Then choose to read the energy of what is working well for this person. If your readee verbally objects to your clairvoyant suggestions and insists that whatever you are suggesting will not work, then create a rose and ask it to show you what is keeping the person stuck. Communicate whatever you are seeing and then let it go.

It's important to remember that you "can lead a horse to water, but you can't make him drink." Energetically, many psychics try to make their clients "drink," and these well-meaning psychics end up exhausted, depleted, sick, and overweight. It's not your responsibility to solve your readee's problems or anyone else's. You are merely there to give them insight. Remember, there is really no such thing as a problem; a problem is merely a cognitive definition of how someone is emotionally reacting to a certain situation. One person will label a certain situation a problem, while another will label it a challenge, and another will think it's funny or exciting. Problem energy is stuck energy.

Ending the Reading

The reading will be over either when you have reached the end of the predetermined time for the reading or, for a structured reading, when you have completed each predetermined step; or when it feels like you have covered all the information that needed to be addressed and you find yourself repeating the same point over and over again.

Suggested Action

I like to end every reading by giving the readee a suggestion for action they can take in order to help them reach their goals. It might be a solution to an issue previously discussed in the reading, or it may be a new piece of helpful information. Throughout the reading, it is helpful to take an action-oriented approach and to always be clairvoyantly looking for actions the readee can take, but it is especially beneficial to give some "next steps" at the end of the reading so the readee will walk away feeling empowered. Giving the person two or three simple steps or actions will help them realize that while you gave them some answers, they are really the one who has the ability to change their life. It also signals to them that the reading is wrapping up.

Technique

Simply put up a rose on your reading screen that represents a helpful action. Look to see the color. Describe the color and the images.

Say a Closing Prayer and Wish the Readee Good Luck

I always end every reading with a short and simple prayer that goes something like this: "Thank you, God, for all the help you gave us during this reading. Now I invite all of my energy to come back to me and all of (Readee's name) to come back to her. May it be with the blessings of the Supreme Being that this reading be completed."

Saying a prayer of gratitude coupled with the words "the reading is completed" helps both parties (and any guides in the room) know that the reading is really over. Stating out loud that you are taking back your energy and giving the readee back their energy lets the readee know that any energy exchange that was occurring is now ending. You are reinforcing and teaching them about boundaries. In effect, you are saying, "The reading ends here and I'm not going home with you." Following the closing prayer, you can thank the readee for the opportunity to read them. You can give them your business card and receive your payment if you have not already (see chapter 23). Physically escort the readee to the door. Now you are ready for a psychic shower.

Psychic Shower Time

At the end of a clairvoyant reading, it is imperative that you separate your energy from your readee's energy; otherwise your physical and emotional health and that of your readee could become compromised. The cleaning-out process utilizes visualization techniques that remind your body and spirit that you are in fact a separate entity from your readee, so that you don't continue to read and heal that person forever. These techniques help you call back your energy from your readee, and vice versa, and even assist you in bringing your karma and other energies into present time. They also help you work through your matching pictures and release any of your emotional energy that may have gotten stirred up during the reading.

It is best to run through the clean-out process immediately following the reading. A sign that you have not thoroughly made separations from your readee is if you continue to think about or worry about the reading or the readee. As mentioned in earlier chapters, any time you have a thought about someone or something, it is because on some level your energy is engaged with that person or thing. When you have successfully completed the cleaning-out process, you will find that you will be more in the present and will have very little need to rehash the reading. Minutes later it will seem like a distant event.

Taking a Psychic Shower

Cleaning Your Grounding Cord

First, take a clairvoyant look at your grounding cord. Has it changed in any way since you last created it? Are there any holes in it or any parts that are hard to see? Are there any colors in it that don't seem to be the ones you originally chose? Has your grounding cord matured and grown stronger and more vibrant? Make some observations about your grounding cord and then say goodbye to it. See it exploding into a trillion pieces and create a post-reading grounding cord in present time. Write your name on it with your imagination.

Cleaning Your Reading Screen

On your reading screen, create and destroy at least twenty roses as fast as you can. Start at the far left upper corner of your reading screen and work your way across and then down. Postulate that this is clearing out your sixth chakra and moving out any excess energy that accumulated on your reading screen or elsewhere in your system during the reading. Destroy your reading screen and create another one.

Clearing Out the Center of Your Head

Check to see where you are in your body. Imagine that you are sending a rose to the center of your head. Have your spirit follow directly behind the rose so that it lands in the center of your head, behind your sixth chakra. Notice where the rose and you came from. This is where you were performing the latter part of the reading. Notice the difference between how you feel sitting in the center of your head versus wherever else you just were. If you find that you are having difficulty coming back from that place, create a large yellow sticky rose and use it to clear out the center of your head. Imagine that it is inside your head sucking out grime like a vacuum cleaner. See the yellow sticky rose circulating around in there as if it were inside a washing machine or dryer. Look to see what colors have accumulated in this sticky rose. Once the rose seems full, destroy it and create another one. Repeat this process again if necessary.

Making Separations

From the center of your head, on your reading screen, create a rose that represents your readee. In the center of the rose, visualize a very strong magnet. This magnet is going to suck up any energy from your aura that really belongs to your readee. See this rose filling up with your readee's energy, growing bigger and brighter. See an image of your readee's face in the rose and say goodbye to it. Thank your readee for the lessons and experience they provided for you, and then tell them firmly that the reading is over. You can further visualize your own body and see the readee's energy and any other foreign energies related to them flowing from your body into their rose. When this rose is completely filled up, destroy it and watch as it explodes into a trillion sparks of light.

Next, create a rose that represents you. Visualize your face inside of it and label it with your name. Again, in the center of this rose place an enormous magnet. Postulate that you are calling back all of your energy that may still be with your readee or anywhere else. See your energy returning to your rose and watch as the rose gets fuller and fuller. Ground the stem of the rose deep into the planet and watch any extraneous energy drain from it. Then take that rose and place it above your head. Explode it into a million sparks of light, and watch as this light flows into your crown chakra and down to the very bottom of your toes. Watch as it fills up your feet, ankles, calves, thighs, torso, neck, head, shoulders, arms, hands, fingers, and hair, and spills out into your aura and down into your grounding cord.

Find Five Physical Differences

Next, on your reading screen, visualize your readee and yourself and notice at least five physical differences between the two of you. Make a note of these. For example, notice that you have a different hair color, different facial features, a different body size, or even a different voice. Maybe your readee has freckles, a mole, a missing tooth, bigger or smaller feet, etc. Describe these differences either in your head or out loud. Then imagine that you are taking a pen and making a list of these differences. See each item on the list and then tear it up in your mind, set it on fire, and watch it disintegrate. By noting the physical differences, you are reminding yourself that you are yourself and not your readee. If you are ever having extreme difficulty making separations, you could physically go through this exercise by using an actual paper and pen to make your list and then burning it in a real fire.

Working with Karma

Create a rose that represents the relationship between you and your readee. Visualize that there is a golden ring hovering slightly above the rose. Imagine that there is a piece missing from this ring. Postulate that you are bringing all of your karma with your readee and any of their spiritual guides or family into present time. You are essentially completing your karma with them. See the energy of this karma as it fills in the missing piece in the golden ring. When the golden ring is complete, drop it into the rose.

Ending Your Communication

Next, imagine that there is a telephone on top of the rose. You are ready to end your telepathic communication with your readee and anyone or anything in their space. Imagine that you are breaking the phone into many pieces and cutting the phone cord. Toss the phone into the rose. Take the rose and watch it as it gets smaller and smaller until it is only a tiny dot. Then imagine that you are looking at it with a magnifying glass. Imagine a bright sun shining through the glass. This sets the rose on fire, and it burns until it is merely ashes. Imagine a gust of wind blowing the ashes into the heavens.

Moving into Present Time

Now imagine a new rose. Write the current date and time on this rose. Imagine that it is sitting in your heart chakra and that it expands outward to the point that it is encompassing your entire body. Know that you—your body, spirit, and mind—are in the present and are now ready for your next adventure.

Revisit Your Intention (Optional)

On your reading screen, put up the rose that you created at the beginning of the reading that represented your intention or wish for the reading. Next to it create a rose that is labeled the "after reading rose." Notice if they look the same or are different. You can give the "after rose" a reading to see what changes might have occurred in you. Then create a new intention for the rest of the day or your future (see chapter 12).

CHAPTER 15

Relationship Readings

A relationship reading is a reading where the focus is on the relationship between your readee and another person who is not physically present during the reading (to perform a reading on a couple who are both present, see chapter 18). Eighty percent of the questions people ask me in my readings have to do with relationships. Sometimes the readee wants to know when they will meet someone special, and sometimes they want to know where their current relationship is headed or why they are having a hard time letting go of a past relationship. People want to know about their relationships with their children, parents, coworkers, husbands, wives, lovers, mistresses, bosses, enemies, teachers, etc. No matter what the nature of the relationship, the same technique can be used to clairvoyantly access information about a past, present, or future relationship.

Tuning in to the Readee and the Person in Question

Tune in to your readee using the technique outlined in the preceding chapter. On your reading screen, create a clear glass image of a rose. Invite your readee to say their present name and date of birth, and see the color of the readee's vibration/spirit flow into that rose. Match your crown chakra to that color, and then imagine that you are writing the readee's name under that rose. Move this rose to the far left side of your reading screen.

Next, create another viewing receptacle, also in the form of a rose, and ask the readee to say the person's name in question. Have your readee say the person's first and last name out loud. If the readee does not know the full name or does not want to say the name out loud (which may seem strange but happens more than you would think), then just postulate that the energy of the person in question will enter into the rose. Then look for a color in that rose. Once you see a color, write that person's name under the rose, if you know it.

Because people have so many different kinds of relationships in their lives, it is sometimes challenging to know if you are looking at the exact person in question. Oftentimes you will find, particularly as a new reader, that you are not reading the person they verbally asked about, but that you are reading another person who has played a prominent role in their life. It is for this reason that it's helpful to ask the rose representing the absent person to show you a symbol so that you and your readee will know you are tuned in to the correct person. This symbol will most likely have no meaning to you, but it will to the readee.

Reading the Relationship

On your reading screen, the two roses should stand side by side, about four inches from one another. Postulate that the way in which these roses interact will symbolize the nature of the relationship in question, and then patiently watch to see what happens to the roses. Notice any changes that occur to the individual roses or to the distance between the two. Watch how they interact. Notice if the colors change, if the size of one rose grows larger or smaller, whether the leaves fall off, whether they entwine in a passionate embrace or scatter away from one another to the far ends of your reading screen, etc. Just sit back and watch; you don't need to make anything happen. Share your observations with your readee. Then destroy these roses and create a new receptacle and ask it to show you an explanation for the most notice-able change or behavior of the roses you just observed.

Answering a Readee's Question about Someone They Know When the Question Does Not Have to Do with Their Relationship

Some of your clients will ask about everyone else in their lives except themselves, despite the fact that they are in greater need of insight and communication than those they are inquiring about. In my clairvoyant training, we were taught to pretty much ignore a readee's question about another individual (e.g., "How do you see my son's relationship with his girlfriend turning out?" "How is my father's health?") and in-stead say, "This is your reading, so let's focus on you." From my own experience both as a student and a professional reader, I have found that at times this approach is appropriate, while at other times it could feel patronizing and totally alienate the readee.

Recommended Approach

I suggest that as a reader, you spend a couple minutes directly address-ing the readee's question about the other person, and then clairvoy-antly look to see what it is that motivated the readee to ask that ques-tion in the first place. You can also look at the relationship between the readee and the person in question, even though the readee isn't asking about the relationship. This is a gentle way of bringing the focus back to the readee while allowing them to feel satisfied that their initial ques-tion has been addressed. Some people are initially very nervous about being clairvoyantly "examined" by a stranger. As they realize that you can offer helpful information in a caring and insightful manner, they will enthusiastically open up to having themselves be read.

Occasionally you may read someone who is so resistant to hearing about themselves and is so into controlling the reading on an energetic level that you realize it is pretty useless to tell them anything about themselves. In these cases I am more than happy to read other people for them. I will match my crown chakra to the person they are asking about (usually their children) and do mini readings on each person. Oftentimes it's the children (or whoever the person is) who need their mother to understand something, and I can help them by reiterating what they have been telling her for years; e.g., "I am a talented artist and will never be a doctor," "Get your own life and stop bothering me," etc.

CHAPTER 16

Navigational Tools

Using a predetermined format for a reading is especially helpful for beginning students because it allows them to control the direction of the reading; it helps them focus on the elements that will provide the most helpful information to the readee regardless of the readee's awareness of energy and other unseen forces. Beginning readers have little to no certainty or confidence and they are vulnerable to getting sidetracked by questions and concerns of the readee that might not have anything to do with the real issues affecting the readee.

Reading the Aura
(60 to 70 minutes, 10 minutes per layer)

Every layer of the aura contains energy that has an effect on the physical body and mind. During a clairvoyant reading in which you merely answer the readee's questions, you are viewing information through color, images, and thoughts. Images and thoughts give you answers, but they don't reveal the underlying energy that is affecting the readee's body and mind. When you see colors, you are seeing the color of the underlying energy, which helps move the energy. However, you are still not seeing exactly where the energy is located within the person's energy field or body. During an aura reading, you can focus on one layer of the readee's body at a time. You look for the color of their energy and foreign energy, and then you ask these colors to show you information in the form of images. By seeing exactly where color/energy is located, you can move it more easily than if you merely see the color. Aura readings are an intense form of energetic healing, even though your underlying intention may be just to read the aura as a means to structure the reading.

Technique

First, take an overall look at the readee's aura. Ask the general shape and size of it to appear on your reading screen and describe what you are looking at. Then take a look at the first layer of the aura closest to the body. Create a crystal ball or rose on your reading screen and invite the color of the first layer to enter your viewing receptacle. Ask this color to show you something helpful about the readee in the form of an image or picture, and then communicate this information to your readee.

Next, look for a color in this layer of the aura that doesn't belong to your readee. Ask this color to show you images or pictures that illustrate how this foreign energy is affecting your readee. Communicate this information to your readee. Then move to the second layer of the aura. Repeat this process with all seven layers, ending with the outermost layer, which is the seventh layer.

Male/Female Aura Reading

During an aura reading, you can focus on the readee's female and male energies in each layer of the aura. This can be accomplished by creating four viewing receptacles per layer. One viewing receptacle will show you the readee's own male energy, and another one will show you their own female energy. The other two will show you foreign male and female energies that are lurking within a particular layer of the aura.

Following a male/female aura reading, I also like to perform a relationship reading (see chapter 15) on what I call the readee's *inner male* and *inner female*. This is done by creating a viewing receptacle for the readee's inner male, as well as one for their inner female, and then watching to see how these two receptacles interact with each other. Or you can create a third receptacle in between the two and ask it to show you a color and some images that represent the relationship. Your inner male and female will often manifest in the physical form of a relationship with another person, so if you are having conflicts with a boyfriend, girlfriend, or spouse, it is likely that your own female or male energies are weak, unbalanced, or in conflict or competition with one another.

Reading the Chakras (10 to 15 minutes)

The chakras contain a plethora of information. When reading them it helps to limit the focus to a particular category of information. Many clairvoyant training programs teach students to focus on the readee's psychic abilities, which are located within the chakras.

Beginning with the first chakra, put up one gauge on your reading screen to show how open the chakra was at birth. Then create another one that shows how open the chakra is in present time. Compare the two to see whether the particular psychic ability associated with that chakra has diminished or increased. If there is a drastic difference, you can put up a viewing receptacle and ask it to show another color that represents the reason for this change. Then ask the color to show you an image that will give you insight into how this color affects the readee in general and what the readee needs to do in order to turn up or turn down the psychic ability that is associated with the chakra.

The chakras can tell you lots of other things about your readee. You can look to see how open each chakra is in terms of the readee's level of personal power/self-esteem and how this affects the health of their physical body. You can clairvoyantly investigate how the openness of each chakra influences the readee's ability to relate to others and to themselves, and you can look to see how the openness of each chakra affects the readee's ability to create and manifest goals in their life.

Answering Questions

Even when performing a structured reading, it is always a wise idea to leave at least ten to fifteen minutes at the end to address the readee's specific questions so they will feel satisfied that their direct concerns were addressed. Often, their specific concerns and questions do get addressed during the course of the reading, regardless of whether or not the reader consciously knew what these were. However, your readee will appreciate having the opportunity to ask questions, whether they are merely seeking clarification about information that was already brought up in the reading ("You said you saw a red energy in the third layer of my aura. What does the red mean?") or they are asking a question that they had been wondering about prior to the reading ("When will I meet my true love?").

Some schools allow for questions during the last ten or fifteen minutes of a reading, while other schools allow the readee to ask questions upfront, with the idea that the readers will go through the aura with the questions in mind and see where these issues are located. For more information about answering questions clairvoyantly, see chapter 14.

Formatted Daisy Drawing Reading

In this reading, you will create a transparent image of a daisy. First, take a look at the overall daisy, including the stem going into the earth. This will represent the physical health and grounding of the readee. Notice if the daisy is firmly planted into the ground, whether it stands straight or droops, whether it is firm or withered, etc. Draw a picture of this on a piece of paper and communicate what you are seeing to your readee.

Next, look at the entire bloom of the daisy, with its pistil/stamen and surrounding petals. This will represent the readee's self-esteem, sense of personal power, and communication with their inner voice. What color is it? Does this part seem to hold its head up high, or hide itself in its petals? Is it open or closed, turned toward the sun or away from it? Again, choose the appropriate color of crayon, marker, or pencil and then draw a picture of this while you communicate it to the readee.

Next, read the petals. Start with the petal on the top. This petal represents how the readee likes to have fun, what activities they enjoy and are good at, etc. Going clockwise, look at the second petal. This petal represents their education, learning potential, level of spiritual knowledge, etc. The third petal represents the readee's romantic relationships, and the fourth petal represents their family relationships. The fifth petal represents their work and career, and the sixth petal represents their finances. If there is time, you can perform a mini reading on each petal. If not, then merely look for the color of each petal and notice whether there is anything unusual about any one petal that makes it stand out from the others; e.g., it may be brighter, darker, misshapen, larger or smaller, torn, etc. Ask whatever feature that stands out to show you an image that explains the feature.

Now look at the pistil or stamen of the daisy. Notice whether the petals are fully connected into the middle or if some are pulled away. If the petals are not symmetrically connected into the pistil, then it means that the readee's various life goals (represented by each petal) are in conflict with each other. If so, look for the color that sits in between the pistil and the petal(s) and ask it to show you an image that represents the energy that is causing the readee's goals to compete with one another.

Next, look at the leaves on the stem, which represent the readee's overall strengths. If the leaves are torn or bent, then look to see what is blocking the readee from utilizing their strengths or accessing their sense of personal power.

The stem represents the readee's spiritual path and evolution. Notice if it is very long or short, or if it is broken in any parts. Clairvoyantly investigate any oddities you observe.

In this template, any rings around the stem have to do with past lives. Any bugs on the stem have to do with the readee's spirit guides (ladybugs are helpful, cockroaches are not), and any thorns have to do with challenges or limitations to be overcome. Use the clairvoyant process of investigation that, by now, you are becoming quite familiar with.

Using Mini Templates—
Archetypes and Predetermined Symbols

As discussed in chapter 5, soon after I began doing clairvoyant readings, a series of images began spontaneously reappearing in my readings. These images acted as shortcuts to help me know immediately what type of subject or issue I was looking at. (When other clairvoyants read me, these same archetypal templates often spontaneously appear to them for the first time). Eventually, I learned to consciously and purposefully manipulate these images (which I call my personal archetypes) to help me navigate my way through readings. I present several of these here and offer simple suggestions for how to best utilize them in your own readings. Eventually, through clairvoyant reading practice and experience, and paying attention to symbols in your dreams and your waking experiences, you will accumulate your own personal library of symbols.

The Piano or Harp

The piano or harp represents your readee's communication with their innermost voice. This is the voice of that individual's heart and soul that knows exactly what the individual longs for and needs.

On your reading screen, visualize a piano or harp. Now, in your imagination, see your readee standing next to the piano or harp. Notice how they relate to the piano or harp physically and emotionally. How are they playing the piano? Notice whether they look peaceful or distressed, whether they play it with grace, zest, or enthusiasm or are afraid to even touch the keys or strings. Once you make your observations, ask these observations to show you a color and some accompanying images that will provide further insights into the relationship between the readee and the innermost voice of their heart.

The Window

The window represents the readee's ability to envision personal goal(s) and their potential to achieve these goals. The readee's spirit longs for these goals, but their ego may be in resistance to and unaware of them.

The window often signifies a major life change or the lack of one. It will show whether a person is willing to make a necessary change or whether life circumstances are forcing them to make the changes that they are resisting due to fear. This archetype or template deals with unconscious factors that your readee is struggling to bring into their awareness.

On your reading screen, visualize a window. Place your readee on the left side of the window and patiently watch to see how the readee interacts with the window. Notice whether the readee turns away from it or whether they earnestly look out of it. You may see any number of responses. The readee may confidently open the window and step to the other side, or may be unexpectedly blown out of the window by a gust of wind. You may find the readee standing on the opposite side of the window looking back inside or trying to get back inside. Once you make your observations, create a viewing receptacle, ask it to show you a color, and then ask the color to give you insight into your observations.

The Tree

The tree is another image that represents your readee's goals and how close your readee currently is to obtaining these goals. These goals tend to be tangible ones that the readee is conscious of and is actively pursuing and/or struggling with.

On your reading screen, visualize a simple tree. Visualize your readee standing next to the tree. If the readee has asked you a question regarding a particular goal, you can postulate that these images will interact in order to give you insight into how close the readee is to obtaining this particular goal. Or you can ask the image of the tree and your readee to show you where the readee is at with any major goal. You don't need to know the goal in order to see the readee's success with it. Eventually, if the readee wants you to understand the exact goal, it will be revealed by the clairvoyant images during the course of the reading.

Using your clairvoyance and the clairvoyant techniques we have described in previous chapters, observe how the readee interacts with the tree. Does the readee climb effortlessly to the top of the tree, or remain on the ground, jumping up and down? Is the readee stuck somewhere halfway up the tree, or crawling slowly but surely? If the readee is at the top of the tree, are they taking a nap, or looking out over the horizon with binoculars? Is the readee sweating and out of breath, or do they look like they are used to standing at the top?

The Room

The archetype of the room represents the readee's sense of personal freedom and potential within a particular structure or organization. It often demonstrates whether they will be allowed to reach goals related to the organization. This image will often appear when reading someone's career or looking at their participation and status within a company, spiritual group, organized community, etc. Many people who operate within an organization overlook the fact that their ability to achieve their personal goals is directly proportional to the support they receive from the other members of the organization. No matter how hard an individual works or how brilliant they are, they will be unable to achieve their goals if there is a lack of permissiveness or attentiveness from whoever runs the organization. Also, they may be operating within a structure that they have outgrown, that is keeping them from their true spiritual goals, or that is dominated by others who possess a lower level of "havingness." Havingness is a term that describes a person's level of permission to obtain or possess a particular thing or state of being. So, for example, even if you are the most talented salesman and are given the best leads and resources to do your job, if the person you are working for repels money because they maintain a deep-seated, unconscious belief that it's selfish to have money or that they don't deserve it, then it will be harder for you to create or hold onto the money. The archetype of the room will provide insights into these factors.

I recommend using this template in order to answer a readee's questions regarding their workplace, potential promotions, career goals, their participation within religious or community organizations, etc.

On your reading screen, visualize the readee standing in a room. Patiently watch to see what happens next.

The Mirror

The mirror is a symbol that demonstrates how your readees feel about themselves and their body. The way in which they interact with the mirror reveals their level of self-esteem and aspects of their relationship with themselves that could use some healing.

On your reading screen, visualize your readee standing in front of a mirror. Then sit back and patiently watch to see how they interact with the mirror. Does the readee give herself a big smile, or does she look displeased as she checks out her body? Does she stand there for a while, looking deep into her own eyes, or does she turn away from the mirror in disgust? If it looks like she is not happy with herself, ask a color to appear that will represent the energy that is causing this unhappiness, and then ask the color to show you an image that will help you understand the root of her feelings. You can also ask a color to appear that will show you steps the readee needs to take in order to improve her self-esteem.

Using Your Own Symbols for Navigation

Creating your own template is a simple and fun way to help yourself navigate your way through a clairvoyant reading. You can use any symbol to represent an issue in a person's life. This symbol can be any object as long as that object has meaning to you. Simply visualize the symbol on your reading screen along with an image of your readee, pose a question to the symbol and the readee, and then see how the readee interacts with the symbol.

For example, let's say your readee wants to know if a friendship with a particular man will blossom into a long-term romance. Since a wedding ring symbolizes a long-term commitment, you can visualize your readee handing a wedding ring to an image of the man, and watch to see what he does with the ring. You can then watch her response. Out of the infinite number of possible responses, the images you see will be those that reflect the subjects' actual feelings, intentions, and behavior.

CHAPTER 17

Reading with Other Clairvoyants

There are many advantages to reading with other clairvoyants, particularly when first developing your clairvoyant abilities. One of the best ways to gain certainty and confidence as a clairvoyant reader is to read with other clairvoyant students. This is because they will often see exactly what you are seeing. You may be looking at a particular image, wondering whether it's too silly or insignificant to mention, when suddenly the clairvoyant sitting next to you describes the same image you are looking at. This, of course, is extremely validating and exciting.

Reading with other clairvoyants takes some of the pressure off you. It allows you to read at a more leisurely pace. If you are having difficulty accessing information, you have the luxury of working with your tools and focusing more on yourself while the other clairvoyant(s) communicate with the readee. Another advantage is that your fellow clairvoyants can be quite a good support system both during and after the reading. They can identify energies that are affecting you and the other readers. They will be reading through their own pictures and therefore will often arrive at the same conclusions as you, but will come up with their own unique way of arriving at these conclusions. If you lose your neutrality, become ungrounded, or start to heal in an out-of-control sort of way, your fellow clairvoyants can gently point this out to you.

Reading with Two or More Clairvoyants

Both or all of the clairvoyant readers should sit together, shoulder to shoulder, in a line. Choose one person to be the lead reader before the readee arrives. Designating a leader is not essential, but is helpful for beginning students so they can feel secure in whatever role they are adopting. Usually the reader with more experience or more confidence will be the lead reader. Each person should take the time to individually run through the psychic tools. Then the lead reader can lead the other(s) through a short meditation and group prayer.

Next, the lead reader should bring his crown chakra to a neutral gold color and ask the other readers to match their crown chakras to his. They can do this by visualizing their own crown chakra and watching it turn to gold, or they can put up a clear glass neutral rose or viewing receptacle, place it over their head, and ask the receptacle to fill with the same vibration as the lead reader. The lead reader can clairvoyantly check to make sure everyone is at the same level of gold, and let the other readers know if it needs to be darker or lighter. We use gold here because it is a neutral high-vibration color. We avoid white because white is used for channeling; it is too easy for other spirits to attach themselves to this color or for our own spirits to depart through it.

The readers then should all send a hello in whatever form they choose to the spirits of all the other readers. The hello can be in the form of a rose with the word "hello" inside, or any other kind of neutral gift. Then the readee should be brought in to the room. The lead reader will sit directly across from the readee, with the other clairvoyants on either side of the lead reader. The lead reader can introduce himself and the other readers, and explain the process of the reading. Next, the lead reader can lead the other readers in a group prayer. The lead reader will be the one to tune in to the readee's vibration and set a color for the reading.

The lead reader will visualize a clear crystal viewing receptacle and then ask the readee to say her name as he watches the energy of that person's spirit go into the rose. Once the lead reader chooses a color, he should communicate that color to the other readers. The other readers should let their crown chakras match that color, again either by using a rose or by viewing their crown chakra directly. They should notice how that feels. If something feels wrong or a reader feels they are having a hard time holding that energy on their crown chakra, they can ask the lead reader to double-check the color. It may need to be adjusted.

Depending on the format of the reading, it should be determined beforehand whether everyone will read together or if the lead reader will do a certain part of the reading and the other readers will do other parts. If it is decided that all the readers will read every part, then the lead reader should still have the privilege or responsibility of being the first reader to communicate. Predetermining the role of each reader provides an organizational structure that allows the readers to read more harmoniously and confidentally. At the same time, it's important to be flexible with these roles so that the clairvoyant information can flow and be expressed through whomever it needs to be. During the final clean-out stage, readers should make sure not only to make separations between themselves and the reader, but between each other as well.

Reading with a Monitor

One option for a group reading is to appoint someone to perform the role of a monitor. This person does not sit down with the other readers; instead, he stands behind the line of readers and clairvoyantly watches everything that is happening in the room with his eyes open. The monitor's job is to watch the energy of the room and how it is affecting the readers, rather than focusing on the readee. This person uses his seventh (crown) chakra and the ability of his knowingness.

The monitor takes over some of the responsibilities of the lead reader in terms of bringing the readee into the room, explaining the process, and doing the introductions. He also leads the readers through the various stages of the reading process. The monitor reminds the readers to use their tools, and offers suggestions or poses questions to the readers to help them navigate their way through the reading. The monitor acts as the conscious logical mind of the group of readers.

This allows the readers to feel free to go further inward into a deeper trance where they just access the information without worrying about the process. Readings can be performed with or without a reader acting as a monitor.

CHAPTER 18

Reading Couples and Groups

A couple's reading is one in which the clairvoyant reads the dynamics of a relationship in the presence of both partners at the same time. It is very similar to couple's counseling in which two people attend a therapy session together to work on or enhance their relationship with the assistance of a counselor.

If a couple requests to be read together, you should first determine if they are really seeking information about their relationship or if they are merely trying to avoid having to pay for two individual readings. If the couple wants you to address their relationship or joint projects and issues, I recommend reading them together. If they explain that they each have their individual issues and are not interested in hearing about the relationship itself, then I recommend reading them separately for the same reasons that you would not want a readee's companion to remain in the room during the reading, as discussed in chapter 14.

Even if a couple states that they are more interested in hearing about their combined interests and projects rather than the relationship itself, I will address these specific questions, but I will still look to see how their relationship is affecting the outcome of their creations/endeavors and how these in turn will affect their relationship. If any specific information spontaneously arises about the relationship itself, I will not hesitate to share it, because oftentimes the couple does want to hear about their relationship, but they are afraid to admit it or are worried that whatever I tell them will be too embarrassing to hear in the presence of their partner.

Reading couples can be rewarding in that it will teach you about your own relationships and about male/female energies and dynamics, but it can also be very challenging. One of the greatest challenges is being able to match information about one of the partners with the correct person. For example, you may see an image of one person doing a lot of housework while the other person sits in front of the television. Sometimes you will clearly know whom this information applies to, at other times you will think you know due to your preconceived ideas about gender roles (which you'll soon discover is a big mistake), and at other times you won't have a clue. Often, one person's energy is occupying the other person's aura or body so that at first clairvoyant glance they are virtually indistinguishable. If you are not sure whom you are talking about, you can be honest with your readees and tell them, "I'm not sure whom this applies to, but I see that one of you tends to do all the work around the house while the other one does all the relaxing. The one doing all the work is feeling resentful and the one doing all the relaxing is feeling left out of the household decisions." Most of the time the partners will know exactly whom and what it is you are referring to. If they don't, you can create a new viewing receptacle and ask for a symbol to appear in it that will demonstrate exactly which person you are referring to.

Another challenge of reading a couple has to do with maintaining a balanced perspective of both individuals and avoiding the potential to "side" with or focus on whatever individual you have the most in common with or are most sympathetic to.

As a young clairvoyant student, I performed a reading on a couple with another clairvoyant reader, Michael, who just happened to be a guy I had recently started dating. The couple sat down in front of us at a psychic fair. Michael began speaking first. He talked in totally positive terms, saying that he saw their relationship was perfect, that they were so happy together, and that everything was just peachy. This alarmed and confused the heck out of me because I was seeing images of the woman chained to a chair with tape on her mouth and crying. I knew Michael was an excellent reader, and I in no way wanted to question his clairvoyant competency since our own relationship was still on somewhat shaky ground. However, I could not ignore the images flashing across my own trustworthy screen, particularly since I felt that I had an ethical and personal responsibility to state what I was seeing. Despite my fear that I was about to totally invalidate Michael's reading ability, I shared this image with everyone. As soon as I did this, I heard a sigh from the woman who was sitting directly across from me and opened up my eyes to see what was happening with her (something I usually avoid doing since getting validation from the readee is not always conducive to the reading process and it pulls you out of your trance/reading space). She was nodding her head and her desperate eyes pleaded with me to continue.

Further exploration of this image showed that she was feeling helpless, passive, controlled, and very stuck in the relationship. The man was startled at my comments and verbalized that I was wrong. However, the women finally turned to him and admitted that this was how she was really feeling. I realized then that the discrepancy in the assessment of the relationship had nothing to do with my or Michael's lack of competency, but rather that we were looking at two different things. I was reading the woman and her perspective of the relationship, and Michael was reading the man's perspective.

This reading taught me how clairvoyant images are not always based on an inherent truth; instead, they can be coming from the biased perspective of the readee. It also taught me how, in a couple's reading, I must purposefully focus my attention on both people and see how their unique perspectives and attitudes interact to form the dynamics of the relationship. It showed me the value of reading with another clairvoyant, and it also demonstrated to me how a couple's reading can be a powerful form of therapy that opens up or even establishes new lines of communication and honesty. Furthermore, it provided an opportunity to work through my own relationship issues and MEI pictures that actually arose during this reading in terms of trusting myself enough to speak my truth even if it meant potentially upsetting my partner or losing the relationship itself.

Reading Same-Sex Couples

One-fourth of the couples I have read have been same-sex couples, either two men or two women. These readings have taught me a lot about male/female energies and how these dynamics are played out in same-sex couples in the same way they manifest in partners of the opposite sex. When there is conflict in the relationship, it is often due to the differences between the male/female energies and qualities that are dominant within each person. One person tends to be more passive, more attached to their home, and more interested in commitment, fidelity, nurturance, and intimacy, while the other person may seek more freedom, more excitement, more independence, and more individuality (these are often the same qualities that attracted the partners to each other in the first place, and that each partner is unconsciously lacking, searching for, or exploring within themselves). There is no difference in reading couples of the same sex or of the opposite sex, other than the fact that sometimes it is a bit trickier to determine whom you are talking about when you see images that could logically apply to either person.

The Reading Technique

The couple should sit in front of you in chairs about a foot apart. Visualize your reading screen and see it growing bigger and moving away from you until it is encompassing the couple. Notice who is on the left of your screen and who is on your right. Then explode your reading screen and create a new one that is only a few inches from your sixth chakra. Imagine a viewing receptacle in the form of a clear crystal rose on the left side of your viewing screen and postulate that this rose will represent the person who was placed on the left side of your previous screen. Then create another receptacle on the right side of your reading screen and postulate that this rose will represent the person who was placed on the right side of your previous screen.

Ask each person, one at a time, to say their birthday and their current name, and watch for the color of their spirit to appear in their assigned rose. Ground each of the roses into the center of the planet, and in your imagination write each person's name under their respective rose using a crayon that matches the color of their energy. Now imagine that you are matching your crown chakra to both of the readees' crown chakras. You can see the two colors nestled side by side on top of your head, or see the two colors stacked on top of each other. Or you can swirl both colors together into one.

Technique 1

This is the same technique that you would use to read a relationship when one person is not present, as taught in chapter 15. Simply invite the two roses on your reading screen to show you how they interact together. Relax and observe any changes or activity within or between the two roses. Then create a new receptacle and ask it to show you further images that will explain these changes.

Technique 2

Imagine that there is a third viewing receptacle that represents the couple in between the two receptacles that represent the individual people. See a clear glass rose and invite the energy of the relationship to enter into it. Underneath this rose, imagine that you are drawing the word "relationship." This rose represents the actual relationship, which is a separate entity from the individuals you are reading but is, of course, influenced by their individual traits. Give this rose a reading. This technique is helpful because on an energetic level it sends the picture to the people that they are not their relationship, but rather that their relationship is a separate entity that deserves attention but is not any more or any less important than their individual selves.

CHAPTER 19

Reading and Healing Children

I love reading children and teenagers. They still dwell in the magical world of imagination, and thus they believe that anything is possible. Their wide-eyed wonder and belief in miracles, in the unseen, in extrasensory perception, has not yet been poisoned by the atheism, skepticism, and pessimism of their parents, teachers, or other adults. Even children as young as seven or eight seem to approach a reading with great reverence and awe, as if they somehow know that they are participating in a sacred experience that touches upon the divine. Many children sit on the edge of their chair, afraid to breathe or even bat an eyelash for fear of missing a single word. Much like their adult counterparts, they are there to receive hope, validation, and direction. They want to know that they will be somebody important in the world and that they will be happy. Unlike so many adults, they still believe this is possible.

A clairvoyant reading is an experience that these young people will re-live over and over again in their minds, and describe time and again to their friends. While the exact words and sequence of events of the reading will become cloudy or distorted over time, many of the clairvoyant images that are relayed to them will forever be inscribed in their memories and imagination.

When a child or teenager comes to me for a reading, I view this as a unique opportunity to bring inspiration and hope to a young life, while teaching that child, through example, about their own psychic abilities and potential. For a clairvoyant reader, an opportunity to read a younger person is a special gift and a challenging responsibility. Children can so easily be programmed and their enthusiasm so severely crushed by negative input. Also, they have selective hearing; they are prone to misinterpret words and fill in the blanks with their own hopes and fears. Children and young teenagers don't yet know how to discriminate between information that is really relevant to them and information that is not. If a psychic tells them one thing that seems to be true, they will likely believe that every other word from the psychic's mouth is a proven fact. Furthermore, children and particularly teenagers often don't know how to responsibly handle the information they receive during a reading. They may use it as a weapon against their parents or others.

In this chapter, I offer suggestions on how to approach a clairvoyant reading and communicate clairvoyant information to children of varying ages. These suggestions will help you empower and inspire the children you read, while minimizing the possibility of detrimentally programming or upsetting them during the reading. I also offer specific techniques and age-appropriate reading formats that I have personally developed to help you navigate your way through a reading.

General Pointers

Always focus on the positive.

When reading children, focus on their strengths, their successes, and their positive relationships with others. Look at their dreams and how they can best achieve these. Acknowledge problems and challenges that the child is struggling with, but help them redefine these problems as opportunities for growth. Help them see how their strengths will get them through difficult periods in their lives.

Be honest, but don't feel compelled to tell everything.

As clairvoyant readers, I feel that we must be honest with our clients, no matter what their age. We should never make anything up just to make someone feel good. Luckily there is no reason to do this, because there is always a bright side to anything. That being said, when reading children, I feel that it is all right to sugarcoat potentially upsetting information so that the child can deal with the situation at their own pace.

For example, if you see that the child's grandmother is dying, rather than stating, "Your grandmother is going to die very soon," you can clairvoyantly ask the grandmother's spirit if she has any messages for the child, e.g., "I see your grandmother loves you very much and will always be by your side, even after she has gone to heaven. She loves taking walks with you and how you laugh at her funny faces." Or, "You are a very strong and brave boy and know how to take care of yourself. Someday your grandmother may have to leave and go to heaven, but she wants you to know that you will be fine no matter what. She loves your stories and knows you will be a great writer someday. She knows that you will always have lots of friends near you."

When looking into a child's future, let them know that you are merely looking at one or two of several different possibilities.

Many kids have a fantasy about what they want to be when they grow up. They want you to tell them what you see for their future, but if you see something different than this fantasy, they become very upset. Looking at your own life, you probably can see where you have worked in many different jobs and held many different roles, and the same will be true for these children when they reach adulthood. If the child is upset by your answer, ask them to tell you what they want to be when they grow up and then clairvoyantly look to see if this is a transitory dream or if it is one they will ultimately pursue. There is no reason to take away their fantasy, even if it looks very unlikely. You can say, "Well, I see clairvoyantly in your future that you will be really good at working with computers, and lots of people are going to depend on your help and pay you a lot of money for it, but that doesn't mean you can't also be a famous baseball player if that's what you really want."

Always counterbalance a negative statement with a positive one, and always give the child proactive steps to take to change their future if it looks bleak or difficult.

Instead of saying to an eight-year-old, "It looks like you will become an alcoholic and end up in jail by the time you are twenty," you can say, "I see you are vulnerable to the problems that drinking alcohol can cause. If you want to have a happy life and enjoy your freedom, then you should stay far away from alcohol. I see you are a very strong runner, and if you stay away from alcohol, you have a good chance of becoming a very successful athlete." Again, only say what you honestly see.

Tell the child about their personality characteristics that will help and those that could present challenges throughout their life.

For example, "I see you are a great speaker and are very funny. You will always have lots of friends because you know how to make them laugh. I also see you don't like people to tell you what to do and you have a strong stubborn streak. This could cause problems at school and at your work unless you learn to give in during arguments that aren't that important to you."

Give the child hope that a current problem they are dealing with will eventually be resolved or will lessen with time.

Look to see how time will heal their wounds. For example, perhaps when you sit down to read a child you see an image of the child standing over a motionless dog. The child drops to his knees and hugs the dog, crying, trying to get it to stand up. It's clear that the child has recently experienced the death of a favorite pet or will soon experience this (be aware that you may see the pet as a dog because you had a dog yourself as a kid, or you prefer dogs, when in reality the child's pet might be a cat). In this scenario, I would verbally ask the child if he had recently experienced any kind of loss of something or someone he loved and if he has been feeling sad, or if something unusual had recently happened with a pet. If the child says yes, then you can clairvoyantly look into the present to see what might make the child feel better, or into the future to see the soonest point in time when the child will be happy again. Maybe you will see the child hitting a home run at a baseball game, or getting a new pet, or going to Disney World. If the child doesn't seem to know what you are talking about, you might say something like, "I see that at some point in your life something difficult might happen that will make you feel sad for a while. But then I see you looking happy again." Or you may just decide not to say anything and go on to the next topic because the child really isn't ready to talk about or deal with this subject, and you don't want to make him apprehensive about a future even he can't control. Most of the time, however, you will be picking up on the past or present rather than the future.

Take advantage of this opportunity to see how the child is already using their psychic and healing abilities and which ones will help the child in their life.

There is a reason why the child or teenager has come to a clairvoyant reader as opposed to another kind of reader, so tell them something about their own clairvoyance, how they can develop it, and how they can overcome any obstacles to accessing this and any other ability. You can also look to see whether the child is tuned in to their own inner voice, higher self, etc., and clairvoyantly give the child some tips about how to connect with their own spirit. You may see a specific technique for the child to practice, or you may see that they would benefit from going to Sunday school at their family church. Remember, this is not you spouting advice, it is you giving a reading to see what that particular child needs. This may be the only opportunity the child has for a very long time to receive communication on the level that you can give, so make full use of your time together. You are one of the child's spiritual mentors, even if you only spend five minutes together.

Always address a child with the same level of respect as an adult.

Use simple words the child can understand, but don't talk down to them in a condescending manner. Many children are hidden within the shadows of their parents and long to be seen as the sovereign spirits that they are. As clairvoyant readers, this is one of the most important gifts we can offer them.

You must respect the child's confidentiality, but don't expect them to do the same.

Let the child know upfront that you will not repeat whatever is said during the reading, even to their parents, but that they should feel free to share the information with anyone. Children need to know that they can trust you and that there will not be any negative repercussions from being honest or allowing a clairvoyant reader to see into their lives and feelings. On the other hand, it's important that you don't ask them to keep secrets from their parents, because the conflict between not wanting to disappoint you but wanting to share with the people to whom they are closest could be traumatic. Some children view a secret as something that is shameful or bad, and if they feel that there is something secret about the reading, they may feel that they have done something wrong.

Help the child understand the dynamics between himself and his parents, but know that whatever you say about a child's or teen's parent could and likely will be used as ammunition against the parent.

When reading a child or teenager, issues concerning their relationship with their parents will frequently arise. Sometimes you will see information about the parents that the parents will not appreciate. This is the information that the child will bring up later at the first sign of conflict with their parents. This is a sticky situation. Children are obviously dependent, physically and emotionally, on their parents, and yet even the most nurturing, best intentioned parents may not have a clue as to what their child's spiritual destiny entails or how to provide the proper experiences or education that will help their child move along on their own unique spiritual path. So many parents are consumed with fears, judgments, and limitations that the more they love their children, the more they suffocate and poison the children with their own doubts and lack of faith in the ultimate perfection of God's plan and the universe.

As a clairvoyant reader, you can see the child's spirit and tune in to the blueprint of their spiritual path, and often you will see where there is a clash between the child's desires and needs and those of their parents. On rare occasions, you may read a child who is being physically or sexually abused by a parent, in which case I recommend that you talk to the child about this and see if they are open to you speaking to the other parent or another family member, and possibly calling the police or child protective services.

However, most of the time, struggles at home have more to do with differences in personalities, desires, and goals between well-intentioned parents and their children. Most parents think that because they are the parents, they have the right to make all the decisions for the children. They want to control their children, and when the child asserts her own will or attempts to control the situation, the parent labels the child as being "bad" or "naughty" or even as having attention deficit disorder.

A child may come to you for a reading because she desperately needs to know that she is all right, that all the labels that are being placed upon her, all the crazy-making around her, has much more to do with the dysfunction, blindness, or self-centeredness of her parents than the flaws within herself. A child also needs to know how he can best cope with his parents until he is old enough to physically take care of himself. When you give him honest and clear communication about who he is, you will empower that child in a way that he has never been empowered before. Many parents don't want their child to be empowered because this could lead the child to become even more disobedient and outspoken.

As a clairvoyant reader, I recommend that you be honest with children about their family dynamics, and at the same help them see their parents or family members with compassion and forgiveness. Always clairvoyantly look to see how what actions and philosophies children can adopt that will help them peacefully coexist with their parents for as long as necessary, without having to sacrifice their own sense of self.

Should the parent be present during the reading?

Personally, I always prefer to read a client in privacy, whether they are an adult or child, unless the reading is going to focus on the child's relationship with their parent or I am reading a very young child who is nervous about being separated from their parent. Most children cannot clearly see themselves in the presence of their parents because even the most loving of parents are constantly projecting roles ("You are the child, I am the parent"), expectations ("As a child, you are unable to care for yourself, unable to speak for yourself, and dependent on me") and judgments ("You can never sit still, you talk too loud, you misbehave in school") onto the child. The energy behind these projections is so intrusive that the child may feel like, and therefore become, almost a totally different person when they are around their family versus when they are not.

Have you ever noticed how, as an adult, you feel different about yourself when you are around one or both of your parents? Your self-esteem and sense of independence may suddenly plummet, or you may feel generally cranky and irritated but have no idea why. This is because your parent's projections continue to persist far into adulthood, even when it is logically clear that they have nothing to do with reality.

These projections interfere with the relationship between the clairvoyant reader and the child as well as the overall accuracy and ease of the reading itself, in that the reader will be more inclined to confuse the parent's projections with the true nature of the child. Even when the parent is not present, there is always the risk that a psychic may confuse the parent's energy, in the form of projections, thoughtforms, and emotions, with the child's energy and true characteristics, but this is much more likely to happen when the parent is present. Furthermore, both the psychic and the child may feel greater inhibitions in the presence of a parent in terms of their communication.

At times it may be appropriate, with the permission of the child, to speak to a parent after a reading and to share with them the information that you obtained clairvoyantly and communicated to the child. Some parents may be open to your communication, while others may be totally opposed to it. By the time you have completed the reading with the child, you will have a pretty good idea whether or not you and the child should even consider this possibility. If the parent and/or child insists on the parent being in the room, ask the parent to sit as far back in the room as possible.

Due to the prevalence of lawsuits and accusations of child abuse and molestation, some readers, particularly men (although women need to be concerned with this as well), will insist that another adult be present for the reading or at least within eyesight of the reading. From a legal standpoint, this is a prudent practice to adopt. It is also for this reason that I recommend avoiding physical contact with a child, with the exception of shaking their hand. When an adult shakes a child's hand, they are saying to that child, "I respect you as an equal," and this may have more of an impact than even a hug. If a child hugs you, accept the hug for just a moment and then offer them your hand.

Reading Younger Children

A few months into my clairvoyant training, while performing readings at a psychic fair, one of my teachers approached me and asked me to read a little girl who was about five years old. He was reading her mother and the girl kept interrupting them, so the mother offered to purchase a reading in order to keep her daughter occupied. Before I could protest, the little girl was seated across from me, impatiently banging her feet on the metal chair. Having no children of my own at the time nor any recent experience with them, I had no idea how to talk to a child, much less read one. I decided that I would read her like any adult. I closed my eyes, said a prayer, directed her to say her name, and asked her if she had any questions. Her response seemed very far away and I opened my eyes to discover that she had already vacated her chair and was now exploring the neighboring tarot card booth. "What's that?" she asked, picking up a deck of Rider-Waite tarot cards. She pulled out the Tower card. "This card looks scary. What's that?" she asked, pointing to the tower.

At this point I decided to abandon any idea of giving her a reading. Her mother was really just looking for a babysitter anyway. I recalled that babysitters read stories, so I decided to tell her a story about the cards.

"See this tall building?" I asked, pointing to the tower. "That is a house. And the people sticking out of the windows are kids. They are upset because one of the boys set fire to the house and it is burning down." What a charming story to tell a five-year-old! I thought to my-self. But I was shocked by her response.

"Yeah, that happened to our house. My brother was playing with matches and set the grass in our backyard on fire. My mom was really mad. He always does bad things." I realized I was on to something.

"See this person on the card?" I asked her. "That is you. She looks to me like she is angry at the other people in the house."

"Yeah," the girl responded. "My mom is always too busy watching my brother to play with me. He doesn't want her to play with me. He makes me so mad."

"Well, let's see if things are going to change soon. Show me another card in the deck." She handed me the Sun card. "This looks like a happy card to me," I told her. "See the child's face? She's smiling. The sun is shining on her and she is having fun. She looks like she is on vacation."

The girl's face lit up. "Yeah, we are going to Disneyland for my birthday, on an airplane!"

The girl's mother later confirmed that her son had set their back-yard on fire the week before and that they were going to Disneyland the following week.

Tarot Card Reading Technique (ages 3 to 7)

My experience with that little girl taught me not only how to read a young child, but also how to utilize tarot cards to read people of any age. First, ask the child to pick a card and then start talking about the card without censoring yourself. Don't think of the experience as a reading, just tell the child and yourself that you are merely making up a story with the help of the cards. This will eliminate any feelings of pres-sure or responsibility. Use the images in the card as springboards for the plot and events of the story. Ask yourself what these images remind you of. As you talk, pay attention to new images or thoughts that pop into your mind and then describe and incorporate these into the story.

PART 4

Clairvoyant Healing

CHAPTER 20

Basic Clairvoyant Healing

What Is Clairvoyant Healing?

If you have attempted any of the techniques in this book, then you have already performed a clairvoyant healing. Whether you grounded yourself, ran your energy, or created a viewing receptacle and invited someone else's energy into it for you to read, you were engaged in healing because you were moving energy. The moment you clairvoyantly look at energy, it changes. The degree to which it changes is dependent on many factors. The most significant factor is the intention of the person receiving the reading or healing and their receptivity to change, followed by the intention of the person conducting the reading or healing. The degree to which energy can transform is also dependent on factors such as the type of healing methods employed and the experience and nature of the healer or healing guides, counterbalanced by the degree of resistance from family programming, friends, lovers, coworkers, disembodied spirits, etc.

As discussed in previous chapters, emotions, thoughts, memories, pain, information, etc., are all energy. Our physical bodies are made up of and surrounded by energy. So when energy moves, changes, transforms, or releases, transformation occurs in our bodies, minds, feelings, and ultimately our spirits. This transformation is called healing.

Basic Clairvoyant Healing Technique

There are countless techniques that can be employed to facilitate transformation and healing. Touch, sound, acupuncture, chanting, prayer, and herbs are just a few methods that have been proven to be effective sometimes for some people. Oftentimes these techniques are accompanied by visualization. It is natural for people to visualize their desires and intentions. You are hungry and for a moment you may visualize a hamburger. You hear about someone winning the lottery and you lose yourself in images of driving around in a convertible BMW, soaking in the hot tub outside your new mansion with a glass of champagne in your hand, rolling around naked in a bed full of dollar bills . . . (don't tell me I'm the only one!). When you have the desire to heal yourself or someone else, it is natural to visualize the person getting better and/or see the illness leaving. Even if you don't realize that this desire and visualization will have any effect at all, you may be enacting powerful changes in yourself or someone else, because nothing more is really needed.

The preparations for a healing are the same as the preparations for a reading (see chapter 14). Once you have prepared yourself through grounding, running your energy, and getting into the center of your head, you will be ready to begin the healing.

Begin by visualizing the person you wish to heal. This person could be seated a couple feet across from you, or could be a million miles away on another continent. There is no such thing as space or time when it comes to performing readings and healings, so regardless of the physical distance, the results will be the same. If your healee is present, have them sit a few feet away from you in a comfortable chair. Ask them to say their current name a few times. If your healee is not physically present, then visualize that person and repeat their name and address to yourself, if you know that information. Some healers like to have a picture of their healee if they are performing a long-distance healing. Personally, I have discovered that while having a picture may help me concentrate or visualize the healee, I don't really need to have or know anything other than the readee's name. Even the name is not essential. This is because healing and reading have to do with intention.

If a woman comes to you and says her grandmother is ill, as long as you intend to heal the grandmother she was referring to, you can energetically connect with the grandmother, without knowing her name. All you need is a symbol, which in this example is the word "grandmother." If you hear about a missing child on the news but don't catch her name, you can choose to give her a healing by saying, "I now chose to heal the missing girl I heard about," and you will instantaneously be connected with that girl. Again, the value of knowing names and additional information, like the date of birth, address, and what your healee looks like, is that this information helps you, as a reader, improve your concentration, and when the readee/healee is present, stating their name out loud can help bring them back to their body if they become ungrounded or unfocused.

Whether your healee is present or far away, visualize that both of your crown chakras are turning to a bright blue or purple color. Next, give the healee a grounding cord. See their entire body grounded into the center of the planet. Then imagine that you are holding a jar of cobalt blue or glowing purple energy that looks like paint. This is neutral healing energy. First match your crown chakra to this color. Then take the energy in the jar and throw it all over your healee's body. Patiently watch to see what happens. Any area that is not healthy will light up as a different color.

You can either perform a reading on this color to understand what it represents, or you can merely watch as the color releases down the healee's grounding cord. If you wish to read the color of the unhealthy energy, first create a viewing receptacle, invite the color into the receptacle, and then perform your reading as you would any other. Destroy the receptacle when you are finished. Even if you plan to merely help release the energy, you can still create a viewing receptacle and fill it up with the color of the unhealthy energy until it grows very large. Then imagine you are sending this rose into the middle of the ocean or desert and see it exploding. Repeat this process until you feel the energy has been released.

Recharging the Readee with Their Own Healing Energy

When a person cuts their finger or bruises their knee, within a few days or weeks that injury will heal on its own, regardless of whether any care is given to that part of the body. This is because the bodies of human beings are designed to heal themselves. They possess a life-force energy that is a healing energy. Whatever energy created our body in the first place remains with us until we die, helping recreate any part of our body that may become injured or diseased. During a healing, you may be activating, complementing, or speeding up this force within your readee with the use of your visualization methods. After helping your healee release unhealthy energy, you will want to help them fill up the area of concern with their own healing energy so that it will continue to repair the damaged or diseased area and prevent the foreign energy from returning.

I recommend that you first look for the color of the healee's energy, and then ask the healee to tell you the color that they believe represents their healing energy. For those who hesitate, rephrase the question and ask them to describe their favorite color, the color that is the most soothing or comforting to them, or the color that gives them the greatest sense of peace and happiness. If the color they choose does not match the one you saw, or if it doesn't feel right to you (some people become very comfortable with foreign energies even when those energies are destructive, as in codependent relationships), then put the color into a viewing receptacle, give the receptacle a grounding cord, and look to see if the color has changed. Whatever color you see will be the correct color of the readee's healing energy.

Once you have determined the correct color, run this color through the area they just released as well as through their chakras and aura. Then ask the healee to join you in running this energy through their body. This not only empowers them, but also teaches them a handy healing technique they can independently use anytime, anywhere.

Cellular Healing

All illness begins on an energetic level before it manifests in the physical body. When an unhealthy energy invades the body, or when energy within the body becomes stuck or stagnant, it will glob onto the cells of the body first before going on to affect the glands, organs, muscles, and other parts of the body. If there are enough healthy cells already in the body, these healthy cells will fight the infected cells and eliminate the unhealthy energy from the body.

As clairvoyant healers, we can use visualization to stimulate and enhance this process by working with both the unhealthy and healthy cells of our healee's body. The healing technique discussed here is very simple, yet extremely powerful. It is particularly helpful when healing people who have been diagnosed with cellular diseases such as cancer. It can be used in conjunction with any of the other healing techniques discussed in this book. As with any type of reading or healing, it's important to first have your separation objects up, be well grounded, and have your energy running before beginning your healing.

Once you are tuned in to your readee, create your reading screen and clairvoyantly look for the unhealthiest cell in the body. Let this cell appear on your screen. Look to see what colors are in it. Give the cell a grounding cord and ground it into the center of the planet. See the unhealthy energy leaving the cell. Right beside this cell, ask the healthiest cell in the body to appear. This cell will be called the *teacher cell*. Patiently wait until it appears on your reading screen and then observe the size, shape, and colors in this cell. The job of this teacher cell will be to "teach," or reprogram, the unhealthy cell(s). Take this cell and lay it on top of the unhealthy cell until the unhealthy cell takes on the exact proportions and colors of the teacher cell. Continue to check in with the grounding cord of the unhealthy cell to see if any further energy or colors release from it. Know that these two cells represent all the cells in the body, so that all of the unhealthy cells are instantaneously being transformed by this one teacher cell.

Once you are fully satisfied that the previously unhealthy cell has been transformed into a healthy cell, then imagine that the teacher cell is splitting off into two teacher, or healthy, cells. See these two cells splitting off into two more cells. Continue this process until you see so many healthy teacher cells that they fill up the entire body. Command these cells to go forward on their own and seek out any final stubborn unhealthy cells that may still be lurking within the body.

Healing Your Relationships

Healing your relationship doesn't always mean that all problems will be solved or that things will work out exactly how you want them to. Performing a relationship healing could result in the termination of the relationship, if that is what is in the highest good of each party. What is guaranteed is that the communication between the parties will become more honest and peaceful and that any outside influences that may be negatively affecting the relationship will diminish or cease.

Just like individuals, relationships are vulnerable to all sorts of energies that affect the health of the relationship over time. The two people involved in the relationship are constantly bringing all sorts of thoughtforms, emotions, and energies to the relationship that can make it stronger or tear it apart. Then there is the energy and resulting influence of both individuals' families, friends, and spirit guides as well as society in general that have an effect on a relationship, regardless of whether these people are even aware on a conscious level that the relationship exists.

To perform a relationship healing, create a new reading screen after running through your meditation tools. On the screen visualize two clear glass crystal roses (or two wine glasses), which will represent the individuals in the relationship. Assign a name to each rose and write the name across the rose. Give each rose a grounding cord. See a color for each rose and notice the differences and similarities between each rose. Next, create a space between the two roses, and inside this space create another crystal rose. Write the word "communication" inside this rose. Next, conduct a quick mini reading on this communication rose. What colors do you see? Give the rose a grounding cord and command any foreign energy in this rose to exit through the grounding cord. Watch the energy release and notice the color of the releasing energy. Then do the same to the individual roses.

Once all the foreign energy has fully released, choose a vibration(s) that you would like to bring into the relationship that will positively influence the communication between the individuals. This vibration could be peace, happiness, enthusiasm, amusement, fun, love, passion, etc. Then choose a color for this vibration and see the color filling up all three roses. Watch to see if any further energy releases as you fill up the roses, and notice if there is any change with any of the roses. Then you can go a step further and visualize images in the communication rose that express the vibration or general feeling you just set in the rose. For example, if you chose peace, then you could visualize a peace sign or see the two people holding hands, watching a sunset together and looking serene and comfortable. If you chose passion, you could see the couple wildly making love to each other.

For this exercise, I recommend that you choose to see a state of mind, such as happiness, peace, love, etc., rather than get too specific about an outcome, because the outcome might be one that you think you want but that is not really in the best interest of yourself or the other person. This simple technique is so powerful that it easily creates exactly what you have visualized. On the other hand, if the outcome you choose is really what you want but not what the other person wants, it could result in the breakup of the relationship. This is because when you perform this exercise, the individual involved will subconsciously and telepathically receive the images you have just created. If the images and desires expressed in the rose are not in alignment with the other person's desires or life path, they will either break off the relationship or life circumstances will create a rift in the relationship so both of you can go on to have the type of relationship your hearts really desire.

As a final step, create an image that represents God. You can visualize this image as a glowing star, a shining sun, a sparkling ball of light, a grandfatherly looking face, or even your dog Fred! Visualize this image as being suspended above the three roses. Choose a color that represents God's compassion, love, and all-knowingness. See the color glowing brighter and brighter until it glows brighter than any light you've ever seen. Then draw columns of this colored light from each rose to God and from rose to rose, forming the shape of a triangle with a line in the middle. See the color travel from your symbol of God down into the communication rose, filling it up completely. Then see the color travel to the individual roses on either side, and watch as these fill up. See the colored light travel back up to God. Watch this circulation for a few minutes. Know that whatever is in your best interest and the best interest of your partner will come to pass. When you have completed the healing, destroy all the images on your reading screen and commence with your usual clean-out routine.

Techniques for Handling Troublesome Entities

In your readings, you will undoubtedly encounter troublesome spirits at some point. These entities may be bothering your readee, or they may be pestering you as you attempt to read. Some of these spirits may have the highest intentions. They may wish to heal or help the readee, but are behaving in a way that is not conducive to the readee's well-being (as in the case of a loving but overbearing or controlling parent who erroneously thinks they know what is in the best interest of their child). Some spirits in this category are deceased relatives who don't realize they are dead or are not willing to let go of the readee (or vice versa). Many people erroneously assume that any spirit that has passed on is now enlightened, or at least wiser than they were before they were dead. From my readings I have discovered that some of these spirits do gain wisdom upon their passing, but many others do not. If your Uncle Fred was a jerk when he was alive, there is a strong possibility that he may still be one now that he has passed on. Even if he was a saint, if he is hanging on to you too tightly (or you to him), both of you could encounter a number of problems.

There are many types of spirits that have a strong desire to experience life as a human being on earth. They are desperately seeking parents who will bear them, and they will stop at nothing to achieve their goal. Some of these beings are in fact meant to be born, while others are not. These beings can have substantial positive and negative effects on a person's relationships, self-esteem, sex drive, desire (or desperation) for children, etc. Some beings will attempt to invade or possess an existing body instead of being born into a new one.

Another class of troublesome beings are those that lack the ability to understand and respect human life. These beings often show themselves as insects, worms, snakes, spiders, or ugly/scary faces. These beings are highly antisocial. Some seem to be human, while others are like animals or aliens. They feed off pain and fear. They can interfere with and destroy relationships, crucify a person's self-esteem, and even incite suicidal feelings and behavior.

Regardless of a being's intention, nature, or propensity for love or evil, the basic technique and approach for dealing with any spirit is the same. First, it's important to always remind yourself (and the spirit) that you always have the advantage over disembodied spirits because you have a physical body that is connected to the earth. Sometimes you may fear a spirit because you don't understand them. Other times spirits may use scare tactics to control you because fear brings you down to their vibration. If you are not scared, they ultimately have no power over you. Some spirits are like bullies: they put up a good show of being tough, but the moment they understand that you really do see them, they get scared and flee.

When you see a spirit (clairvoyantly or with your physical eyes), always first say hello to them. Let them know that you do see them. Ask them if they have a message for you. If their message is unfriendly or it scares you, you would be wise to end the communication right there. Acknowledge their presence, but don't try get them to understand you or attempt to reform them. Don't argue with them. Trying to change their nature is like trying to reason with a hungry man-eating tiger. If you try to talk sense into them, you will merely make yourself more vulnerable to their tactics.

The high vibration of amusement is your greatest weapon. When you see or sense an unpleasant, serious, or determined entity, use your great imagination to dress them up in funny clothes. Pretend that they are wearing a sparkly pink baby girl's dress with a matching frilly bonnet and sunglasses with little birdies on the ends. Throw them into a pink baby carriage, plop a bottle of milk into their homely mouth, and take them for a ride through a lovely garden while you tell them silly monster jokes and then transport them into outer space. They will often run screaming from you before you actually move them away! They won't be able to handle the vibration of amusement that you are creating. Laughter and beauty will melt them. When you raise your vibration, they won't be able to match you there and they will usually disappear.

If you are having trouble finding your amusement, there are several other tactics you can apply. On your reading screen, see this spirit connected up to God with a cord of brilliant light, and connected into the planet with a strong grounding cord. Imagine that God has giant hands and that you are gently placing the spirit into God's hands. Thank God for helping the spirit and taking this spirit away. Continue this visualization until you have a strong sense that the entity is gone.

As you do this, feel free to call in help from an ascended master, such as Buddha, Jesus, Mother Mary, Archangel Michael, or one of your spirit guides. Whether or not you consider yourself to be a Christian, the name of Christ is a powerful symbol that has been used for centuries in exorcisms (I'm Jewish and it works for me!). In the name of Christ, demand confidently, with every ounce of your being, that this spirit be banished from your kingdom. State this demand out loud.

When working with spirits, handle them in your imagination as you would handle a physical person. If an intruder were in your home, you might yell at them to leave, you might call the police, or you might shoot them, and while doing all of this you might be praying or yelling for assistance from your neighbors. In the same way, if you are performing a clairvoyant reading and discover that there is a spirit invading your aura, tell it to leave, ask God and your spirit guides to take it away, see yourself forcing the spirit to leave and go far far away, or, as a last resort, see yourself destroying the entity by shooting it, or merely taking the end of a pencil and erasing it.

PART 5

Professional and Personal Considerations

CHAPTER 21

Psychic Ethics

As a clairvoyant reader, you are going to need to develop your own personal code of conduct to help you wade through a wide range of ethical dilemmas that will arise both during readings and in your relationships with people in your everyday life. The Webster's New Collegiate Dictionary defines ethics as "the principles of conduct governing an individual or group" and "the discipline dealing with what is good and bad and with moral duty and obligation." Professionals such as psychologists, doctors, social workers, and attorneys all are governed by licensing boards that have developed and actively enforce a strict code of ethics by which these professionals must abide.

In the United States, there is no governing board that regulates the behavior of professional psychics and healers (which ultimately is a good thing, given all the misperceptions the majority of people have about psychic phenomena—government regulation at this point might resemble the Salem witch trials!). Therefore, each psychic must develop their own moral code, which will determine certain choices they will have to make during the course of a reading or healing and in their everyday life.

As an undergraduate psychology student and a graduate social work student, I was required to take several classes regarding professional codes of ethics and the law for these two disciplines, which are closely related to each other as well as to psychic reading, which also involves an element of counseling. Some of the principles stuck with me and helped me understand the importance of behaving in a certain way so as to minimize the suffering of both myself and my clients in my readings. These principles have also served to strengthen my relationships with my clients and to resolve various dilemmas that involved conflicting values. Two of these principles that have been most relevant in my readings have to do with confidentiality and setting boundaries with clients. Unfortunately there have been many other issues that are unique to psychic reading for which there were no guidelines. As a result, I have had to learn through experience and, occasionally, painful mistakes how best to handle these dilemmas.

In this chapter, I will discuss my own code of ethics governing psychic readings and healing, which at the very least will initiate a dialogue or get you to start thinking about certain issues and options of how to handle them. While I do not wish to push my personal values on anyone, there is a definite possibility that these will emerge, so you can do with them as you please. I feel a discussion concerning ethics and common ethical dilemmas that arise in readings is essential both to readers who are certain they want to learn to do readings and to readers who are still sitting on the fence, because these ethical dilemmas and your resistance to or fear of dealing with them could be the very things that have stood in the way of your awareness and application of the God-given spiritual and psychic gifts that have been with you since the beginning of your existence.

Confidentiality

The American Psychological Association and Social Work code of ethics stresses the importance of confidentiality between the practitioner and their client. This agreement is vital to the client/practitioner relationship because it creates an environment in which the client can feel secure and safe enough to be totally honest. When confidentiality is breached, the client and others could not only suffer damaging consequences, but could suffer severe emotional trauma from realizing that perhaps the one person in the world they thought could be trusted, a role model whom they greatly admired, has betrayed them.

As a psychic, people are going to come to you with issues that they have hidden from others, and from themselves, for their entire lives. There are times when you will see images depicting behavior that your client is extremely embarrassed about and ashamed of. The client ultimately needed to have these issues addressed, but never consciously expected they would arise during the reading and never dreamed you would have the ability to see the details so blatantly. For example, during one reading I saw a man having sexual intercourse with a blow-up doll. While he ultimately desired help with his relationship problems, he certainly didn't expect me to see this aspect of his sexual behavior! You can imagine how devastating it would be to him if I were to share this information with someone who turned out to know him.

A few years ago, a man and his wife came for readings. I asked them if they wanted a couple's reading, but they said no and explained that they each had their own issues they were working on. I read the man first and discovered that he was thinking about having an extramarital affair. I helped him understand his feelings of guilt and responsibility that were tormenting him. By the end of the reading, he felt so relieved that I had treated him with compassion rather than judgment that he asked me if I'd like to become his mistress! Before I could say no, his wife entered the room for her reading. Talk about pressure! Did I maintain confidentiality, or did I let this poor woman know that her husband had just asked me to have sex with him and was planning on leaving her the first chance he got?

The first thing I did was ground myself and get into the center of my head. Next, I reminded myself that I was not responsible for these people's lives. They were coming to me to access information, not to hear my moral judgments. I decided that it was not my place to violate the man's confidentiality and instead gave the woman a reading, which turned out to address her issues of dependence on her husband and how she could enhance her own life so she could feel more fulfilled as an individual. The information I gave her might have potentially helped her relationship, but more likely helped her cope with the strong possibility of the marriage ending in divorce.

Some people might argue that I should have told her what had occurred with her husband because this information would have helped her make the appropriate decisions in her life. To be honest, I still wonder if that would have been the best course of action, since I know that if I were in her shoes, I'd want to know the whole truth. Had the question of her relationship or her husband's fidelity come up during her reading, my dilemma would have been easily solved, since my clairvoyant images would have given her the same information that was revealed during her husband's reading. However, the subject never came up, so perhaps it was not meant to.

This example demonstrates the confusion and difficulty of choosing the right course of action when one ethical value (confidentiality) collides with or opposes another value (telling the truth, fidelity). When it comes to maintaining confidentially, social work and psychology codes of conduct offer some clear guidelines, which provide that confidentiality can be broken if there is a likelihood that a person's life could be in jeopardy. In fact, social workers and psychologists are actually mandated by law to report a threat of intent to harm if there is an identifiable victim. Infidelity, as emotionally damaging as it is, falls short of this requirement.

The very first reading I ever did on my own, without the assistance of another student or teacher, involved a threat of violence and demonstrated to me the particular dilemmas psychic readers are faced with as opposed to traditional counselors who access information purely through discussion or observation on a physical level.

I had been reading all day outside at a psychic fair sponsored by my clairvoyant training school. I was sunburned and thirsty and preparing to make the two-hour drive back from Sacramento to my apartment in Oakland when a teacher I didn't know approached me and asked me to read a man who had been sitting for some time in the past-life booth. I told her I had never done a reading by myself and her response was, "You'll have to do it sometime, it might as well be now. Besides, reading past lives is easy, because they are not something that the readee can affirm or deny."

I greeted the man and sat several inches across from him on a warm metal folding chair. He did not speak other than to tell me his name. I began looking at his earliest life, most of which was spent on the floor of a filthy dungeon. He was having sex with a guy who was whipping him. His next life was not much better. In fact, life after life I saw images depicting the sadomasochistic torture he endured as a sex slave. I had only intended to look at a couple lives, but I was on a roll.

Next, I saw the man as a boy standing in the kitchen with his father, who was beating the crap out of him. He was wearing fairly modern clothing. And then I saw him as an adult once again, also wearing modern clothes, but this time there was a child with him. He was beckoning for the child to get off his bicycle as he rubbed his hands over his crotch. Next, I saw another child, even younger, crying, as the man unbuttoned the child's pants. And suddenly, I knew beyond all doubt that I was reading a child molester.

At that moment, I did the only logical thing I could think of. I panicked, silently. And then I grounded myself. And then I told the man everything I had seen. I left out not one single detail and he never said a single word. When I ran out of words, we sat there in silence and I prayed for God or anyone to help me know what to do. Seconds turned into minutes, and then finally I asked the man if he wanted me to look to see what actions he should take that would help him and his situation. He did not respond. I opened my eyes for the first time since I had sat down and repeated the question. He lifted his eyes for a brief moment and I saw gratitude in them. He nodded his head yes. I closed my eyes and I created a viewing receptacle in my imagination. I then connected it up to God with a cord of golden energy and again prayed feverishly for an answer to appear in the rose, an answer that would not only help this man, but that could stop him from hurting any more children.

The first image I saw was of a little boy talking to his mother and to a police officer. It looked as if there was already an investigation going on. I then saw an image of a church. The man was walking into the church and speaking to a pastor, who had a concerned look on his face. I sensed that this man in particular would feel more comfortable with a pastor or spiritual counselor than any other kind of therapist. Next, I saw an image of this man standing before a mirror, slicing the veins in his wrists. The look of self-loathing on his face is one I will never forget. I described this vision and told him that I knew he was in pain from his own childhood abuse and the abuse he was inflicting on these children, and that his own self-hatred was something he could not bear for much longer. He had to stop the cycle of abuse in this lifetime or it would merely continue into the next. I encouraged him to immediately go to his church, whatever church he was comfortable with, and ask for guidance. I opened my eyes one last time. He stood up and walked away. He never said a word.

I sat there for several minutes, not knowing what to do. Should I go to the police? I couldn't recall his name. Should I follow him? I went up to a teacher and told her what had happened. Her response made me furious: "It's not your responsibility." On an energetic level she was right. However, on a moral level, I feel to this day that she was dead wrong.

This example illustrates a dilemma that is unique to psychics. I knew this man had done harmful things and that it was very likely he was going to continue to hurt children. But what evidence did I have? I didn't even have a statement from the man other than a nod of his head. What would the police say if I told them about my reading? What could they do?

Now, years later, I feel that if this happened again I would go to the police. Because even if they laughed at me and threw me out of the station, I would have planted a seed. And when a child's parents called with the same description of the man I had told them about, someone in that office might remember and check into things a little more thoroughly.

Today, there are many more police officers who do welcome the assistance of psychics. These officers may joke about psychics to their buddies or even to your face, and they may never admit publicly that they took you seriously, but you can be sure at the end of the day, particularly after they have made some progress based on your clairvoyant information, or even solved their case, that they are going home to their wives or husbands and saying, "You know, I can't explain it, but the strangest thing happened today . . ."

These examples further illustrate that as clairvoyant readers/healers and counselors, it is not our business to judge our clients, because their biggest problem, which usually is at the core of their questionable behavior, is their own self-judgment and hatred. The only way a person can heal and transform is through acceptance. This acceptance does not mean that we condone their behavior and praise the readee for cheating on their spouse or molesting children. What it does mean is that, as readers, we maintain our neutrality at all times. We navigate our way through the reading so as to help the readee understand their motivations and feelings for their behavior, and we help them find alternative ways of behaving that in the end will help them find peace and happiness in their life. The information we provide does not come from our logical minds or our code of ethics, but from neutral clairvoyant information.

What sets psychics apart from other counselors is that we know we have access to information from a higher source and we know how to access it. This higher source could be God or a person's spirit guides, their higher self, or their inner voice. This higher source has the answers that we do not. We think it is wrong for a man to cheat on his wife, but our logical minds do not know that she actually cheated on him in several past lifetimes and now the karmic scales are being balanced. Our logical minds do not know that as spirits, before they were born, this couple agreed to marry and then divorce in order to learn lessons about love, commitment, and independence.

People grow, learn, and develop as human beings and as spirits by having life experiences that involve all sorts of breaches of commitments, contracts, laws, and commandments. As clairvoyant readers and healers, the more we can put aside our judgments and neutrally look at the spiritual blueprint or path of a readee in distress, the better equipped we will be to help our clients, and the more forgiveness we will have for our own transgressions. The more forgiving and neutral we are, the more clearly they will hear us. Neutrality and forgiveness bring light into the world, while judgment brings, and is, darkness. You must decide which path you are going to choose as a reader and a healer. That decision will form the basis of your ethical code.

As a clairvoyant reader and healer, you need to know that you are not alone in your readings or healings or at any moment of your life. There is a larger force, whether you call it God or the readee's higher self, that is ever present. Whenever you encounter anything that is too difficult, too challenging, or too overwhelming for you to deal with, it is okay, because no matter how great the illusion, it is not all up to you. Any problem that is impossible for you to solve is not your problem to solve. Otherwise it wouldn't feel impossible!

As a reader, you have the ability to communicate with God, the universe, or your higher self through visions, prayer, mantra, your mind, your voice, and your heart. You can ask for help and then use your clairvoyance to receive the answer. Sometimes the answer will come and other times it won't, no matter how hard you try to force it.

As a reader, you will not always be given an answer, because your readee or healee is supposed to discover the answer on their own, through their own actions. It is important for clairvoyant readers to remember that our job is to look for answers, but also to be okay when they don't appear. We are not God, we are merely aspects of God. No matter how good a clairvoyant we are, we are not all-knowing, we are not all-powerful. We are human beings doing the best we can. Out of the purest of pure intentions, many psychics and healers forget this fact. You will not.

Common Dilemmas that Psychics and Healers Face

Once you know that you are not expected to have all the answers, it is easier to deal with the plethora of questions or dilemmas that can arise during a clairvoyant reading or healing. Several of these are presented here, in a question-and-answer format.

1. What do I do if I see something upsetting about my readee's future?

One of the main reasons people avoid going to psychic readers is that they are afraid to hear potentially "bad" news about their future.

Many people avoid developing their own psychic abilities because they are afraid they will see and know "bad" things about the future. Clairvoyant readers do occasionally pick up information about other people that has the potential to cause an emotional reaction. The following discussion offers some helpful insights into how to cope with this information.

The future often can be changed based on present behavior.

For example, you are told that you will be make a mistake on your job and be fired. This happens because spiritually your job is no longer serving you, and you even hate your job but are afraid to leave it willingly. As a result of this news, you take steps to start your own business and you voluntarily retire. You are given early-retirement pay that you would have lost had you been fired.

Knowledge of unpleasant future events can help clients make physical and psychological preparations.

For example, you are told that your mother may not have long to live. This makes you so sad, but it motivates you to throw her a party, videotape her life story, visit her more often, and tell her you love her.

"Bad" things are teachers, blessings in disguise, or part of one's spiritual path.

For example, you are told that your body is rebelling against your workaholic behavior and that you have the beginning of a serious illness (which is true). This illness requires you to take a leave of absence and depend more on friends and family to help you. At first this is very difficult, but eventually you discover that others really care and you are not alone. You work through issues you were avoiding but that were blocking you from living your dreams. You begin writing a book and eventually become a well-known author. You also have more time to spend with your children.

You would not be receiving the information if you or someone else didn't need to hear it. What you consider to be bad, your readee may think is good, and vice versa.

I don't know how many times in my own readings I have been nervous about revealing what I considered to be upsetting information, but once I did share it with the readee, they blurted out, "I knew that" or "That's what I thought, but everyone has been telling me I'm crazy." The greatest thing you can do for a readee is validate what they already know and feel, even if it's something they consider unpleasant. When everyone else in their life is trying to tell them that they are wrong, or that they shouldn't think about it, or that it will be okay when it will not, this is far more frustrating than hearing the truth. Keep in mind the following points when considering whether or not to disclose information to a readee:

- Some people need to undergo certain life experiences; they will ignore your warnings and learn from them in retrospect.
- Some people are very programmable, and a reading could affect their feelings and perceptions.
- Your reading may have been written into the script of the readee's life to alter the course of events.
- Most clairvoyant information will concern the present unless you choose to focus on the future.

Potential clients need to understand that you are there to validate and explain their current feelings and experiences.

The purpose of looking at the future is to see what action needs to be taken or altered in the present to achieve desired goals.

Your client may not be emotionally ready to hear your information now, but may need to hear it on a spiritual or intellectual level.

A sad or angry emotional response from a readee does not mean that you made a mistake.

2. *What should I do if I spontaneously receive information about someone I know, when this person has not asked for a reading?*

I have learned from experience that when you spontaneously receive information about a person you know in your life who has not solicited a reading from you, that it's important to look at your own motivation for desiring to share this information and to question why you are the one receiving the information, and then to clairvoyantly look to see how it might affect the person. You may be receiving the information for any number of reasons, many of which may have more to do with you than with the person.

Many beginning clairvoyant students will be so excited about their clairvoyance and will not yet have learned when it is appropriate to share information and when it's invasive or simply annoying. They may be motivated to share information by their desire to showoff or prove that they are capable psychics to their friends and to themselves. Some readers who feel uncomfortable in social situations will fall out of a conversation and into a reading space as a means to escape or to feel superior to other people. I have known some clairvoyant students who, at a party or social event, would abruptly turn a casual conversation into a reading in which they brought up issues regarding my personal life that were none of their business and that I didn't care to address at that time.

Occasionally you will spontaneously receive information about someone because they are searching for an answer in their life but are unable to hear it on their own. This information could come to you in the form of clairvoyant images when you are fully conscious, during a meditation, or when you are dreaming. In this case, sharing the information with the person could be very helpful.

Any time you are not sure whether to share unsolicited information, particularly information concerning death or illness, I suggest that you clairvoyantly look to see how it will affect the person, and ask God to show you, through your clairvoyance, how to proceed.

3. What should I do if I have agreed to give someone an hour reading, but I don't feel it's going well and want to terminate it (or they do)?

Occasionally you will find it necessary to end a reading prematurely. Your clairvoyant reading is a gift, not an obligation. You should never read anyone at any time if you have a feeling that it might harm you in any way or that the person is disrespecting you or the gift you are offering them. As a clairvoyant reader, your personal health, safety, and well-being have to be your top concerns.

Likewise, there will be times when your readee will decide to terminate the reading. Some people become very anxious at the start of a reading because they are experiencing the energy that they are about to release. They will immediately attribute their uncomfortable feelings to you, which will lead them to conclude that there is something wrong with you or that they are not meant to be receiving a reading from you. Some people will walk out of the reading because they don't like what you are telling them. I've had a few people leave a reading because they felt uncomfortable getting a reading from a person younger than themselves.

When a readee voices displeasure with a psychic or the reading and terminates the reading prematurely, it is so easy for the reader, particularly a newer one, to blame themselves, lose their certainty, and obsess over what went wrong. Many readers could do a hundred brilliant readings followed by one reading where the readee voiced displeasure, and they would question whether they should be doing readings at all. The best thing you could ever do for yourself if you have a difficult, unpleasant, or disastrous reading is to jump right into another reading as soon as possible to remind yourself that you are clairvoyant, you do have something to offer other people, and that reading is fun.

Unless I end a reading out of fear for my own safety or because the readee is being rude, I will usually refer the readee to another reader. I do this for a few reasons. First of all, I like to be helpful. I know certain people will feel more comfortable with other types of readers due to age, personality, or the reading methods and approaches. Providing referrals is also a good business practice because it demonstrates to the readee that you do care about them, that you don't feel any animosity toward them, and that you are a professional.

I believe that one of my duties as a clairvoyant reader and teacher is to do what I can to reverse the misperceptions and stereotypes that the general public has regarding psychic readers. The best way for me to do this is to serve as a positive example. It's for this reason that I usually don't charge a readee if they or I terminate the reading early. I don't want to give anyone the impression that this is another case where a psychic was taking financial advantage of a client. I also don't want to engage in an ongoing battle over money, whether on the physical or spiritual plane.

Other professional readers have far different approaches. Some readers even have a policy that unless a readee gives twenty-hour hours' notice of their desire to cancel a reading, they will be charged the full price of the reading, regardless of the circumstances. This policy helps them establish and maintain personal boundaries and their own sense of self-respect. However, I have seen some of these people get into huge battles with clients who felt they should not have to pay, and it seemed like the extra energy they had to exert to get their way or resolve the dispute was not worth the money they were fighting for. I think that whatever approach will bring the greatest amount of peace to one's life is the best one to take. Some people cannot be peaceful if they feel that even a minute of their time was undervalued or uncompensated for. Others are far more peaceful when they know that everyone has left the situation feeling good.

Sexual Ethics

The licensing boards and codes of ethics that govern healthcare professionals, whether they be doctors, dentists, psychologists, psychiatrists, or social workers, strictly forbid these professionals from becoming sexually involved with clients because of the psychological and emotional trauma that the client would suffer. When a psychic or healer violates a client's sexual boundaries by making advances or exchanging sexual energies during a session, it is just as damaging as if a gynecologist asked his patient on a date or expressed his attraction for her while she lay naked, vulnerable, and exposed on the examination table.

Many of your clients, whether they be men or women, are not used to being in the presence of someone like yourself who can see them as spirit and who can validate their feelings and life circumstances. Many clients are desperate for attention and kindness. They will feel gratitude and admiration toward you and this can easily turn into feelings of attraction. Many psychics and healers don't know how to handle this admiration any better than young rock stars. They begin to see their clients as groupies. Others try so hard to be the perfect healer that they repress any feelings that they think a "spiritually advanced" person should not have, and as a result become disconnected with their sexual energy. This sexual energy then takes on a will and a life of its own.

As a clairvoyant reader or healer, it is imperative that you monitor and control your own sexual desires, behavior, and energy to make sure they are not interfering with the reading or the readee. If you are unable to do this, don't beat yourself up about it, just seriously consider avoiding reading and healing anyone whom you are sexually attracted to, which may mean all people of the opposite or same sex, depending on your sexual orientation.

When performing a reading and especially a healing, you need to be aware of what you are doing with your energy, because during this time, the walls between the physical and the spiritual will become permeable and transparent. Your client will feel your sexual energy as it penetrates her aura, she will hear your lascivious thoughts as if you were whispering them in her ear (or shouting them into a microphone), and if she is particularly perceptive, she may even see the images of your fantasies as clearly as if you had just thrust a pornographic photograph in front of her eyes. Some clients will consciously know when you are leaking sexual energy and will feel violated or slimed, while others may confuse your energy for their own. Those that do have an awareness of the situation are placed in a precarious position—they know they are being sexually slimed and energetically assaulted by the very person they are relying upon for healing and guidance. Because all of this is occurring on an energetic level, the client may not feel justified in confronting you and will likely feel, for the rest of the session, uncomfortable, trapped, and angry at themselves for remaining in this situation.

Those clients who confuse your energy for their own may actually end up forming a crush on you or becoming obsessed with you. They may even make an advance toward you and later (immediately following the session or months later) realize their mistake, at which point they will become overwhelmed with feelings of shame, remorse, and even self-hatred for letting themselves be manipulated by someone else's thoughts and feelings that really had nothing to do with them.

Even if your readee makes advances toward you, it is your responsibility as the psychic and healer to set and enforce boundaries and to help the person understand the reasons for their feelings. The readee is not acting on their own accord if it is your energy in their body that is driving them to act out sexually. Furthermore, you are the expert, the professional, the parent, so to speak. If a patient blatantly comes on to her psychiatrist and he responds by having sex with her, he could lose his license and face a serious lawsuit, because as a professional it is his responsibility to conduct himself in a way that is in the best interest of his patient, even when she is not acting in her own best interest.

As a psychic/healer, there is no governing board to punish you nor any license to take away, but there is your own conscience and the karmic laws of the universe that you cannot evade. If you desire a date with someone, then ask them out on a date. Don't offer to give them a reading or healing as a way to get closer to them or get to know them. This is the coward's way of handling romance.

If you find yourself feeling sexually aroused during a reading or healing, put up a separation object and ground yourself. Then check to see if your sexual energy is running solely through your own body or if it is also running through your readee's body. Sometimes you may be feeling their sexual energy, and if that is the case, then use your clairvoyant healing abilities to cut any cords that might be joining the two of you together, and watch as the readee's sexual energy returns to them.

If you feel extremely attracted to a client and believe that this is someone with whom you are destined to have a significant relationship, then I recommend the following:

1. Terminate a reading, and especially a healing, if you realize that you cannot control your sexual energy or realize that it's getting in the way of your neutrality. You have lost your neutrality if you become jealous when your client asks about a relationship with someone else, or if you are seeking information about her to determine whether she is available or will be a viable partner, or if you tell her she doesn't have to pay for the reading because she is so attractive.

2. Do not express your feelings of attraction to your readee during the reading or immediately after the reading or healing.

3. If you terminate a reading before the agreed-upon time has ended due to your feelings of arousal or attraction, refund the readee's money. Explain that you are working out some personal issues and are not mentally focused enough to continue the reading.

4. Give yourself time away from the readee to explore your feelings. Once out of the readee's presence, you may feel totally different. If you still desire contact with the readee, then call her, tell her you are calling her as a potential suitor rather than as a reader or healer, and ask her out on a date. Regardless of her answer, make the determination that you will not see her on a professional level again.

5. If you are afraid to be so direct, get over it or give up. Your client should not have to be manipulated or mislead just because you don't have the guts to be direct with her.

Unsolicited Astral Advances Are a Form of Rape

There are many healers, psychics, and spiritual teachers who use their spiritual knowledge and abilities to interact sexually with clients (or anyone they are attracted to, including students, teachers, friends, etc.)

on the astral plane. They will consciously send their astral body over to her (or his) home, enter her bedroom, and actually have sexual intercourse with the client or student without her consent. Many of these astral travelers do not feel they are doing anything wrong because their physical bodies are not involved. However, I have read far too many people and counseled far too many friends who suffered tremendously from these unwelcome, unsolicited visitations, which are nothing less than rape. Having sex with a client on the astral plane is no different from physically having sex with a client. If you have sex with anyone, energetically or physically, without their consent, then you are violating and molesting that person and you have no right to call yourself a healer.

CHAPTER 22

The Psychic Minority

It isn't easy being psychic in a society filled with people who aren't even conscious of their own psychic/spiritual abilities. This lack of consciousness causes many of these well-meaning people to misunderstand, judge, criticize, fear, stereotype, and persecute practicing psychics as well as laypeople who have a casual interest in metaphysics. Many psychics and healers in the Western world struggle with feelings of loneliness, isolation, and alienation until they learn how to successfully coexist among a majority of people who experience their lives from a denser state of consciousness.

In this chapter, I offer some suggestions that will help you cope with the challenges of being awake in a slumbering world. *It's important to understand that there are both people who will accept and understand you, and those who can't. Get out of judgment with those who can't, and seek those who can.*

In the same way that there are entities that you cannot see because they vibrate at a different frequency and on a different plane or dimension of existence, there are people out there who cannot see or hear you. They may see your physical body, but beyond that they are only experiencing their own projections when they look into your eyes. Some of these people literally will not be able to hear you when you speak of clairvoyance; others will only hear jumbled words that their conscious minds won't allow them to process, no matter how intelligent they are. You can tell this is happening when the only response you get is a blank stare and a quick, almost frantic change of subject.

The best way to deal with people who can't understand you is to get out of resistance to them; that is, don't try to change them or control what they think about you. If you want them to treat you with respect, then do the same thing for them: let them be where they are. Treat them with the same compassion you would have for a child whose brain doesn't have the synapses and pathways to understand certain things. Don't try to make them see you, understand you, or like you. Don't prove yourself to them. It's like trying to prove yourself to a scared bunny rabbit who leaps away from you when you are offering a fresh carrot. If they are meant to break through the veils of consciousness from their plane of awareness to yours, it will happen in their own time.

Forgive Them, For They Know Not What They Do

Of course it will hurt if the people whom you have been closest to and dependent on all your life, such as your parents or siblings, don't seem to care about your spiritual interests or appreciate what you are trying to do with your life. It will be frustrating when a neighbor says you are doing the devil's work by reading and healing people, or when a co-worker warns you that you may lose your job if you ever again mention seeing a spirit in the bathroom, or when your boss forbids you to do readings during your lunch hour on company premises. Just know that these people are speaking as much out of concern for you as they are out of ignorance and fear.

Some people are very afraid of clairvoyance because practice of their own abilities in other lifetimes resulted in violent persecution and death. When you speak of your clairvoyant abilities, experiences, or training, their MEI death pictures become stimulated (see chapter 4) and they literally feel like they might die unless they can get you to shut up!

Other people are not meant to understand clairvoyance because their spirits are striving to gain other experiences in this lifetime, and knowledge of this ability could steer them on a whole different path. In these cases, forcing your clairvoyant knowledge or spiritual convictions on these people would be interfering with their spiritual destiny. What is so right for you is not right for everybody.

There are a small number of mentally unstable people who would topple into madness if their psychic centers opened any further. Then there are those individuals who have misused their abilities and authority in past incarnations and are therefore banned by certain guardian spirits and councils from having any awareness of these abilities. I have a theory that most hardcore skeptics fall into this category. The karmic sentence they must live out to the end of their days is having tremendously strong psychic abilities but being completely cut off from their awareness of them. This causes an inexplicable anger and frustration that fuels their passion to debunk other psychics.

Teaching Through Example

I have discovered through my own experiences and those of many of my clairvoyant or spiritually oriented friends that the most effective and least painful way to impact other people's lives is through living your life honestly, with grace. As you follow your heart and your dreams, you will create an exhilarating life filled with peace and joy. Others will want to know your secret and will begin to question why they are living their lives the way mainstream society told them to, but they are not nearly as fulfilled as you are.

Teaching through example means that you don't beat people over the head with your convictions, but also that you don't hide in the proverbial closet. Many psychics, even practicing professionals, hide their abilities from their closest relatives in order to avoid judgments or uncomfortable confrontations. They live a double life and give away their power to people who don't know what to do with it. Most of these psychics are very stuck in their lives and tend to get trapped in a pattern of creating jobs and romantic relationships in which they feel victimized and disrespected, primarily because they continue to put other people's ideas and feelings ahead of their own.

One of my favorite quotations comes from *A Course in Miracles* and was made famous in a speech given by Nelson Mandela. Marianne Williamson paraphrased it in her enlightening book *A Return to Love* (pp. 190–191):

Who am I to be brilliant, gorgeous, talented, fabulous? Actually, who are you not to be? You are a child of God. Your playing small doesn't serve the world. There is nothing enlightened about shrinking so that other people won't feel insecure around you. We are all meant to shine, as children do. We were born to make manifest the glory of God that is within us . . . and as we let our own light shine, we unconsciously give other people permission to do the same. As we are liberated from our own fear, our presence automatically liberates others.

Seek Your Spiritual Family; Forgive Your Birth Family

Understand that your family of origin may not be your spiritual family. Be grateful to your birth parents for bringing you into the world and nurturing you to the best of their abilities, and for all the lessons they have taught you. But if you don't feel that they understand or accept you, or see you in the way you long to be seen, then you would do well to seek out your true spiritual family.

Your spiritual family is a group of souls that are on the same level of consciousness as you. They usually originate from the same soul grouping as your own. You will recognize members of this family because they will automatically understand, accept, and honor you. Understanding the difference between your birth family and soul family helps you lower your expectations of your birth family and motivates you to seek out individuals who have a greater potential to love you for who you really are.

Seek and Ye Shall Find; Ask and Ye Shall Receive

Growing up in the suburbs of Chicago, I knew no one, except for me and my twin sister, who exhibited psychic abilities or had an interest in

psychic phenomena. Decades later, when I began my clairvoyant training in Berkeley, California, for the first time in my life I was surrounded by hundreds of people who were exploring their own spiritual
abilities. What was even more mind-boggling than the number of psychics I encountered was the fact that so many of these people existed
for so long without my knowledge, despite the hundreds of metaphysically oriented books I had read since I was a child.

After a couple years, I realized it was time for me to leave California, which not only meant leaving my clairvoyant training schools and
built-in support systems of classmates, teachers, and staff, it also meant
abandoning all of my clairvoyant friends and acquaintances who lived
within those particular communities. Since I did not yet know that
there are spiritual and metaphysically oriented communities all over
the world, I was forced to contemplate the possibility that I would
never find another place where I belonged. The idea of once again
being a lone psychic in the world was not a comforting one.

Then one of my clairvoyant friends gave me a reading and reminded me that I had the ability to create the kinds of people I wanted
to be with, simply through having faith and determination that I would
find them, and through visualizing my positive interactions with future
friends. This reading helped me decide that my departure from this
community would serve as a signal to the universe that I did in fact believe in my own ability to create that which would ultimately serve my
soul.

From that point forward, wherever I have lived, I have found myself
surrounded by other metaphysically minded folks within a matter of
weeks if not days. For about five years, I lived in Sedona, Arizona,
which has the largest population of psychics and healers of any city in
the United States. During my time there, I knew so many people, including my hairstylist, my son's babysitter, my car repairman, many of
my friends, and even my cleaning lady, who were not only believers or
practitioners of psychic phenomena, but exhibited a depth of understanding, faith, and wisdom that one would expect only a great sage or
yogi to possess.

If you wish to find people who will understand and respect you
(this includes romantic partners as well!), then you must make the

commitment to yourself to find and associate only with people who are on your level of consciousness (with the exception of a few family members you can't bear to let go of). You must have faith that you are not alone even before you have any hardcore evidence that this is true. As you meet more and more like-minded people and develop friendships that are truly fulfilling and joyful, you will know that you are on the right path.

While you may be in the minority in terms of the entire country, know that there are many, many people like you all over the world and in almost every major city of the United States. Sedona, Arizona and Berkeley, California are only two of the many cities with communities where psychics, healers, massage therapists, acupuncturists, channelers, yogis, etc., are the norm. Other places that are populated by psychics include Cassadaga, Florida; Salem, Massachusetts; Marin and Santa Cruz Counties, California; and Taos, New Mexico.

In just about every metropolitan area across the United States, there are communities of psychics and healers. You will only meet people of a higher consciousness when you are near or at that level yourself, whether these people are located on the other side of the globe or in the house next door.

Within most cities, there are certain locations, businesses, and activities where you are more likely to meet fellow psychics and healers. Obviously, metaphysical bookstores attract people who are metaphysically oriented. Other popular places to meet like-minded people are at yoga and meditation centers/schools and massage and acupuncture schools.

Most of these metaphysically oriented shops and centers offer classes or information about workshops where you will meet other psychics, healers, astrologers, or people who at the very least are interested in and accepting of what you do. Most of these places have public bulletin boards and offer free metaphysically oriented magazines or newspapers that list local practitioners and events.

CHAPTER 23

The Business of Spirituality

To Charge or Not to Charge

Early on in your clairvoyant training, the issue of compensation will arise. This is because most of the people you work with will recognize that you are providing a valuable service that requires you to devote your personal time and energy that could easily be spent elsewhere. Many of your clients will feel an instinctive need to balance the exchange by giving something back to you.

Ironically, you may be so excited to practice your new skills on real subjects that you may feel that you should be the one paying them! Many clairvoyant students and graduates do actually pay a fee to their schools in order to be given the opportunity to read clients in a supervised and grounded setting.

Hopefully you will always feel blessed to have the opportunity to read people, but most likely, after having gained some experience and confidence and realizing how much work some readings can be, you will feel the need to receive some form of compensation for your efforts. Obviously, psychics and healers have to eat. In societies outside the United States, such as in India or Southeast Asia, healers may not be paid with money for their services, but instead are given food and shelter and are cared for by their devotees who could number from a few to a few thousand. In the United States and Europe, the primary form of compensation is money. Many clairvoyant students and practitioners also exchange services, such as doing a reading in exchange for receiving a reading, healing, or massage.

There are pros and cons to charging for your readings and healings and these can change according to your development in these areas. As a beginning student, charging for your readings and healings can have a detrimental effect on your learning process. Money creates expectations for both the reader and the readee. When you are reading merely for the sake of learning, you will feel greater freedom to explore and experiment with your clairvoyance. You will also be more likely to give yourself greater permission during a reading to use your psychic tools and to release your own matching pictures.

When payment is involved, you may fall into the trap of feeling like you need to give your reader their money's worth, which translates into delivering the correct answers in an efficient manner. If you feel that you are reading too slowly (in that your images are taking a while to display themselves, which is common when you are first learning to read) or giving the readee unpleasant information, you may fear that the readee is going to feel cheated, disappointed, or angry. This will create performance anxiety, which will not only make it more difficult to access clairvoyant images, but will damage your ability to read in a neutral and honest manner, and could cause a tragic decline in your enjoyment of and enthusiasm for clairvoyant reading and healing.

Whether you have been reading for two hours or two decades, eventually you will begin accepting money for your readings and the above issues will arise. However, as a beginning clairvoyant student, you are more vulnerable to losing sight of what is important in a reading because you have much less certainty and confidence in yourself as a reader. With every image or slice of information that comes to you, your certainty will increase until one day you will know that you can trust the validity of your clairvoyance more than you can trust any other part of yourself or anyone else. When you get to this point, you will be able to recognize more easily the feelings of pressure and responsibility that come with money and will be better able to cope with them. The longer you have been doing readings and utilizing your psychic tools, the better you will understand how important it is to continue using your readings as a self-healing process and to always honor yourself as much as the readee, no matter who they are, how serious their issues are, or how much they are paying you.

Despite the pitfalls, there are definitely some good reasons to charge for readings, even as a beginning clairvoyant student. The most significant reason has to do with the readee's level of commitment to the reading. People who are willing to pay for readings are often more invested in the reading process and their own personal growth. Those who will only come for a reading if it is free or very cheap tend to take the reading less seriously and may be there only to play "test the psychic" or as a curious observer. I am not saying that these motivations are bad; in fact, some people's lives are transformed when they experience what a psychic can do because they become more fully aware of their own potential. However, clairvoyant readers invest so much of their time and energy in their readings that to spend time with a client who is not taking the reading seriously can be quite frustrating and even degrading. Imagine if you spent hours painting a beautiful portrait for someone in which you painstakingly recreated every detail of their face and emotional expression. Imagine then that the person glanced at it for less than a moment and then threw it in the trash can. That is how it feels to read someone who is not respectful of you and your clairvoyant ability. Charging money for readings, even a small fee such as twenty dollars, will help weed out readees who are just curious onlookers or skeptics from those who are really open to communication.

The more money you charge, the more you will attract people who seriously want your help. However, those who "seriously" want your help tend to be more "serious." They may have more urgent and difficult issues that are not as fun to look at and require more of your energy. It seems to be a basic spiritual law that you will attract what you can handle. As your certainty and neutrality increase, you will be presented with more challenging readings for which you will receive greater compensation. If you go for the big money before you really can handle it, you will only create problems for yourself in the long run. On the other hand, if you fail to honor your abilities and experience as you progress on your clairvoyant path by refusing compensation, you may become exhausted, frustrated, and unbalanced. Receiving money for readings is a way to honor your self-worth, to celebrate your abilities, and to validate the progress you've made through discipline and courageousness.

Practically speaking, charging for your readings often makes it possible for you to devote more time and energy to your readings/healings and less time to jobs that have been paying the bills but are not as fulfilling or fun.

The Incremental/Experimental Pricing Approach

I suggest that you begin your clairvoyant training by practicing on people who seem to be the most supportive and nonjudgmental. Let them know you are wishing to gain practice, and ask them not to have high expectations of you (then they will be pleasantly surprised at how much they get out of the reading). I suggest accepting tips during your first several readings if they are offered to you rather than charging a set price. Let yourself enjoy the freedom of being a clairvoyant student for as long as possible. Once you begin to feel the urge to charge, adopt an experimental approach. Start off with a small fee and notice how this feels. You may feel very satisfied with this amount or you may feel undercompensated, at which time you could raise your rate and again notice how it feels to receive this amount of money. When you increase your rate, notice whether you attract more or less clients, and pay attention to any changes in your level of enthusiasm. These will be your barometers to tell you whether your rate is appropriate for where you are in your life. Some psychics charge hundreds of dollars and have so many clients that they must turn them away, so if you raise your rate and find that suddenly you are not getting any clients at all, realize that this state of affairs has more to do with your own issues regarding money, your clairvoyant certainty, and/or your self-esteem than with the rate itself.

If you live in an area where there are several other psychics, it will be helpful to inquire how much these readers charge. Some people think that if they charge less than the going rate, they will get more clients. However, this is often not the case because potential clients may sense that the person charging less is not as talented or qualified.

My prices also reflect how busy I am, how much energy I have to devote to my readings versus other projects and people in my life, the location where I am living and practicing, my relationship to the readee, our financial situations, etc. Because clairvoyant reading is such a personal and intimate experience, you need to allow room to consider personal factors of both the reader and the readee. I offer a sliding fee scale for people who can't afford a reading and will never turn someone away from a reading if the only consideration is that they can't afford one.

Exchanging Services

In general, exchanging clairvoyant readings is an excellent way for beginning clairvoyant students to gain practice and experience in a supportive environment and at the same time to feel as if they are receiving some form of compensation for their readings. There is value in exchanging readings with students or readers who have or are studying similar methods taught in this book or through clairvoyant training schools, as well as with psychics, channelers, and spiritual counselors who employ different methods or are versed in other traditions of psychic development. Psychics and healers are usually very open and receptive and therefore easier to read than the general population. They tend to be compassionate and caring people who will be supportive of your efforts and your learning process. You will share many matching MEI pictures, which will make the readings more intense but will provide you with greater opportunities to work through these pictures and to gain a deeper level of understanding about your own and other people's psychic abilities. Through exchanging readings with other psychics, you will learn new reading techniques and approaches. When reading psychics who are not familiar with the information in this book, you will have a chance to observe the detrimental effects of reading a person who is not as aware of how to maintain neutrality or energetic boundaries.

When doing exchanges, you will want to discuss expectations beforehand. Decide who will be the first to receive a reading, and whether the exchange will happen immediately following the first reading or at a later date and time. Unless the readings are kept to a short time limit of thirty minutes or less, I recommend that the readings or healings be scheduled for two different days in order to allow the person receiving the reading to fully relax and have time to process the information and energy redistribution that may be occurring within their body and energy field. The tone of the first reading usually sets the tone for the second reading, in terms of time and effort expended.

There are some factors to be aware of when doing exchanges with other psychics or healers. Beginning clairvoyant students are often naive in that they think that anyone with similar interests in metaphysics can be trusted. Unfortunately this is not always the case. Occasionally you may encounter another psychic or healer who is in competition with you or your abilities or your method of practice. Competition is connected to feelings of insecurity and resentment about not being where a person thinks they should be or wants to be in their life.

If you agree to an exchange and then become aware that you may be exposing yourself to unfriendly energies, do whatever is necessary to avoid doing the exchange or terminate it immediately, particularly where healing is involved. Your health and well-being are far more important than being polite or having someone like you. I have made the mistake of allowing people to heal me who, after getting to know them better, I would not even allow through my front door! Whether the healer is an energetic healer, a chiropractor, an acupuncturist, or an allopathic doctor or surgeon, it's important that you consider what kind of person they are. For that matter, do you even like them?

It amazes me that we let doctors who are complete strangers examine the most private parts of our bodies, and even cut open and remove parts of our bodies that will determine whether we live and die, but we don't even question for a moment who this person is, or whether we like them or feel that they will respect us. We have been socialized to respect the knowledge of mainstream medical professionals and to not ask these questions. We need to be careful not to make the same mistake with alternative healers.

I always opt for the honest approach to communication. If you feel uncomfortable letting someone read or touch you, or vice versa, let them know this. It will be harder for them to argue with your true feelings than with your excuses, particularly if they are psychic! If they take offense, this is not your responsibility.

If hardcore honesty is not your style, or you have to deal with this psychic/healer on a regular basis, or you fear they may seek revenge in the form of black magic or voodoo, then politely tell them you have a general rule of not receiving readings and/or healings from anyone other than your teacher; or you don't allow people of the opposite sex to heal you; or you just realized that you are at a point in your life where it's not appropriate for you to do exchanges with other readers or healers so you are changing your mind. If you have already received a reading or healing from the person but don't wish to reciprocate as agreed, you can offer them financial compensation in return in order to make a clean energetic and karmic separation.

On the other hand, if you have carried out your part of the exchange but they seem to be backing out, then gracefully let them go. When I worked at one of the New Age centers in Sedona, some of the psychics and healers there were intimidated by my level of training and certainty. They sought readings from me, but then came up with excuse after excuse to not read me. At first this felt unfair, but then I realized that they were really doing me a favor. As with any agreement, if someone is not living up to their end of the bargain, this may be because they are not capable of it, or because ultimately it would not serve either of you. If someone doesn't want to complete an exchange, allow them to gracefully bow out of it; otherwise you may become chained to them in a karmic battle for the rest of infinity!

Regardless of the lightness or darkness of the person you are reading or healing, you will always want to make sure you use your tools, keep your energy running, and clear the readee's energy from your energy field, and vice versa, at the completion of the exchange.

Embarking on Your Professional Career of Psychic Reading

Good Business Practices

Some clairvoyant readers in business for themselves do quite a bit of marketing and advertising, while others depend solely on referrals and repeat business from former clients.

Many professional psychics find that taking care of the business end of their practice can be challenging if not downright disastrous. Clairvoyant reading involves one part of the brain, while marketing and financial planning involve the other. A successful reading practice requires a marriage of the two. Observations and conversations with financially successful readers reveal some common business practices that have contributed to their success in terms of attracting clients and repeat business.

It's always wise to take care of the business end of a reading prior to the commencement of the reading. At the beginning of a reading or healing, have the client sign your log book, which should include an area where they can write their name, phone number, mailing address, e-mail address, and the date. This will help you at a later date when you wish to send out a newsletter or mailing in which you offer discounted readings or gift certificates. It will also help you keep track of the number of clients you are reading and will give you a means to contact your clients in the event that they inadvertently leave something behind in your office, or their check bounces, or you remember an important piece of information that you forgot to share during the reading.

As discussed in chapter 14, you will want to discuss expectations for the reading, the cost of the reading, the format and methods employed, etc., prior to the commencement of the reading. You may want to handle payment for the reading at this point as well, since after the reading you are likely to be much more spacey and less capable of performing mathematical calculations or negotiating payment. The only disadvantage to this is that many more readees request that their readings be extended when they have not paid beforehand compared to when they have already paid prior to the reading. Therefore you are more likely to conduct a longer reading, which is deserving of more money, if you wait to receive your payment until the reading has been completed.

Working with a Promoter

Some of the most successful psychics in business for themselves have business managers, agents, and promoters who take care of the business end of things so they can invest their energy solely in their readings and healings. Finding a talented business manager whom you can trust and who will stay through the slow times is a challenge. This is a case of which one came first: the chicken or the egg? It is always easier to attract promotional help once you have already established a strong reputation, or have the funds to pay a manager a regular salary. Most psychics who work with agents or managers have already published books and conduct workshops with large numbers of attendees. However, it's a lot easier to establish yourself with the assistance of someone who believes in your work and has strong marketing and managerial skills, since marketing in itself can become a full-time job.

Whether or not you can afford or find a promoter, managing your own business affairs can teach you skills and lessons from which you may greatly benefit in the long run. It's nice to have help, but it's also nice to know that you don't have to depend on outside assistance for your survival.

Marketing Strategies for Beginning Professionals

If you are in business for yourself as a clairvoyant reader or healer, you will need to develop a feasible marketing strategy that will help you attract clients. This strategy could include advertising through written materials; offering introductory lectures, classes, or group demonstrations; offering free mini readings in populated places; reading at psychic or Renaissance fairs; developing a website; or appearing on television and radio shows.

As with most business endeavors, the old saying "It takes money to make money" is true even for psychic readers who intend to read out of their homes. Starting your reading practice may not require a lot of money, but it does require some. Even the least expensive form of advertising, such as creating a one-page flyer, can become expensive. For example, you will need to have access to a computer or word processor to type up and print your flyer, you will need to have a good picture taken of yourself, and you will need to make copies of the flyers. If you choose to hire someone else to create your flyers, this could cost anywhere from fifteen dollars for the original copy to hundreds of dollars. Or perhaps you would like to place an ad in the newspaper. This could cost anywhere from ten dollars a week to several hundred dollars a week, depending on the size of the ad and the number of colors and pictures in the add. Renting a space to give an introductory lecture could cost anywhere from ten dollars a hour to hundreds of dollars an hour.

Libraries, churches, and some metaphysical centers tend to offer the lowest rates for public room rental, while hotels and retreat centers are often the most expensive. If you are in need of a room for a lecture, class, demonstration, etc., find out if any advertising will be done on your behalf. For example, the Sedona Public Library rents out rooms to groups and individuals. They permit you to post your flyer on their bulletin board and will list your event in their calendar, which is mailed to the public and is seen by library patrons upon entering the library. This type of free marketing obviously increases the value of the space.

Optimizing the Value of Written Materials

The basic written materials needed by a professional clairvoyant reader are a business card and a one-page flyer. Other materials may include larger posters and newspaper ads. Your business card demonstrates to potential clients that you consider yourself to be a professional and also serves as a reminder and as a means to contact you. Your flyer is literally and symbolically a portrait of who you are as a person and professional reader. You can post your flyer around your neighborhood on bulletin boards located in or outside metaphysical stores and centers, health food or natural food grocery stores, massage schools, yoga centers, health clubs, etc. You can also give them to individuals such as hotel concierges or tour guides who are in a position to promote you. Many psychics who work for or out of metaphysical bookstores or centers are required to supply a flyer, which is placed in a book or on a bulletin board for potential customers to view.

Your flyer is the quickest and easiest way for a potential client to assess you. It will help them determine whether they wish to receive a reading from you versus another reader. Therefore your flyer must stand out in some way to attract attention, to announce who you are, and to demonstrate what makes you special.

One of the most important items on a flyer is your picture. Potential clients want to know what you look like so they can determine whether you seem trustworthy or caring or fit into their stereotypes of an authentic psychic. From your picture, they will consider and evaluate your age, your gender, your attractiveness, your physical size, and your sexual appeal. Some people will be attracted to a reader with a young beautiful face while others will be intimated by a reader who is better looking or younger than they are. From my own observations, most heterosexual males will consider a reader's beauty and sexual appeal over other more practical qualifications. Attractive male readers with long hair and crystal necklaces, particularly men of Native American descent or appearance, tend to attract a lot more women than their older, more conservative or homely counterparts!

For those of you who don't look like Brad Pitt or Marilyn Monroe, I suggest that you choose a picture for your flyer that reflects your charisma and enthusiasm for life, since people are attracted to happy, enthusiastic people. This doesn't mean you need to have a toothy goofy grin on your face, but you certainly don't want to look overly serious or morose, even if that is your natural state of being. Color photos are more expensive, but are usually more noticeable and complimentary.

The content of your flyer is also important. You will want to include a description of the types of reading/healing you do and your methods employed. You will also want to include a personal biography that describes your experience and ability. People who have similar experiences or backgrounds will naturally be attracted to you, so I suggest being as honest as possible about yourself. People are looking for clues to assure them that you are honest and nonthreatening and that you are grounded in the real world. Any mainstream-world credentials, such as educational degrees or impressive professional experience, should therefore be included. Several of my own flyers mention that I was a former federal probation officer and have a Master's degree in social work. Numerous clients have told me it was one or both of these qualifications that convinced them to seek a reading from me rather than other readers. These clients usually held degrees and professional jobs themselves, and were excellent mirrors for me in terms of working through my own issues and MEI pictures.

Some psychics, such as myself, also include the prices for sessions on their flyers. Some people will immediately dismiss your flyer if it doesn't include a price because they will either think a reading costs more than it actually does or they will feel that you are not being honest by not including it. Other people will call you and ask you your price and then become belligerent when they hear it exceeds their budget or expectations. Personally, I feel it is important to be upfront about costs and that in the long run it saves both the reader and the potential client time and energy. I don't have the interest or the energy to seduce or manipulate people into getting readings. Either they want one or they don't. Other readers with a more sales-oriented approach to life may prefer to operate differently, and through their sales pitch and charm they could end up convincing potential clients to purchase a reading that ultimately will benefit these people despite their original misgivings.

A successful marketing campaign can help you bring in clients, but there are other forces at work that will ultimately determine your success. I know people who spend thousands of dollars on full-page newspaper ads, their business cards are works of art, and they are very good psychics. However, they are lucky if they attract even one client a month at the most. I know other psychics who do no advertising and they attract several clients a week. The ability to attract clients has more to do with your level of enthusiasm for reading, your karma, your Mental Emotional Image pictures surrounding readings and money issues, your present energy level, the appropriateness of your reading location, and your personal life circumstances than anything else.

If you are having difficulty over a period of time attracting clients, I suggest you obtain a reading from a competent clairvoyant who can look to see what is keeping you from doing readings or receiving compensation for them. It's possible that perhaps you don't really want to be reading professionally, or that you don't have enough of your own energy in your body to do readings on a full-time basis, or that you are not ready to look at or release the MEI pictures that would arise from doing so many readings. You may have also had a few unpleasant reading experiences (out of hundreds of positive ones) that you are weary of repeating.

Determining the Proper Situation/Location

Once you have decided to take the plunge, you will need to find an appropriate location in which to receive clients. Many psychics read out of their homes, others rent office space, and still others opt to read out of metaphysical centers or bookstores. Some psychics make house calls or, in heavy tourist areas, read visiting clients in their hotel rooms. Other options for reading are through psychic hotlines, at psychic fairs, or at parties.

If you desire to work independently, reading out of your home may be appropriate if you have a particular room or area that you can devote to your readings (an office with a separate entryway from the rest of the house is ideal) and if your home life is conducive to receiving strangers without attracting a lot of notice. The advantages of reading out of your home are that you have no commute and you hopefully are comfortable there. The disadvantages include safety concerns, the time it may take to clean your place prior to the client's arrival, the effect your work will have on family members and their level of interference with the reading, and the extra energy you will have to deal with following a reading.

During a reading, both you and your client release a lot of energy. No matter where you are, you will want to ground the room and do your best to clear out the energy, but you may not always be thorough. Long after the client has physically departed the location, their emotional energy and the energy of all their spirits guides and their family members will continue to return whenever they think about you or the reading. When this energy is deposited in your home, which is your personal sanctuary, it can create problems for you and your family that will range from increasing emotional tension, to disrupting relationships, to disturbing sleep and meditation patterns. Locations away from home may also become contaminated with foreign energies, but since you will not have to spend as much personal time there, you will not be as adversely affected.

Promoting Yourself Through Local Businesses

A great way to promote yourself is through the concierge desk at local hotels, resorts, health spas, and tourist information booths. Some of these establishments will keep your card, flyer, or brochure on file and refer clients to you who are seeking readings. The reader will then give the concierge a commission, which is usually about 10 percent of the cost of the reading. Sometimes the concierge will call and say, "I have a guest who would like a reading tomorrow morning. Are you available?" At other times, the guests themselves will call for a reading. If you are not available, the concierge will call someone else on their list or refer a client to a local center where psychics are available. As long as they have other options, they have little investment in whether or not you choose to do the reading.

Many psychics who don't have an adequate space to receive clients will go to the client's hotel room, a service that most clients appreciate. Others will give the guest the option of meeting them at their home or office. The more you can help the concierge understand your readings and what you have to offer, the greater the likelihood that they will recommend you. Offering a short, complimentary reading is usually the best way to accomplish this. Many of these people will be thrilled to experience your readings while others will politely decline, usually due to fear or resistance to the changes they might have to make if they receive your clairvoyant communication.

Safety Concerns

Your physical safety and well-being always need to be your top concerns, whether you are reading from your home, your office, your client's hotel room, etc. I recommend that you prearrange to have a friend or family member be close enough to hear you scream, but far enough away not to interfere with the reading. If this is not possible, or if you are visiting a client in their home or hotel room, leave the client's address and the time you plan to be finished with a friend or even the front desk of the hotel. Make arrangements to call them once you are finished, or have them call you if they don't hear from you within thirty minutes of the scheduled time. If at any moment, whether before you begin the reading or during the reading, you feel that your readee may become violent, then do whatever is necessary to extract yourself from the reading without inciting an emotional reaction from the readee. Of course, you may choose not to make house calls at all.

Working Through a Metaphysical Center

Many psychics choose to work out of a metaphysical bookstore or center that offers readings to the public. These places tend to operate in a few different ways.

Option 1—Renting or Leasing a Space

Some of the larger businesses rent or lease space to readers, healers, and massage therapists. These practitioners are employed as independent contractors. As long as they pay their rent, the owner gives only minimal input into how they conduct their readings or how often they show up to work.

When I first moved to Sedona, I worked out of the largest and most successful metaphysical center in the area. It consisted of a bookstore, a crystal and clothing shop, and approximately twenty rooms of varying sizes that were leased to readers. Upon my arrival, I signed a lease that required me to pay eight hundred eighty dollars every month for an eight-by-eight-foot room as well as a security deposit that would serve as my last month's rent providing I gave thirty days' notice prior to my departure. Downstairs by the front door was a bulletin board that displayed the flyer and business cards of all the practitioners renting rooms. Tourists would visit the center to explore the store or to seek out a reading and eventually choose a reader based on the flyers.

During the first six months, I earned just enough money to pay my rent at the center, my living expenses, and child care expenses (which averaged five hundred dollars per month). However, during the slow season of summer and early fall, fewer tourists came through the door and I was unable to pay these expenses, even though I was still doing several short readings a day (mostly fifteen-minute readings that brought in about twenty dollars each). When I realized I was so burnt-out that I was dreading even the thought of doing another reading, I gave notice and opted to find a regular nine-to-five job in the field of social work. Some readers who had been in the business longer had more repeat customers or referrals from former clients and were more financially successful; however, in general there was a constant turnover because there were always too many readers for the amount of clients that came in. The owner did her best to advertise the center, but she was never willing to lower the rent, or the number of readers, because there was always a new reader to replace any of those who left due to lack of business.

I value my time there because it made it possible for me to do a lot of readings on a lot of different kinds of people without having to do my own advertising or marketing except for creating a flyer. At times I had a lot of fun meeting and working in close proximity to other psychics and healers with similar interests. However, there was a lot of competition to deal with. I choose to believe that the clients who are meant to work with me will find me, so I don't have to worry about other readers "stealing" my business. However, this seems to be a rare perspective among readers and healers who, despite their claims of being enlightened and well versed in the laws of creativity, are some of the most competitive and envious people I have ever encountered. There would be days when I was very busy and no less than five or six readers would make a snide remark about my success. When I was not doing so well, they were as compassionate as anyone could be! Many of the readers seemed particularly curious and intimidated by my strong clairvoyant abilities, since none of them had any formal training in this area and most did not know how to call forth their own clairvoyance at will. Most of the readers in Sedona use spirit guides and their abilities of clairaudience or clairsentience (knowingness) to conduct readings.

Despite these pitfalls, my time at this center helped me make the transition from being a sheltered student at a clairvoyant school (where I read under supervision in a completely protected environment) to becoming a self-reliant professional. Many students never go on to make this transition due to their own fears and lack of encouragement from their clairvoyant training schools whose staff encourages students to enroll in their advanced programs or remain involved in the school as graduate readers or teachers.

Option 2—Giving a Split of Your Earnings to the Store Owner

Another common option for psychic readers is to work for a metaphysical shop or bookstore where, rather than paying rent, you split a percentage of your earnings with the owners of the store. The advantage to this arrangement is that during slow times you don't have to worry about making your rent, and the owner is more likely to be motivated to advertise or solicit business for you so you will both make money. The downside is that you make less money per reading, since the owner is likely to price the reading competitively and then take a commission (which could be anywhere from 20 to 60 percent). Even if the overall monthly amount you earn is equal to what you would earn at a business where you pay rent but make more money per reading, when you receive less per reading you may feel that you are putting out more energy than you are getting back. This may lower your enthusiasm for reading out of that establishment and decrease your motivation for showing up to work.

Psychic readers and store owners often run into conflicts with one another. Psychics tend to let their intuition and feelings direct their actions. When a reader doesn't show up for work, perhaps because her intuition told her that she needed some time to reconnect with herself, the store owner earns nothing and understandably becomes very upset. Most owners of stores that employ psychics are more concerned with the success of the business than with a reader's energetic well-being. They don't understand if you turn down a reading because you are feeling too "low on energy" or because you have a "bad feeling" about the readee. They don't understand why you may feel the need to take a half-hour to meditate after a particularly challenging reading before you are ready for your next reading. Most shop owners will also not appreciate it if you complete a reading in a half-hour because you feel your client got all the communication they needed or could handle, when the client originally told the owner that they were interested in an hour reading, which would yield more money.

Another issue that frequently arises between business owners and readers is that of who has the right to repeat business or referrals. I have encountered owners who forbade me and other readers to pass out business cards even when the client requested them, because they were afraid the client or someone referred by the client would contact me directly and the owner would miss out on a potential commission on that future reading. It seemed to me that the store owners were already getting a large percentage of the profits from my reading. So for them to expect to get a cut of any future readings I did for that person or their friends outside of the store was not only unreasonable, but impractical and invasive of the reader/readee relationship, especially because these same business owners usually refuse to provide a reader's forwarding address once they have left the business. If a reader and client are forbidden to exchange information, they could easily lose track of one another. This is an issue that many readers and business owners grapple with and should reconcile prior to acceptance of employment by either party.

Option 3—Reading at Local Businesses

Some local businesses, such as coffee shops, restaurants, or night clubs, may welcome your presence in their establishment and will ask nothing from you in return other than that you show up at a regularly scheduled time each week. Owners of these businesses feel that the presence of the reader and the opportunity to receive a reading will attract customers. The owners will not make any money directly from the readings or the reader, but rather will make money from the food or drinks that are purchased by these customers. Some of these businesses (most of which are located in areas where psychics are not as numerous or common as in Sedona) are incredibly successful, largely because they offer readings from talented and charismatic readers.

This situation is therefore financially ideal for readers, since they can earn more money per reading and have minimal expenses. The downside is that they may be placed at a booth or table in the corner of the establishment where they have no privacy or control over the noise level. Some psychics thrive under these conditions. They learn how to use the outside noises and distractions as a tool to bring them into a more focused inner state. Others soon crumble under the distractions and attention from curious onlookers.

Option 4—Reading at Parties

A fun and educational way to earn money as a psychic is to perform readings at parties, either by getting your own gigs or by working for an agency that contracts readers for parties. As the former owner of one of these agencies, Sedona Psychic Entertainment Services, and a former employee of two others, I have read at every type of party imaginable, from small intimate cocktail parties to corporate functions with over a thousand attendees.

At the majority of parties, the psychic will sit at a table and guests will line up to receive a five- to ten-minute reading, depending on the number of guests versus the number of readers and the number of hours the readers have been contracted for. At very large gatherings, psychics may be instructed to roam through the crowd, offering one- to two-minute readings. Most agencies request their readers to dress up in a gypsy-style costume for entertainment value, which usually goes over extremely well with the guests at parties and is usually fun for the readers as well.

Professional psychics can expect to make anywhere from seventy to two hundred dollars an hour for reading at parties, depending on whether they are working through an agency or are self-employed. Expectations should be discussed between the reader and the host or co-ordinator of the party or event prior to the event. When a psychic is working through an agency, that agency will be the one to pay the psychic and will often provide a representative of the agency to be present at the event to supervise the psychic and oversee the readings. In this case, the reader and the agency should discuss expectations prior to the event. These expectations include the amount of money the reader will receive per hour; how many hours they will be expected to read; how overtime work will be handled (will they have the option to refuse working overtime; will they be paid extra); whether the psychic will be permitted to accept tips or should do anything to encourage tips; whether they will be seated or expected to stroll among the guests; whether they will be served food and beverages or need to bring their own snacks; whether they are expected to wear a costume; whether they are permitted to hand out their own business cards or must give out the business cards of the agency; whether they are encouraged or forbidden to socialize with guests following the readings, etc.

Reading at parties can be challenging and rewarding at the same time. It's imperative that readers stick to their time limit to ensure that all the guests receive a reading (something I still find to be extremely difficult!). The readers usually are placed in an environment that is not particularly conducive to reading in terms of noise, activity level, and amount of privacy. They must read numerous people back to back, with little time for cleaning out or meditation. The psychic must therefore exert extra energy to remain focused, grounded, and neutral, and to continue on with the readings no matter what occurs. Reading numerous people over the course of several hours can be exhausting, and it is important to continue to call back your own energy as frequently as possible (see chapter 8). This is actually an incredible opportunity for psychics to challenge themselves and to realize that they can really read under any circumstances, provided they continue to use their tools and practice the techniques taught in this book.

Most of the time, guests at parties are very excited to receive a reading. This is a great opportunity to expose people to clairvoyant readings and help them examine their stereotypes and misconceptions of what a psychic reading is all about. However, many of the guests will be quite skeptical, which always makes a reading more challenging.

Another challenge that psychics must grapple with when reading at parties is the question of how to deal with serious or difficult issues that arise during a reading that could put a damper on the guest's experience at the party. I encourage my employees to read from a space of validation (see chapters 14 and 19) so that they will look to see what is working for the person in their life and remain as positive as possible. However, there will always be instances in which a guest has been grappling with a certain issue, and during the reading they receive information that not only gives them insight into this issue, but that could potentially transform or determine the course of events of their entire life. This is information they need to receive, even though it may result in tears or even cause a premature departure from the party.

One of the most difficult things about reading at parties is the alcohol factor. As the party progresses, so do the effects of alcohol on guests and on the readers. Many readers are so clairsentient that they will actually absorb the effects of the alcohol into their aura and experience feelings of drunkenness, which could include feeling dizzy, tired, nauseous, giddy, and confused. When a person is intoxicated, they are flying somewhere outside of their body and this makes it very difficult to read them. Since there is no way to limit the guests' use of alcohol at parties, preparation can be made prior to the event to minimize alcohol-related problems by scheduling the readings during the early hours of the party.

If a reader is approached by a guest who seems to have been drinking alcohol, I suggest that the reader clairvoyantly look at the outer layer of the guest's aura, which contains some very basic information about the guest's personality or how others see this person's personality. The reader should tell the guest about these personality traits and then conclude the reading as quickly as possible. This will satisfy the guest's desire to receive a reading while preventing the reader from having to delve into deeper issues that would require more energy and time. Of course, if a guest is belligerent or so intoxicated that they are unaware of their environment, the reader has the right to refuse the guest a reading or to immediately terminate the reading at the point the reader begins to feel uncomfortable.

Reading at Psychic Fairs

Many readers earn money and gain experience by performing short readings at psychic fairs. These fairs are usually organized by someone else or a group of people. The fair may be a very large one, located at a convention center, with thousands of attendees and hundreds of attractions besides the psychic readers (such as the popular Whole Life Expo, which travels around the United States), or the fair may be a small one, held in a conference room of a hotel, where the main attraction is the psychic readers.

Most clairvoyant training schools hold their own fairs, in which students, graduates, and staff perform readings and offer workshops for minimal prices. Readings can be as low as five dollars, and aura healings may be offered at no cost. The school keeps the profits while the students gain experience under the supervision and protection of their teachers. Attendees of the fair may or may not pay a small entry fee for workshops.

At most other fairs, psychics from diverse backgrounds are available to perform readings of varying lengths and at higher rates. Psychics will rent a booth for either one day or for the course of the fair. The rent will reflect the value of the booth in terms of the booth's size, its proximity to the flow of foot traffic, and whether the psychic is selling products in addition to performing readings. In rare cases, the psychic will not pay a fee for a booth upfront, but rather will share or split their earnings with the fair's organizers. Booth rates could range from twenty-five to hundreds of dollars a day, depending on the anticipated attendance of fairgoers.

Since there are only so many readings that one psychic can perform in a day, if the expense of the booth is very high, the reader will need to charge higher prices for shorter readings, or may choose to bring other readers into their booth, which may or may not be permitted by the fair's organizers. Another option is to sell related products, such as books, audio or video tapes, etc., which may increase the cost of the booth. Many psychics tend to just break even at psychic fairs, but find that it is an excellent marketing venue to network and meet clients who will come to them at a later date for longer, more lucrative readings.

Many readers have found financial success and have a wonderful time reading at medieval or Renaissance fairs, which are becoming more and more popular every year. These fairs often make a circuit around the United States and come to a rural area once a year, for a period of time that could range from a single weekend to a few months. Besides psychic readers, these fairs also employ actors, musicians, singers, dancers, artists, etc., all of whom are required to dress up in period costumes and pretend that they are living in the Middle Ages. Psychic readers usually rent a booth and in exchange are able to keep their earnings. They are required to decorate their booths, and the more elaborate, attractive, or authentic their booth and wardrobe are, the more clients they will attract. Because there are so many attendees roaming around, psychics who read at Renaissance fairs often do very well financially, even if the initial rent of the booth is fairly high. The downside is that they are required to man their booths for long hours. Reading continuously every day for weeks or even months can be extremely exhausting, if not downright impossible. Many readers solve this dilemma by subleasing their booths for a day or week to other psychics.

Working for a Psychic Hotline

Obviously, from the many television ads and infomercials you have seen, there are quite a number of telephone psychic hotlines out there. Readings can be performed as effectively over the telephone as in person; however, from my own experiences and discussions with numerous psychics who have worked for or investigated these hotlines, it appears that most of the larger ones that can afford to advertise on television employ people who have little understanding of their own abilities and are more versed in how to keep callers on the line than in psychic reading.

When a person is initially employed as a reader with one of these hotlines, they are specifically told that their mission is to keep the caller on the line as long as possible. Many of these hotlines charge anywhere from three to five dollars a minute (which totals anywhere from one hundred eighty to three hundred dollars an hour). Callers often tell themselves that they will only stay on the line for a few minutes, but lose track of time because of the sales tactics employed by the "psychic readers" and because of their own desperation. Many of these callers are already facing serious difficulties in their lives, which prompted them to call the hotline in the first place, and the last thing any of these people need is to discover a three-hundred-dollar charge on their phone bill that they will either have to pay or will have to fight with their phone company to dismiss.

Occasionally a "real" psychic and/or caring person will go to work for one of these hotlines, but they usually last only for a short period of time because they realize that there is no way to maintain their integrity when working for a person or company that is cheating and deceiving its clients.

I was once invited to audition for the same company that produces the omnipresent "Miss Cleo" infomercials. In these commercials, Miss Cleo conducts several readings for callers who are delighted and amazed at her psychic abilities. She encourages people to call her on the hotline and gives the distinct impression that she is the person who will answer the phone, even though in reality she does not work the hotline. There are currently legal actions being taken against this company and Miss Cleo due to this misrepresentation. During the initial audition I attended, I was informed that this company was searching for authentic readers to perform readings in similar infomercials in which they encourage viewers to call them directly on the hotline. However, we were told that we would not actually be required to work on the hotline once we were chosen for the commercials.

Although there was the potential to earn a lot of money, I realized that it would be a huge personal mistake for me to represent a company whose practices I find to be not only unethical but downright criminal, and I happily dropped out of the audition process soon after it began. However, there were a lot of authentic psychics in Sedona who did pursue this "opportunity." A few of them justified their participation by explaining that their presence on the infomercial would spread "light" and positive energy to the millions of viewers who watched these commercials, and therefore they would be serving humanity by counterbalancing the darkness of the greed of the company that hired them. It continues to amaze me how so many self-proclaimed "light workers" can so easily delude themselves about their own motivations when it comes to the promise of money and fame!

Telephone hotlines do exist that are run by people who practice the utmost integrity. Most of these are privately owned by individuals who are in touch with their own spiritual abilities. The Berkeley Psychic Institute runs its own hotline in which student readers and graduates hone their long-distance reading skills by volunteering or earning a small hourly wage for reading over the hotline. Callers receive authentic and reasonably priced readings in which the readers do not benefit any more from a one-minute reading than a two-hour reading. For some psychics, working over a hotline offers them an ideal work situation, because often they can work independently from the safety and privacy of their own home, and they can avoid the costs of commuting and enjoy a flexible working schedule.

Many psychics who would never work for a psychic telephone hotline do offer readings over the phone in addition to reading clients face to face, and are able to reap the same benefits. They charge the same predetermined fee for reading over the phone that they would in person. Some of these readers have their own credit card processing machines so they can accept payment by credit card over the phone at the time of the reading. Obtaining the capacity to process credit card payments can initially be quite expensive and requires good credit. Many psychic readers opt for payment by personal check or money order. They usually request that first-time clients send them a check or money order prior to the reading, while occasionally permitting repeat clients to send their payment following the reading.

Reading over the Internet

More and more psychics are advertising their services on personal websites and even do readings through e-mails. A website offers an ideal format in which you can creatively market yourself through text, pictures, images, color, and even sound. In order for a potential client to see your website, they need to know that it exists. Accessibility and awareness of your website will depend primarily on its placement on search engines and through other types of advertising that expose people to your website address. This advertising can be done through other websites and through your own written materials, such as flyers, posters, business cards, radio or local television ads, etc. I recommend searching the websites of other psychics to see how they are using the Internet to promote their businesses.

CHAPTER 24

Finding and Choosing a Psychic Reader

How to Find a Psychic Reader

There are many ways to find a psychic reader. If you are looking for one in your area, I suggest going to a metaphysical bookstore, which will usually have a bulletin board advertising local psychic readers and healers, or will offer free local magazines and newspapers that have many advertisements for readers. In most areas other than the San Francisco Bay area, the majority of psychic readers use their abilities of clairaudience or transmediumship rather than clairvoyance. This is not a problem, since many of them will be able to give you excellent readings; however, if you are interested in experiencing a clairvoyant reading, then you will need to find someone who specifically states that they receive information in the form of images or pictures. Some people erroneously use the term clairvoyance to cover any psychic ability, so even if someone says they are clairvoyant, you should inquire further and ask them whether they see information, hear it, or feel it.

Finding a Clairvoyant Reader
Through a Clairvoyant Training School

Due to the number of clairvoyant training schools in the San Francisco Bay area, there are hundreds, if not thousands, of pure clairvoyant readers there. You can locate many of these schools through the Internet. The curriculum of all these schools is based on the original teachings of Lewis Bostwick, the founder of the Berkeley Psychic Institute, and are run by either his former students or their students. However, they are not affiliated with one another, and there is quite a bit of competition between particular schools. All schools offer the option of receiving a reading from students, graduates, or staff.

Student readings tend to be very inexpensive and quite in-depth. Students obviously read a little more slowly due to lack of experience and confidence, but oftentimes they can offer information that is just as helpful as that of professional readers. The downside to receiving a student reading is that sometimes the readers are overly vigilant about protecting themselves and maintaining their boundaries to the point that they become paranoid and make the mistake of blaming the readee for "getting in their space." They try so hard to read from a neutral place in their sixth chakra that they close their heart chakras down too far. While I have always had very positive experiences receiving readings from students, I know some people who have left a reading feeling insulted or alienated.

Graduate readings at these schools cost about twice as much as student readings but are still remarkably cheap, while professional-level readings from experienced graduates or staff are on par with the fees of most practicing professional psychics within the United States. Some of the directors and staff of these schools are some of the most talented clairvoyants in the world, even though they have their own neuroses, personality quirks, etc., that may or may not complement or clash with your own! All of these readers offer readings in person or over the telephone.

Take a Proactive Approach

Whether you receive a reading from your local neighborhood psychic or from a clairvoyant reader associated with a clairvoyant training school, I very much encourage you to take a proactive approach when choosing a psychic reader. Find out how much they charge prior to the commencement of your reading, what methods they use, where they received their training, how experienced they are, and whether they will address the issues you are concerned with. Every reader has their own particular talents and weaknesses and it's perfectly fine to ask questions about their competence in particular areas.

It is not appropriate to ask them to prove to you prior to the reading that they are really psychic, or to expect them to spend more than five to ten minutes at the most discussing their reading approach. It's also not appropriate to ask them a question that you want addressed in the reading, prior to the reading, such as, "I know my reading isn't until tomorrow, but could you just tell me really quickly whether my boyfriend is going to leave me? It will just take a minute." Know that it never just takes a minute!

Discuss Expectations Prior to the Reading

Prior to a reading, you should make sure that the reader knows the length of the reading you desire. Also, find out how both of you will know when the time has expired. I know some psychics who will tell a readee that they charge one hundred dollars per hour. The readee will assume that they are getting an hour-long reading, and then two-and-a-half hours later they are told they owe two hundred fifty dollars. During a reading, time goes by very quickly, and both the reader and the readee can easily lose track of it. If a reader goes over the predetermined length of time and doesn't ask you if you would like to extend the reading, then you as a client should not be expected to pay extra.

Look Out for Psychic Scammers!

Beware of anyone who tells you that they can only help you if you give them more money than the price of the reading session. There are plenty of psychic scams out there where a psychic will tell you that there is a curse on you, or you are in need of some kind of healing, and that the only way you will recover is if you pay them a large amount of money that they will supposedly use to purchase materials that will break the curse or reverse your ailments.

Occasionally, a reader may see that you are dealing with a lot of issues or health problems and will recommend additional sessions for healing, either from themselves or someone else. Some serious health problems do take more then one healing session to sort out. Some healing schools, such as the Aesclepion Healing Center in Marin County, California (which I am not currently affiliated with, but have immense respect for), offer healing packages in which you can purchase a combination of healing sessions in advance for a discounted rate. The advantage to receiving a healing package is that not only are you being healed during each session, but a lot of the healing also occurs between sessions due to the strength of your intention and level of commitment invested in your healing process. If a psychic/healer suggests that you return for additional healing, the cost of these sessions should be approximately the same price as your original reading or healing.

Buyer Beware . . .

Beware of anyone who tells you that only *they* can help or save you. No matter what your situation is, this is just not true. Also beware of any reader that encourages you to get readings from them on a frequent basis (I feel that more than twice a month is too frequent and encourages dependency—I tell my clients to wait anywhere from two to six months before returning to me), or who befriends you, offers to do things for you, and then later hands you a bill.

Do Not Idolize a Psychic Reader or Healer, No Matter How Talented They Are

A particular talent or ability is nothing more than that; it doesn't say anything about the individual as a whole who possesses that talent. Psychics are often just as messed up and self-obsessed as anyone else, and if you place them on a pedestal above yourself, at some point they will fall, taking you with them. The expression "The bigger they are, the harder they fall" comes to mind.

There are some people out there who can do miraculous things. They can levitate, manifest objects out of thin air, or read every single thought in your mind. Some of these people are enlightened yogis, while others are thieves, con artists, or rapists. It's a lie that God only bestows special gifts and talents on those who deserve them or will use them in responsible ways. If a psychic ever treats you in a manner that feels disrespectful, condescending, hurtful, or abusive, by all means communicate your feelings to them and, if necessary, terminate communication with that person immediately. When you idolize someone, you give them your power. Whatever qualities you are able to admire in someone else are qualities that you possess within yourself. You— your birth, your life, your existence, your love—are miraculous.

Finding a Clairvoyant Healer

When considering a healer, find out what methods the healer will employ. Does the healer channel energy through you, put energy into you, take energy out of you, or use your own energy? I would be cautious of methods that involve putting energy into you, or of healers who aren't aware of the energies they are using. Find out if the healer is working with healing guides and whether these guides have been taught to respect boundaries or if they may be trying to recruit you into a particular discipline. Through questioning and observation, find out if the healer seems concerned with maintaining and respecting energetic boundaries. Determine the healer's intentions for desiring to give you a healing. Find out if sexual desire or the intention of recruiting you into a particular group or as a future paying client has anything to do with the healer's motivation to interact with you. Former clients of the healer/reader can offer insight into that healer's integrity and methodology; however, it's important to understand that their experience could be very different from your own, particularly if their level of self-esteem, their age, or their level of physical attractiveness varies from your own.

Beware of Sexual Predators

Women need to look out for male psychics and particularly healers who are sexual predators. Unfortunately, there are quite a few of these men in Sedona, Arizona, as well as in Santa Cruz, California, and every other area that attracts healers. These men tend to attract more vulnerable women who are in need of a male's attention and validation.

Most of the sexual metaphysical predators I've known actually do have healing abilities and knowledge in the healing arts, yet are as motivated by their addiction to sexual pleasure and money as by their desire to heal. Many of these men are not conscious of their motivations and how they are adversely affecting their clients. These men are dangerous energetically because they put all kinds of cords into the woman's second chakra, which will cause her to be attracted to him or even to feel as if she is in love with him.

These men are destructive on an emotional level because they intuitively know what a women is needing and desiring most and then they give this to her during her healing session, so by the end of it she feels as if this person has the power to make her feel like no one else has in a long time and she becomes desperate to see him again. This feeling, accompanied by the second-chakra cords and his sexual energy pulsating through her body, are a dangerous combination that lead many women to give the male healer exactly what he wants in terms of sex and money. Many of these men's clients actually delude themselves into believing that this man is their soul mate because they feel both a spiritual and sexual connection with him. The sexual connection comes from his sexual energy that is circulating through her body, which she misinterprets as her own. The spiritual connection may be coming more from the energy that he is channeling during a healing than from himself, and from her perceptions of him as a spiritually aware human being. She projects God-like attributes to this healer because she experiences God through him, even though his mind is filled with thoughts of how to get into her bed or her wallet.

Some of these men actually come highly recommended by their female clients because many of these clients are unaware of the way these men are manipulating them until months or years later. I have seen the emotional and psychological devastation that these psychics, healers, and spiritual teachers can wreak, and feel that there needs to be greater awareness, discussion, and intervention at least in the metaphysical communities where these people operate.

Gender Issues

You may want to consider the gender of a potential reader and/or healer. I know some male readers that won't like to hear this, but there are many issues that come up for women during a reading that they may not feel comfortable discussing with a man. These could have to do with sexual abuse, reproductive issues, relationship concerns, etc. More significant is the fact that female bodies are extremely receptive to male energies; their ovaries are like sponges, ready to soak up any male attention that is directed their way. When even the most caring, considerate male healer works on a female, particularly on her female or reproductive organs, he often cannot help but leave behind some of his male energy in her body or energetic field, particularly if he becomes aroused or is not conscious of maintaining energetic boundaries. This is very similar to what happens during intercourse between a man and a woman, and helps explain why a woman can get so "attached" or become dependent on a man with whom she has been intimate.

CHAPTER 25

Clairvoyant Training Schools

This book will teach you everything you need to know to perform a clairvoyant reading and healing on yourself or anyone else. However, there is one thing this book cannot do and that is create opportunities and experiences for you to practice your skills; you will have to create these for yourself. For some people this will be easy; others will find it more challenging.

While this book offers plenty of suggestions for overcoming many obstacles, challenges, and dilemmas that you may encounter in your readings both as a clairvoyant student and as a professional reader, it obviously cannot provide personalized emotional support to help you through your "growth periods" that will arise as a result of all the energy you are releasing and all the changes that may occur in your life as you practice these techniques. For those of you who learn better and feel more secure in a structured setting where you have direct access to teachers and to experiential opportunities that are already established for you, enrolling in a clairvoyant training program may be the greatest gift you can give yourself.

In this final chapter, I will provide some overall information about clairvoyant training schools and programs, and discuss the pros and cons of participating in these programs. I will not discuss the merits of any particular school, but instead will provide an overview so you will know what kinds of questions to ask when researching the schools, and what to expect from participation in one of their programs.

General Information

There are several clairvoyant training schools in the United States and a few in Canada that offer year-long training programs. Then there are many other schools that offer short-term workshops and classes, ranging in length from a few hours to several weeks of intensive training. The following discussion focuses on those schools that offer long-term programs. Most of these clairvoyant training programs are reasonably priced. They usually require a deposit and then allow you to make monthly installment payments. Some schools require people over a certain age (i.e., forty years old) to spend a longer period of time at the school than younger students due to the belief that older students often have more MEI pictures, programming, and resistances to work through.

Some clairvoyant training programs have prerequisites. Students are required to take and pay for a certain number of short-term classes at the school before they are permitted to join the program. Some programs allow students to take their prerequisites while going through the actual clairvoyant training program. I encourage students to take a few classes before committing themselves to any program so they can get to know the staff and form an idea of how well they will fit into the structure and personality of the school. Since several schools are located within close proximity of each other in northern California, it is feasible to try out a few different programs before settling on one.

Some programs have a tithing requirement in which students are required to tithe or volunteer a certain number of hours of their time to the school in addition to monetary fees. Staff members try to work with the student to assign them tasks that fit with their goals and interests. Schools also have requirements in terms of how many readings a week a student must participate in or how many fairs and outside events a student must attend.

Some schools have a program that is tailored to women and their specific issues. Others are not gender-specific, but do offer additional gender-related classes that are separate from the clairvoyant program.

Some schools have certain entry dates when students can begin a program, while others allow students to begin whenever they desire. Classes may be divided into two categories: students who have been in the program for six months or less, and advanced students. New students learn from the more seasoned students as well as from teachers and staff members who oversee the readings. Some schools only teach weekend or week-long workshops.

Some clairvoyant schools have their own church in order to receive nonprofit status and to ordain students as ministers so that they can be free to practice their readings and engage in spiritual counseling without violating any laws. Some of these churches are wonderful places in which to worship, receive healings and inspiration, and to heal oneself from religious programming.

Pros

Due to the intensity of these clairvoyant training programs, you are likely to make more positive changes during your training than you have ever made in your entire life. You will very quickly access your clairvoyance and become adept at reading. You will have plenty of other students with whom to read, which will help increase your certainty with reading. You will be able to observe and learn from these students. You will have a safe physical environment in which to read. Your clients will be provided for you; you will never have to find them. You will not have to deal with money issues related to reading. You will have staff at your disposal to monitor your progress, answer questions immediately, teach you additional techniques, remind you to use your tools, give you readings and healings, etc.

Cons

Some students who have issues around authority find these schools to be overly oppressive. Some schools have strict policies about engaging in any other spiritual discipline or attending classes outside the school during the duration of the program. These policies were originally established to protect clairvoyant students who are vulnerable to outside influences that might want to interfere with their clairvoyance. However, some of the staff at these schools are competitive with the staff of another school. They fear that you might be recruited by an outside school or teacher. Some schools have rigorous yet reasonable requirements that must be followed in terms of class attendance, punctuality, preparing yourself adequately before a reading, etc. In some schools, staff may have free rein to read you at all times and give you uninvited suggestions for self-improvement. This can lead to personal growth, but can also be annoying, especially if it comes from a staff member who is motivated by their own agenda or MEI pictures.

In some ways, these schools appear to take on cultlike features, although they are certainly not cults. Students learn a certain vocabulary that most of the general public is unfamiliar with, so sometimes "outsiders" have difficulty understanding or relating to the students. Because students are reading so frequently, they are rapidly deprogramming their MEI pictures, releasing foreign energies, and breaking a lot of energetic agreements with family members who often don't understand what clairvoyance is or why anyone would invest time and money learning about it.

Many students who study clairvoyance undergo changes in terms of becoming more self-empowered, more self-sufficient, and more communicative with the inner voice of their heart and with the spirit world or with God. These changes are miracles to the students, but are disturbing to those suspicious family members who don't understand the drastic changes the student is undergoing. As a result, many students tend to minimize contact with their birth families, or in some rare cases cease contact altogether, during the duration of their training program. This is a personal choice that students seem to naturally make and has nothing to do with any mandates by the schools or staff.

Some students of these schools struggle with the fact that they often do not have a choice as to who they will read, or what role they will play in the reading (i.e., center-chair position versus monitoring a reading). The schools have the philosophy that wherever you end up is where you are ultimately meant to be. This may be true, but it can be frustrating if there is a certain position or person you want to read—or avoid!

One of my biggest complaints with many clairvoyant training schools is that they fail to encourage students to read outside the school. I learned nothing in my own clairvoyant program about reading professionally or how to handle reading on my own, except that it was supposed to be a scary and lonely thing to do. I believe the number-one reason for this is that most of the staff members at these schools do not have much experience reading independently. Those who finally venture out of the school to read usually do not return because they get used to making a certain amount of money that far surpasses what they are paid at the school (which is usually very little, if anything), and because their ideology changes to the point where they can no longer fit into the school's philosophy about how classes should be taught. Students and staff who eventually learn how to read on their own gain a substantial level of empowerment that seems to surpass that of staff members who never venture away from the security blanket of the school. These independent readers have a more balanced viewpoint of the world and gain skills and knowledge from the various readers they meet and from their own experiences that they could not have if they had remained forever at the school. In this book I have included information about reading professionally that I would have loved to have learned when I was just a student; information that would have given me far more confidence and peace of mind a lot sooner in my life.

I feel strongly that my own clairvoyant training was worth more than any amount of money. For me, the pitfalls and challenges discussed here are nothing more than a drop in a bucket filled with miracles, fun, excitement, and growth. For other people, their lifestyles, schedules, personalities, or level of personal, psychic, and spiritual development make them incompatible with these schools.

The best way to learn more about clairvoyant training schools in a particular area is to search the Internet by inputting the words "clairvoyant training" or "psychic training institutes" and including a specific state.

Summary

I couldn't sleep. I was obsessing about a relationship turned sour and wondering, as I lay still beside my four-year-old son, Manny, who had already been asleep for several hours, "Was it my fault? Am I to blame?" Suddenly Manny bolted upright in bed. With closed eyes he shouted, "Mommy, stop it! You are thinking too loud! It wasn't your fault!" He then fell backwards onto his pillow and let out an indignant snore.

Despite my years of experience as a psychic reader and teacher, after having written an entire book illustrating how clairvoyance and our other psychic abilities are as natural as our ability to breathe, hear, and speak, an incident such as this one still does not fail to startle and amaze me. While it is my hope that this book will help you recognize, nourish, develop, and really enjoy your own natural psychic abilities, I hope that you never lose your sense of awe over all the gifts that your Creator has built into your being, whether that Creator is God or your own creative soul intent on experiencing the wonders of living here on this glorious planet in the wondrous vessel known as your body. I won't even try to guess how the miracle of our beings, of our bodies, of our everyday struggles and joys, came into being. But as Descartes said, "I think, therefore I am" and if there is one thing the faithful, the faithless, the psychics, the skeptics, the conservatives, the liberals, and everyone in between can agree on, it is that we do exist. There really is nothing more remarkable and nothing more scientifically impossible to explain than this fact.

"Lakshmee!" This word exploded into my head one recent morning before I was quite awake, causing me, this time, to bolt upright.

"Lakshmee? What the heck is a Lakshmee?" I pondered this strange word for a few moments and forgot it by the time breakfast was served. The next day I was painfully combing the tangles from my hair in the shower, when again the word bombarded into my consciousness.

"Lakshmee!" I cleared my mind and again asked what Lakshmee meant. I had the thought, "It is a name." But what kind of name, and what did it have to do with me? When I finished my shower, I wrote the name on my hand with a pen so I would not forget it this time.

My friend Tony Carito from Sedona arrived for a visit that day. (I had recently moved to Los Angeles to begin my career as a screenwriter/filmmaker.) I told him about this strange word that would not leave me alone. His response surprised and intrigued me.

"Oh, Lakshmee. Sure, that's the Hindu goddess of prosperity and abundance. . . Why don't we go to the bookstore and look her up." Tony and I took a drive to the nearby town of Ojai, and stopped at the first bookstore we saw.

"We don't carry metaphysical books. Why don't you try the library down the street?" The friendly salesgirl gave us directions. We arrived at the library and I was excited to see that I was standing at the door of the Theosophical Society. This is a worldwide organization dedicated to the study of spirituality. The first books I ever read on psychic development and on psychic self-defense came from the Theosophical Society Library in Illinois, where I grew up as a child. I had always wanted to visit one of their centers, but this was my first opportunity. We strolled into the cozy dark-paneled building and approached a petite Indian woman at the reception desk. Tony spoke for us.

"We'd like to learn more about the Hindu goddess Lakshmee. Do you have any books on the subject?" With a darling accent, the woman held out her hand graciously.

"Oh yes, yes. So nice to meet you! I am her." Confused, Tony and I looked at each other. He laughed.

"Yeah, I guess we'd all like to be the goddess of prosperity!"

"No, you don't understand," she said in broken English. "I am Lakshmee. My name is Lakshmee." That's when one of the other librarians walked up to her and said, "Lakshmee, you have a call on line one."

Later, as Lakshmee pulled books for us, she confirmed, "Lakshmee is the goddess of prosperity, and of fertility."

Only half-joking, I mumbled something to the effect of, "I don't know about the fertile part, but I could sure use some prosperity right now."

She turned and looked me in the eyes. "Oh, the Indian people know that prosperity does not have anything to do with money. It's what is in here," touching her heart, "and here," touching her forehead.

After reading further about Lakshmee, I wandered into the bookstore attached to the library and walked up to the "Extrasensory Perception" section. Next to one of the very books that I had read as a young teen, *The Power of the Subconscious Mind*, by Joseph Murphy, there was an empty space. As I had done many times at many bookstores, I visualized my own book, this book that you're reading now, filling the empty space. I allowed myself to feel happy about how many lives it would touch and, yes, how much money it would bring in so I would be free to work on my other creative projects. And at that moment, I had no doubt that this book would someday be available in this store, if not stores like this, and I understood completely what Lakshmee had been trying to tell me: It didn't matter whether I had a million dollars or just one dollar in my pocket. What mattered was that I had the certainty, the knowingness, and the faith within me to create the life I desired.

Despite my clairvoyant ability, I did not ultimately know at that moment what the future would hold, but I did know that if all the world crumbled beneath my feet tomorrow, if I suddenly lost everything and everyone dear to me in this physical world, that I would be okay. Even though I would surely have bad days where life really sucked, I would have the tools, the groundedness, the neutrality, the energy, and the ability to see, hear, and feel the boundless guidance within and around me, allowing me not merely to survive, but to prosper.

This faith comes with the practice of the techniques and principles within this book. It is the true gift. It is your gift. Behold.

Glossary

ASTRAL PROJECTION OR TRAVEL: The ability for one's spirit to leave one's body and travel on the astral plane or in other dimensions.

ASTRAL RAPE: A sexual crime committed by force or against another's will that occurs on an energetic or spiritual level.

ATHEISM: A disbelief in the spiritual, including God, psychic phenomena, or the human soul.

AURA: The energetic field surrounding every living organism that contains information about the organism and energies affecting it. The aura can be thought of as the organism's spirit that extends outward from the body.

BOSTWICK, LEWIS: Father of clairvoyant training in the United States and founder of the Berkeley Psychic Institute.

CHAKRAS: Sanskrit word for "spinning wheel," chakras are energy centers that correspond to certain parts of the human body and that regulate the body's overall functioning.

CHANNELING: A psychic ability in which a person receives and communicates information coming directly from a source outside themselves.

CLAIRAUDIENCE: A specific psychic ability in which information inaudible to the human ears is heard inside one's mind.

CLAIRSENTIENCE: A specific psychic ability in which information is received through touch or on a physical body level.

CLAIRVOYANCE: A specific psychic ability located in one's sixth chakra, or third eye, that involves accessing information in the form of images, visions, and pictures.

CLAIRVOYANT HEALING: An act in which visualization is utilized to eliminate or transmute emotional or physical pain or negative energies and to restore one to a healthier state.

CLAIRVOYANT READING: An act in which information in the form of mental images, visions, and pictures is accessed.

CODEPENDENT RELATIONSHIP: An unbalanced relationship in which one person sacrifices their own ideals or ignores their inner voice in order to maintain the relationship or get other needs met within the relationship.

CONTROL FREAK: A person who needs to understand or determine every element in life and interferes with the natural course of things, or who expends energy trying to control that which is out of their control. One who attempts to circumvent God's will.

CORE MEI PICTURES: An MEI picture that is developed early in life and that over time attracts similar clusters of thoughts and emotions that influence our perceptions and behavior. Personal transformation occurs when these pictures are destroyed or deenergized.

COSMIC ENERGY: Energy that originates from the air, sun, atmosphere, the spiritual realm, or God.

COUPLE'S READING: A clairvoyant reading in which a psychic reads the relationship or joint goals between two or more readees who are physically present.

CREATING/CREATION: To bring into being.

CROP CIRCLES: A supernatural phenomenon in which geometric patterns suddenly appear in wheat fields. These patterns range in size from a few feet in diameter to miles long. Some of these patterns appear over the course of just a few minutes' time and register as having unusual electromagnetic qualities.

DESTROY: To eliminate or alter a creation.

DISEMBODIED SPIRIT: A spirit that no longer belongs to a physical body.

EARTH ENERGY: Energy that originates from within the earth.

ENERGY: Life force; the essence of all things physical and nonphysical. Matter, atoms, thoughts, emotions, and pain consist of energy.

ENLIGHTENMENT: A state in which a person has become actualized, has accumulated a certain level of wisdom; when a person's body, mind, and spirit are fully integrated and their being holds more lightness than darkness.

ETHICAL DILEMMA: A conflict in which one must choose between two seemingly opposing values.

ETHICS: The study of rules of right and wrong in human conduct.

EXPECTATION: Having a predetermined set of ideas of how an event will unfold.

EXTRASENSORY PERCEPTION: Perceiving information through means other than the five physical senses.

FAITH: Belief or trust in an outcome before the outcome occurs.

FREE-FLOATING ANXIETY: When one person is anxious, this anxiety can be transmitted energetically to other people, who will experience the anxiety as if it were their own. These people then either have no idea why they are feeling anxious, or they may erroneously attribute this anxiety to a particular issue, thereby blowing the issue out of proportion.

GROUNDING CORD: An energetic connection securing an object or person to the earth. Other energies can be released through this cord.

GROUPTHINK: A phenomenon that occurs among groups of people in which their energies merge and they adopt each other's beliefs, thoughts, and emotions, sometimes at the expense of their individual beliefs and codes of ethics.

GROWTH PERIOD: An intense period of personal transformation during which one's beliefs, thoughts, perceptions, and self-image are altered. This can result in a temporary period of emotional or cognitive turbulence.

IMAGINATION: The act or power of creating pictures or ideas in the mind.

INCARNATION: A lifetime in a particular body.

INQUISITION: A court for finding and punishing heretics, set up by the Roman Catholic Church in the thirteenth century and lasting several centuries. These heretics included women accused of witchcraft, people displaying psychic abilities, or those practicing alternative faiths or religions.

KARMA: Spiritual award system that can include both desirable and undesirable consequences for one's prior conduct either in the present life or in prior incarnations.

KIRLIAN PHOTOGRAPHY: Heat-sensitive photography that can record information not ordinarily registered by the physical eye.

KNOWINGNESS: A psychic ability located in the crown chakra, or seventh chakra, in which a person instantaneously knows information in the form of a thought, without having to go through logical steps to gain that information.

LIBRARY OF SYMBOLS: A collection of symbolic images.

LITERAL IMAGE: An image that is what it appears to be.

MARTYR COMPLEX: A self-defeating set of beliefs and behaviors that causes a person to gain satisfaction and elevated self-esteem by sacrificing their own pleasure and needs for the sake of others.

MEDITATION: Listening to God; focusing attention inward or on a particular object.

MEI PICTURE: Mental Emotional Image picture. This is an emotionally charged thoughtform that influences one's perceptions and behavior and is located within one's body, mind, and energetic field.

MULTIPLE PERSONALITY DISORDER: A psychological dissociative disorder in which aspects of a person split off from the person's awareness and behave and respond independently from other aspects.

NAVIGATING: The science of figuring out where one is heading. Charting a course, a path, or a plan that will lead to an intended goal.

NEUTRALITY: Being neutral; maintaining a state of emotional and cognitive balance that is not invested in a particular outcome.

NONATTACHMENT: Having no emotional investment in an object or in the outcome of a situation.

OMNIPRESENT: Being everywhere all at once.

OMNISCIENT: All-knowing.

PRAYER: The act of talking to God or to a higher power.

PRECOGNITION: Knowing that something is going to happen before it happens.

PROGRAMMING: Beliefs, thoughts, ethics, information, feelings, or perceptions that are passed from one person to another that may or may not be in harmony with the recipient's own information or way of being.

PROJECTION: To see one's own qualities in someone else, often unconsciously; to assign particular attributes to another that really belong to oneself.

PSYCHIC EXPERIENCE: A supernatural experience in which information is sent or received through means other than the five senses.

PSYCHIC TOOLS: Visualization techniques that affect and influence energy that can be utilized for psychic reading and healing and to enhance the quality of one's life.

RELATIONSHIP READING: A psychic reading that focuses on issues regarding the relationship between two or more individuals.

SELF-ENERGIZATION: To call one's life force to oneself.

SEPARATION OBJECT: A mental image or visualization that defines boundaries and serves as protection.

SKEPTICISM: A closed state of mind where one doubts or questions things, sometimes to the point where these doubts obscure the truth.

SPIRIT: The essence of a person.

SPIRITUAL PATH: A course that one's spirit is destined to follow in order to gain certain life experiences while in the physical body.

SUPERNATURAL: Beyond the physical senses; beyond the natural.

SYMBOL: An object or sign that represents another object, idea, person, or quality.

SYMBOLIC IMAGE: An image that is representative of something other than itself.

TELEKINESIS: A psychic ability in which one can move or alter objects with the power of thought, emotion, or other energy, through non-physical means.

TELEPATHY: Transferring information from one mind to another without the use of the physical senses.

THIRD EYE: The center of one's clairvoyance. The third eye corresponds with the sixth chakra and is located inside the forehead, slightly above and between the physical eyes.

TRANSFORMATION: To effect change.

TRANSMEDIUMSHIP: A spiritual ability in which a person's spirit leaves the body and accepts a foreign spirit or energy into their own. This happens both consciously and unconsciously.

UNIVERSAL SPIRIT: God.

VALIDATION: To confirm one's value.

VISUALIZATION: The act of calling forth images, visions, and pictures in one's mind.

VORTEX: A highly charged energy center or chakra within the earth that has an influence on nearby organisms.

YOGANANDA, PARAMHANSA: An influential Indian yogi, author of *Autobiography of a Yogi*, and founder of the Self-Realization Institute.

Bibliography

Choquette, Sonia. *Your Heart's Desire: Instructions for Creating the Life You Really Want*. New York: Three Rivers Press, 1997.

Dyer, Wayne. *You'll See It When You Believe It*. New York: Harper-Collins, 2001.

Gawain, Shakti. *Creative Visualization*. Revised edition. Novato, CA: Nataraj Publishing/New World Library, 2002.

Judith, Anodea. *Wheels of Life*. Revised and expanded edition. Saint Paul, MN: Llewellyn Publishing, 1999.

McArthur, Bruce. *Your Life: Why It Is the Way It Is, and What You Can Do About It*. Virginia Beach: A.E.R. Press, 1993.

Murphy, Joseph. *The Power of Your Subconcious Mind*. Revised and expanded edition. Paramus, NJ: Reward Books, 2000.

Myss, Caroline, Ph.D. *Three Levels of Power and How to Use Them*. Audio cassette. Louisville, CO: Sounds True, Inc.

———. *Why People Don't Heal and How They Can*. Audio cassette. Louisville, CO: Sounds True, Inc.

Williamson, Marianne. *A Return to Love: Reflections on the Principles of A Course in Miracles*. New York: HarperCollins, 1996.

Yogananda, Paramahansa. *Autobiography of a Yogi*. Los Angeles, CA: Self-Realization Fellowship, 1946.

To Write to the Author

If you wish to contact the author or would like more information about this book, please write to the author in care of Llewellyn Worldwide and we will forward your request. Both the author and publisher appreciate hearing from you and learning of your enjoyment of this book and how it has helped you. Llewellyn Worldwide cannot guarantee that every letter written to the author can be answered, but all will be forwarded. Please write to:

Debra Lynne Katz
% Llewellyn Worldwide
P.O. Box 64383, Dept. 0-7387-0592-6
St. Paul, MN 55164-0383, U.S.A.

Please enclose a self-addressed stamped envelope for reply,
or $1.00 to cover costs. If outside U.S.A., enclose
international postal reply coupon.

Many of Llewellyn's authors have websites with additional information and resources. For more information, please visit our website at
http://www.llewellyn.com